Edmond de Pressensé, Annie Harwood Holmden

Contemporary Portraits

Edmond de Pressensé, Annie Harwood Holmden

Contemporary Portraits

ISBN/EAN: 9783337375249

Printed in Europe, USA, Canada, Australia, Japan

Cover: Foto ©Thomas Meinert / pixelio.de

More available books at **www.hansebooks.com**

CONTEMPORARY PORTRAITS:

*THIERS, STRAUSS COMPARED WITH VOLTAIRE,
ARNAUD DE L'ARIÈGE, DUPANLOUP,
ADOLPHE MONOD, VINET,
VERNY, ROBERTSON.*

BY

E. DE PRESSENSÉ, D.D.,

Author of

" JESUS CHRIST; HIS TIMES, LIFE AND WORK," " THE EARLY YEARS OF CHRISTIANITY," ETC.

TRANSLATED BY

ANNIE HARWOOD HOLMDEN.

New York:
A. D. F. RANDOLPH & Co.,
900, BROADWAY.
MDCCCLXXX.

CONTENTS.

	PAGE
THIERS	3
THE ANTECEDENTS OF THE VATICAN COUNCIL ...	39
STRAUSS AND VOLTAIRE	79
THE CULTURKAMPF IN GERMANY	103
ARNAUD DE L'ARIÈGE	125
DUPANLOUP, BISHOP OF ORLEANS	139
ADOLPHE MONOD	149
ALEXANDRE VINET	233
VERNY AND ROBERTSON	283

PREFACE.

THE book now offered to English readers is in great part a collection of articles that have appeared at intervals in various French journals and reviews.

The first part of the volume is devoted to subjects of general interest; especially to a study of the Catholic crisis, as represented in some of the most eminent men of the Catholic Church. A careful consideration of the facts advanced seems to me to lead to two conclusions: first, that the course pursued by the Ultramontanes is one fraught with danger to our social interests; and secondly, that it is both unjustifiable and unwise to attempt to combat Ultramontanism with its own weapons. It seemed to me opportune to draw attention to the testimony of a competent German writer—M. Geffcken—as to the inanity of the results of the Prussian "Culturkampf," though directed by the first political genius of the age, and the strongest will the world has ever known.

The second part of the book brings before the reader three eminent representatives of French Evangelical Protestantism and one great English preacher. It will be observed that I have laid more stress in these papers on the necessity of a theological reformation than on ecclesiastical questions, though I am fully alive to the importance of the latter. It is my growing conviction that Protestantism has greatly suffered of late years from a too exclusive absorption in questions of organisation, to the neglect of deeper and more essential principles. In order to regain its hold of the mind of the age, the Church must come back to the study of these fundamental truths, in the same spirit of free inquiry and devout earnestness which characterised Adolphe Monod and Vinet, Verny and Robertson.

E. DE PRESSENSÉ.

PARIS, *November*, 1879.

THIERS.

THIERS.

A BIOGRAPHICAL SKETCH, DRAWN FROM RECENT WRITINGS AND PERSONAL RECOLLECTIONS.[1]

I.

IN 1821 two young men left their native province and came to Paris. They were sons of Provence, that sunny land which has given so many eminent men to France since the days of Mirabeau. They had just completed their law studies, and one of them had been crowned by the Academy of Aix, for his panegyric on Vauvenargues. Both, however, were poor and unknown. The closest friendship bound them together. They took up their lodgings

---

[1] No complete biography has as yet appeared of this great French statesman. M. Jules Simon has published a graphic and very remarkable account of his presidency under the title, "Le Gouvernement de M. Thiers;" but the history of the principal founder of the French Republic is confounded with the annals of the parliamentary history of France. The speeches of M. Thiers from 1831 to 1836 have been recently published by M. Calmon. For the latter part of his career we draw largely on our personal recollections. We are indebted also to the "Souvenirs" of M. Seignior, in which many conversations of M. Thiers have been preserved.

in two adjoining garrets in a miserable quarter of the city, and at once applied themselves to a great literary task. By a strange coincidence, both had chosen the same subject, the history of the French Revolution,—a subject of dramatic and thrilling interest, stirring men's minds to enthusiasm or hatred, and a very firebrand of discord at a period when Old and New France were at desperate warfare.

These two young men both bore names destined to become illustrious. They were Thiers and Mignet. Thiers, born in 1797, was twenty-four years of age. The bond of affection which united them was most close and tender, and remained unbroken through life. *Mignet, c'est mon frère!* we once heard M. Thiers exclaim. In all the critical moments of Thiers' eventful career, especially in all times of trial and danger, Mignet was sure to be at his side, supporting him with a sympathy as manly as it was tender. Neither of the two had any anticipation in 1821 of the fame and fortune awaiting them. Mignet little guessed that he would be one of the great masters of history, one of the most widely read and deeply respected of thoughtful writers, and that, while keeping aloof from active political life, in which he never sought preferment, he would exert an incomparable influence through the world of letters. Still less did Thiers anticipate that he would hold the helm of his country through one of those stormy crises, in which the safety of a nation may depend on a single man.

Thiers belonged to the petty *bourgeoisie* of Marseilles, although by his mother's side he was related to the illustrious poet, André Chénier, who was dragged to the scaffold under the Reign of Terror in 1794, for having defended true liberty against anarchy and crime. Thiers was, indeed, a worthy representative of those middle classes which had played so important a part in 1789, and which were fully resolved not to allow themselves to be robbed of the liberties won by their fathers. He belonged, body and soul, to the Revolution, and it was for the better defence of its cause that he began to write its history. While Mignet, with a restrained nervous force reminding us of Tacitus, drew the general picture of the Revolution in bold, masterly outlines, Thiers described it in a full, detailed narrative, remarkable rather for clearness than for brilliancy. His men and events pass before us under a strong light rather than in relief, but all his descriptions are characterised by that air of movement and life, which mere study never produces, and which is to a literary work what the quick pulsing blood is to the human body. Finance, administration, the plan of a campaign, a discussion in parliament, all become animated under his pen. Hence every one of the ten volumes of this rapid but complete history, obtained at once an enormous circulation; and the young author, who had at first sheltered his humble name under that of a well-known publisher, soon made himself known to the public, and was raised at once to fame and competence. This popularity was also no doubt partly owing to the fact that his book appealed throughout to the passions of the great Liberal public, which was exasperated by the policy of the clerical Right, then in power. The sole aim of this party was to nullify the most positive results of the Revolution, and their first step was to do violence to it and to belie it. It would be absurd to demand the calm and cool impartiality of a judge, from the historian who is touching on a past so recent and so hotly contested, and who is himself engaged in the same life and death struggle. Nevertheless, the young writer does really glorify only the men of 1789, or the great generals who defended the soil of France against the invader. The sanguinary demagogy is sternly denounced by him, though he has been accused of restraining his severity till the hour of retribution and of defeat had come. He has been also accused of fatalism. This is an exaggeration. He was uniformly the man of action rather than of theory; and, while never belying his liberal convictions, he took fuller cognisance of circumstances than of principles. In this respect he differs from all the great theorists of the Restoration, who, like Royer Collard and the Duc de Broglie, attached the first importance to theories, and were never satisfied till they had reduced their practice to the form of maxims.

Thiers' energies were not exhausted by the writing of his great work. He threw himself at the same time, with all his sparkling vivacity and remarkable fluency, into the daily press. He rose at once to the first rank among journalists, not only on account of his brilliance as a writer, but also from his aptitude in apprehending and making himself master of all questions of art, finance, diplomacy and administration. He found also an unfailing source of inspiration in his sincere devotion to the Liberal cause. Passion is a great muse, especially when it is nurtured in the glowing atmosphere of public opinion, when it is in harmony with the general spirit of a period, and when it has to deal with blind and obstinate opposition. From 1823 to 1830, if we except the short interval of the Martignac Ministry, the Government of France was in the hands of the party of the Emigrants, whose one desire was to erase the grand year 1789 from the annals of history. Supported by a bigoted clerical party, whose services it repaid by most dangerous immunities, the Government of the day was tending to restore the fatal union between the throne and the altar. Charles X. was the true king of the Emigration. As Royer Collard said in 1830, he always remained Count of Artois, of the old Court of Versailles,—a foolish fanatic, capable of risking everything for his imaginary divine right, but incapable of sustaining his temerity by wise measures. To usurp absolute power in spite of his oaths to the contrary, appeared to him simply claiming that which was his due, and he looked to heaven for success in attempts which another must have felt to be criminal, just as the mystic folds his arms and awaits the effect of his prayers. He only needed to have for his minister a fanatic like the Prince de Polignac, in order to bring the old French monarchy to ruin; especially as, in an age of such intellectual fertility as a nation but rarely enjoys, all the great minds of France were arrayed against him.

No one dealt more effectual blows at the counter revolution than M. Thiers, who had just established the *National*, a journal of his own, in which he carried on the most brilliant polemical campaign France has ever witnessed. Those who knew him at that time describe him as exerting an irresistible attraction. This little man, with the flexible face, the glance quick and keen as lightning, the inexhaustible flow of brilliant speech, produced the effect of one of those creatures of air and flame, to which Voltaire has been likened. Only he was no comedian seeking to keep the world amused; he was the soldier of a great cause, and patriotism of the truest type was his ruling principle.

II.

Thiers took a very influential part in the Revolution of 1830. After joining in the famous protest of the journalists against the decrees of the 17th of July which suspended, or rather violated, the charter, he was made the messenger of the Liberal party to the

Duke of Orleans, inviting him to become the substitute of the king by divine right, and to inaugurate a new monarchy, the monarchical form of government being at that time deemed better for France than a republic. From this period Thiers rose rapidly into prominence. He was at once elected to the Chamber of Deputies, was then made Secretary of State for Finance, and afterwards successively Minister of Commerce, of the Interior, and of Foreign Affairs. During the first period of the July dynasty he was the zealous defender of the Government against all enemies, whether they came from the Right, in Vendée, like the unfortunate Duchesse de Berry, who attempted to play the part of another Mary Stuart under very untoward circumstances, or whether they issued from the haunts of the secret societies, always rife with demagogic conspiracies. Thiers vigorously maintained the law of the land. He has been very unjustly reproached with having carried repression to the length of massacre. All that he did was to have the barriers of the insurgents carried by the bayonet. As a practical man, influenced more by facts than by theories, he subordinated his Liberal principles to the exigencies of the struggle against misrule. After Fieschi's attempt upon the life of King Louis Philippe, he accepted, indeed he initiated, severe legislative measures against the press and unauthorised societies. When he took the direction of foreign affairs, he made strenuous endeavours to secure for France a more influential position than that with which the Conservative party of the time was satisfied. During his first ministry he urged direct intervention in Spain, in favour of constitutional royalty. In 1840 he was not deterred by the prospect of a general war, from breaking with the Quadruple Alliance, for the benefit of the Viceroy of Egypt, whom he wished to make the supporter of French power in the East.

This temerity cost him his portfolio, which he was obliged to hand over to his great rival Guizot, who carried out with dazzling effect the policy of peace at any price, and of strict Conservatism. This narrow policy went so far as to refuse the smallest reforms, especially in the electoral law, which made the government of the country the monopoly of an oligarchy of proprietors, around which surged on all sides the rising tide of democracy. M. Thiers was, during the whole of this period, the recognised leader of the Opposition, steadily demanding a more liberal policy at home, and a more manly attitude abroad. In truth, he was the only real Conservative, for it was not possible for the Government of Louis Philippe long to withstand the Liberal aspirations of the nation, reinforced as they were by the material prosperity enjoyed by the country, or successfully to oppose the movement of emancipation which was going on in neighbouring lands, especially in Italy. *La France s'ennuie*, said Lamartine, in one of his famous speeches.

It was perilous for the Government of July, 1830, to stand thus isolated, fenced in by a narrow officialism, while public spirit was in a state of agitation on every hand. It was like a tree whose roots no longer reached the water, and which withered as it stood. At the very first blow, therefore, it fell to the ground, and the king of the Revolution had to follow into exile the Legitimist king. M. Thiers had spent his strength in the tribune, in warning a blind power. It has been justly said that Louis Philippe and M. Guizot were both incapable of seeing an unwelcome truth. Their illusions lasted to the end. We have heard M. Thiers tell how they came to seek him in the night of the 23rd February, the night which preceded the catastrophe. They turned to him as to the only pilot who could save the ship. When he arrived at the Tuileries, the storm which was so soon to burst, was already muttering. The politicians who were to bring him into the presence of Louis Philippe, received him with the entreaty, "Above all things spare the king!" "Spare him?" replied Thiers, in a tone of keen impatience; "he has been spared too much already. Let him know all the truth!" It was too late. M. Thiers was never unjust to King Louis Philippe. He often spoke of him, fully recognising his merits, and his philanthropy worthy of a son of the eighteenth century; but blaming his obstinacy and too lawyerly subtlety. He blamed him also for having always attempted to *govern*, when he ought to have been contented with *reigning;* and for having sought to substitute personal rule for a thoroughly parliamentary administration.

Odilon Barrot, one of the leaders of the Left, chosen at the last moment on the morning of the 24th of February, as Minister with M. Thiers, would humorously relate how, when he wished to remonstrate from the boulevard with one of the leaders of the barricade, the man said to him : "Idiot! don't you see that the king is making game of us and of you too?" "And he was right," said Odilon Barrot. M. Thiers was not so severe. He felt, however, that Louis Philippe had himself made the abyss into which his throne was falling. Yet Thiers was not at this time by any means an extreme Liberal. He would have been satisfied with an extension of the electoral right, stopping very far short of universal suffrage, and with a somewhat extended liberty of the press. He was still an ardent adherent of the system of centralisation, which the Revolution had bequeathed to the Empire, and which the Empire had carried to its extreme issues. " Europe envies us this," he said. To which the Liberals of the *De Tocqueville* school replied : " If that is true, why does she not adopt it ? "

Thiers' admiration for Napoleon I. is well known. To him he devoted his second great historical work, in which he displays, in yet larger measure and maturity, all the eminent qualities of his earlier writings

—clearness, graphic power, lucid arrangement and exposition of military and financial operations. He was completely fascinated by the genius of the most marvellous man of modern times. In conversation he constantly alluded to Napoleon, but occasionally he could pronounce severe judgment upon him. It is said that one day, on one of his journeys, wearied with the senseless raptures over Napoleon I. in which some young man was indulging, thinking thus to please M. Thiers, he interrupted him, saying: "You do not know, then, that Napoleon was a scoundrel?" It was a sally which he would not have seriously maintained, but it sufficed to prove that he had taken the moral measure of his hero. He spoke of him with severity in his last volumes, for he came to see what disasters had been entailed upon France, by this stupendous genius unrestrained by law or conscience.

From this time M. Thiers took his place among the leading orators of the French tribune. He was not at first successful. He used to relate with glee that, on the point of delivering one of his early speeches, he was deeply agitated. "What!" said the sardonic Royer Collard, "you moved in this way? Just look at those heads yonder!" and he pointed him to his hearers. It has been wrongly said that M. Thiers attempted at first the sustained style of the great orator. This is altogether a mistake. From the reports of his first speeches, which M. Calmon has just reprinted, with an exhaustive commentary, it is evident that M. Thiers adopted at once a style of his own, simple, familiar, full of natural humour and freshness. Of this style he was a master, and it was without effort that he afterwards rose to higher flights. His great speeches were always inspired by great themes. He never made any attempt to be great; greatness, as it were, came to him. He could not be compared to any of his rivals in the Chamber of Deputies. He had nothing of the rigid exactness and concentrated force of Guizot, who disguised a policy often timid and paltry beneath magnificent forms of speech. Berryer, of whom at the time of his first appearance Royer Collard said, *Ce n'est pas un talent; c'est une puissance* ("this is not one of your men of talent; this man is a *power*"), made the most striking contrast to Thiers by his magnificent stature, the rich quality of his voice, his expressive gesture, and the passion and brilliancy of his language. The eloquence of Lamartine reminded one of those fairies of the fable, whose mouths dropped pearls, while his thought was none the less deep and full, and in political matters he seemed endowed with all but prophetic prescience. Thiers laboured under many external disadvantages; his height was below the average; his gesticulation rapid and abrupt; his voice shrill. He gave no play to imagination in his speeches, and yet no one exercised a stronger influence over a debate. He flooded it, as it were, with light by a mode of statement which left nothing undefined or obscure, and which brought the driest details of finance or administration within the comprehension of all. The calm exposition ended by kindling into a glow. Underlying the fluent verbiage was a closely woven texture of reasoning and fact. The whole was animated by what the French call *esprit*. A striking point, a well-told anecdote, sustained the interest. And then the life pulsed through his speeches as through his books. The audience had no resistance to offer to this orator who placed himself on their own level; they were charmed, fascinated, carried away, often convinced.

III.

The Republic of 1848 surpassed all M. Thiers' anticipations. He was in theory a Monarchist: constitutional royalty was, in his view, the government best adapted for a great country. Universal suffrage seemed to him an extravagance. It must be admitted that its sudden adoption might appear to the men of 1850 a leap in the dark. The Republic of 1848 was not like that of 1870. It had not been preceded by fearful disasters, by the dismemberment of France. The duty of rallying around it did not appear so imperious as it did subsequently, to all those who put their country above their political preferences. We believe, nevertheless, that if M. Thiers had carried out then the policy which he did adopt afterwards, the shame and disaster of the second Empire might have been avoided. In the National Assembly of 1848, as in the Legislative Assembly, he was one of the leaders of the reaction of the Right. He helped to secure the election of Louis Napoleon as President of the Republic, without any presentiment of his becoming the future Emperor. He imagined that he would be able to control him by his own superior mental power. He did not know that this phlegmatic believer in his star, would be ready to send him to prison or into exile, in order to make himself master of France, and that the most able parliamentary discourse would have no more weight with him than his oath, in hindering him from usurpation. This was the great political mistake of Thiers' life, into which he was led by a patriotic dread of the perils of socialism. Associated for the time with men of the Right in granting to the Catholic Church dangerous privileges, which he supposed to be the only safeguards for social order, he helped to hand over, in great part public instruction to the clergy. He thus became the powerful ally of the Abbé Dupanloup (just about to be made Bishop of Orleans), who was the prime mover of the commission which produced that fatal legislation. The future bishop little dreamed then that he would become one of Thiers' most determined opponents.

Thiers was also at this time one of the promoters

of the great change in the electoral law, which was almost equivalent to the suppression of universal suffrage. Prince Napoleon, who was already meditating his *coup d'état*, strongly approved of this measure. He laughed in his sleeve—he who laughed but seldom —as he thought how easily he could get the upper hand of an Assembly which had lost credit with the people. He reserved it to himself to restore to them universal suffrage, as a gift of his joyous accession. Thus, when on the eve of the crime of the 2nd of December, Thiers, foreseeing too late what was impending, besought the Assembly to forget its divisions for the sake of imperilled parliamentary liberty, his agitated, impassioned pleadings (which ring in my ears to-day) found no echo from the Left; and a few days later, when the agent of police came to seize him in his bed, and send him off to the frontier, he learned how dear it costs to place confidence in men who are fatalists about their own fortunes, and who deem themselves entitled, as the fulfillers of destiny, to wrest the laws to their own advantage.

IV.

During the early years of the Empire, M. Thiers remained in retirement, and completed his history of the Consulate and of the First Empire. From 1852 to 1862 a leaden pall seemed to hang over France. With a fettered press, a tribune almost voiceless, or at least without an echo, since the reproduction in full of the legislative debates was forbidden, public opinion had no longer any organ. The Empire strove to lull it to sleep by encouraging material interests, and seeking to develop the wealth of the nation, though not without recourse to the artifices familiar to speculative adventurers, the *condottieri* of the Bourse, those great thieves who are not incarcerated simply because they filch their millions, but who, if they carried on the same operations for small sums, would not escape judicial prosecution.

The Crimean war and the war in Italy lent some *éclat* to the new *régime*. They were unavailing, however, to arrest the fatal consequences which must necessarily flow from its principle. Personal government, capricious and changeable as the will or the health of a man, must needs share in the weaknesses of the sovereign. Napoleon III. was the most dangerous autocrat who could govern a great country. Capable of a kind of generosity, he altogether ignored the distinction between good and evil. It could not be said that he was immoral; he knew no morality. The sworn enemy of liberal institutions, he had kept from his youth, as a carbonaro, a certain revolutionary or socialist bent which impelled him to flatter the democratic instinct, and to support himself by the masses against the cultivated classes. In this, however, he was but following the traditions of Cæsarism. In his foreign policy he aimed only at theatrical effects; he wished to astonish the world, and to continue the Napoleonic legend, though he could not make the slightest pretension to the genius of the head of his race. He threw his heart only into the Italian cause; to this he subordinated everything except his wild dreams of greatness, which took form now in the establishment of a great Catholic Empire in Mexico, now in the restoration of Poland by means of a Congress, the mere proposal of which made Prussia his enemy for ever.

These dreams, which cost very dear to the country, prevented his paying any attention to the spoliations which were threatening Denmark, and securing to himself the alliance of England. He thus took the most effectual means of clearing the way for the ambitious schemes of Prussia. He was the very man predestined to be the miserable dupe of so skilful a player as Bismarck. The latter, after deluding Napoleon with vain promises, drove him into such a corner after Sadowa, that he might have declared war upon him at any moment, while appearing all the while to be himself the offended party.

From 1860 it became evident that it was a terrible thing for France to bear Cæsar and his fortune, and that the vessel of the State might well founder or go to pieces under such a load. Public opinion awoke under the goad of apprehension. M. Thiers, who had been nominated deputy for Paris in the elections of 1863, became the leader of the Opposition. Every one of his speeches was like the blow of a heavy battering ram upon the citadel of Napoleonic despotism.

He completely demolished its system of internal policy by his great speech on the principles of true liberty; he cast a pitiless light upon the confusion and extravagance of its finance, and rose to an almost prophetic height, when he attempted to show the abyss into which its foreign policy was dragging the country. His eloquence on this occasion, without losing anything of its clearness and homely simplicity, assumed a new dignity and breadth. The effect produced by him on the public mind at this time was very great, and he was supported by such orators as Jules Favre, Jules Simon, and Berryer. In vain did the Empire rear itself like a Colossus, armed with all the material resources of the country; it tottered visibly before this handful of men, who had only right upon their side. The words of Thiers were but a light, impalpable breath upon the lips, but before that breath the giant faltered. Never was there a clearer instance of the influence of purely moral force.

On one point, however, Thiers had separated from his colleagues in the Opposition. He supported, with all his strength, the cause of the temporal power of the papacy, in the first instance, undoubtedly, because he knew that the one-time conspirator of the Papal States (now Emperor), was intensely opposed to it; and secondly, because the pontifical sovereignty was connected in his mind with that concordatory union between Church and State, which he had extolled in his history of the Consulate and the Empire. This was one of the weak points of his political theory. Himself a believer in the spiritual, and very far removed from anything like irreverence with regard to religion, he nevertheless considered it primarily, from a social point of view, as an instrument, if not of government, at least of maintaining public peace and morality, provided it was under the control of the civil power. The Concordat, concluded by Napoleon I. with Pius VII., seemed to him one of the grandest acts of the First Consul. And yet none knew better than he, that this so-called pacification had led to the most fierce and perilous conflicts between the two powers.

M. Thiers never regarded the relations of Church and State in any other than a political light. One day, in the President's palace at Versailles, we heard him make the following remark in reference to Henry IV.: "Was there ever anything more admirable than the sight of this great king, giving peace to France by the Edict of Nantes, while himself turning Catholic? And the best of all is, that while turning Catholic, he still remained Protestant!"

It is evident that Thiers speaks of religion, or rather of the establishment of religion in modern Europe, much as Cicero might have spoken in his Tusculans. The convictions of the individual were lost sight of by him in the interests of the community. The eloquence and zeal which he displayed in maintaining the cause of the temporal power were keenly appreciated by Pope Pius IX. M. Thiers used to tell a very good story which shows that the great Infallible could unbend on occasion, and that beneath the stole of the ardent devotee there still lingered something of the acute Italian diplomatist.

"What gratitude do we not owe to M. Thiers," he said one day to a French visitor, after one of the illustrious orator's great speeches in support of the papal cause. "We have only one thing more to wish for him—that he were himself a believer in Catholic doctrines. And yet," he went on, after a short silence, "if he had faith, he might perhaps do me less service."

Thiers was, in truth, destitute of the Catholic faith; and he sometimes found his client of Rome very embarrassing. At the time of the affair of little Mortara, the young Jew, who was stolen away from his parents to be baptized by force in a Roman Convent, he said to a vehement prelate who was defending the crime in the name of God: "How dare you bring the name of God into such a scandalous affair? If, in order to be a Christian, it is necessary to convert souls by force, then God is no Christian, for He has not yet suppressed the Queen of England, who is the powerful protector of what you regard as most dangerous heresy."

M. Thiers would not, indeed, have ventured from the tribune of the legislative body, on such open criticism of one of the maddest acts of the papacy in modern times. He only expressed himself thus freely in his own *salon*. None but those who heard him there could fully appreciate the remarkable versatility and fruitfulness of his mind. There, surrounded by reproductions of the masterpieces of painting and sculpture, he discoursed on all subjects, from the fine arts, of which he was a passionate admirer, to the most abstruse questions of home and foreign policy, which he illumined by the vivid flashes of his wit. In happy sallies, in *bons mots*, in piquant anecdotes, he was inexhaustible. Standing in the chimney corner, he would go over his recollections, in which all the contemporary men of note figured in turn. He never assumed anything; his *bonhomie* was charming and full of kindliness.

Every evening his *salon* was open to all the eminent men of the country and of the age. It was a great European rendezvous. The most distinguished members of the *corps diplomatique* deemed it an honour to resort there frequently. At midnight, when the circle had drawn closer, the old man still dazzled his intimate friends by the brilliancy of his conversation. This *salon* of Place St. Georges was a veritable political power under the Empire.

We all know what supreme efforts M. Thiers put forth, from love of his country, to save the Empire from its last fatal error. The war against Prussia seemed to him from the first, the most criminal folly. Those who were present at the famous session of July 15th, 1870, will never forget the spectacle of the great citizen exhausting himself in opposition to a furious Assembly, in the attempt to save his country from a mad act, the disastrous issues of which he too clearly foresaw. Railed at by the band of Bonapartists, who tried to stifle his voice in their passionate eagerness for this war, since their only hope was to drown reviving liberty in blood, he fought to the end. One of his friends found him, when the sitting was over, bathed in tears. He had obeyed the dictates of the purest patriotism. He knew, moreover, more than he could tell. Two days later he avowed, in a circle of intimate friends, his certain knowledge that the military preparations of France were inadequate to the struggle. When the first disasters followed one another with the rapidity of lightning, the Empress herself felt constrained to have recourse to him to save the nation in distress. It was too late. He tried, however, after Sedan, to get the Government of National Defence nominated by the Legislative body, so that it might not appear revolutionary. Two days after the movement of the 4th of September, he complained bitterly of the vacillation of that middle party, which in the following years was to do so much mischief to France by its indecision and intrigues. Immediately on the

accession of the new power which had swept away
the Empire, M. Thiers accepted unhesitatingly the
painful mission of seeking an alliance for his unhappy
country. Nothing could be more disheartening than
his unavailing quest throughout Europe; but nothing
reflects more honour on his memory.

V.

We shall pass briefly over the latter part of the life
of the great citizen, for it is fresh in the recollection of
all. We shall confine ourselves chiefly to that which
is least generally known. Brilliant as had been the
career of M. Thiers hitherto as an orator and a statesman, it now assumed a new element of greatness.
Nominated to the National Assembly by twenty-three
Departments, he was designated by France herself to
guide her destinies in her hour of supreme peril.
Whatever might be the divisions of the National Assembly on questions of government, all must yield to
the exigencies of public safety. The situation was a
terrible one. A third of the country was desolated
by the horrors of a most cruel invasion. An army
of three hundred thousand men was held captive in
Germany; another army was scattered over Switzerland. The army of the National Defence, which had
saved the honour of the country by its resistance,
was disorganised. Peace with the foreigner must be
treated for with the knife to the throat; while at

home the spirit of faction was muttering threateningly, especially in Paris itself, the working population of which had been completely unhinged by their brave endurance of five months of siege. The name of M. Thiers was forced upon the Parliament. His first task was to conclude peace with an enemy of unbounded resources, who knew to what a condition unhappy France was reduced. It was, indeed, as we have heard M. Thiers relate, a time of terrible struggle, in which he tried to contest with Germany the possession of a strip of frontier, and, among other places, of that town of Belfort, without which the country would have been left open, and incapable of defending itself against the most formidable aggressions. It was a drama of history. Bismarck appeared at first inexorable. In order the better to defend himself against the patriotic determination of M. Thiers, he called in the Prussian staff, with its illustrious chief, Von Moltke, and finally the king himself. There was one moment when M. Thiers declared that he should withdraw, and that he preferred even the most desperate struggle to a treaty which left the sword of Germany in the side of France. He succeeded, however, in saving Belfort, and signed with bitter mortification the treaty for that mutilation of his country which he had done all in his power to avert by his resistance to the most insane of wars.

Strangely enough, the two combatants in this very unequal diplomatic contest, judged each other favourably. M. Thiers appreciated in M. Bismarck the political artist, so to speak. He admired his genius, the abrupt simplicity of his language, his only tactics being an almost cynical frankness. Bismarck had too much perception not to enjoy the most remarkable talker of his time. It is said that at their first interview at Versailles, in discussing the preliminaries of an armistice in October, 1870, he said suddenly to M. Thiers, " Let us return to civilisation." He wished to resume one of the unrestrained conversations of former times. The representative of conquered France was not in a mood to divert his terrible interlocutor. Bismarck, seeing that M. Thiers was worn out and exhausted, urged him to rest upon his own couch, and himself covered him with a mantle. He remained unyielding, however, on all the great points at issue. France had to cede Alsace and Lorraine, and to consent to a ransom of four milliards.

The treaty being concluded, M. Thiers had next to get it accepted by the Assembly, and then to carry it out. We must refer the reader to M. Jules Simon's book for all that relates to the great financial operation, by which M. Thiers contrived to redeem and to free the territory of France without bringing about any monetary and financial crisis. He was more proud of this than of any other achievement of his life, and never wearied of talking of it.

Hardly had the peace been signed when Paris had

to be rescued from the most formidable insurrection of modern times. The war against the Commune was conducted with as much prudence as vigour, and if there were some terrible acts of reprisal in the first moments of victory, when the incendiary fires kindled by brigands were still raging, when the blood of the hostages was reeking around, and when from more than one house in the faubourgs shots were fired on the soldiers, the Government must not be held responsible for these deeds of vengeance. It passed no condemnations *en masse*, and M. Thiers was always for measures of humanity.

The political question began from this time to present itself in all its gravity to the National Assembly. The majority of that Assembly was Royalist, and it had hoped to find an instrument to carry out its views in the head of the executive power, formerly so bitter against the Republic. His old Orleanist friends, who had recognised him as their head in the struggle against the Empire, had no doubt of his support. He began by declaring that he believed it to be his duty, and the duty of all, to adjourn the question of the form of government. In his memorable speech of the 17th of February, 1871, he said : " Can there be any one here who will dare to discuss learnedly the articles of the Constitution, while our prisoners are dying miserably in distant countries, or while our people at home, themselves perishing of hunger, are obliged to give to foreign soldiers their last remaining morsel of bread? When we have lifted from the earth where he lies prostrate, the noble wounded soldier whom we call France; when we have bound up his wounds, and revived his fainting strength; when he has come to himself and finds he can again breathe freely, then, indeed, it will be time for him to see how he shall live. Then when, under the Government of the Republic, we have effected our reconstitution, we shall have some ground to go upon in deciding our future destinies."

M. Thiers had already arrived at his own decision, and there are few of his public acts which deserve more grateful recognition, than the promptitude with which he sacrificed his own political preferences, and threw himself heartily into the cause of the Republic. He gave a very conclusive reason for this adherence to the Republic, when counselling all good citizens to take the same course. "There is but one throne," he said, "and there are three men who wish to sit upon it, which is impossible!"

This witty sally was unanswerable, and the reason given was undoubtedly that which forced an Assembly, very anti-republican in its majority, to found the Republic. For it was not enough to be simply a Monarchist. The choice had to be made between Legitimists, Orleanists, and Bonapartists, and thus the Monarchical majority became a house divided against itself. It could only agree in the attempt to undermine the power of M. Thiers. It could not prevail against him so long as the territory was not liberated, but it never ceased to place difficulties in his way, and to hinder his work of reparation, entailing upon him arduous conflicts in Parliament, at the very time when he was bearing the burden of the liberation and reconstitution of the country. No one has described better than M. Simon what was at this time the life of M. Thiers. He says : " M. Thiers had to do with everything. All despatches passed under his eyes. He endeavoured to watch, minute by minute, the state of France and of Europe. During all the struggle with the Commune, he was seen every day at the foremost posts. His soul was absorbed in the triple conflict with the Commune, the German Chancellor, and the Assembly. By his strength of will and his remarkable penetration, he proved himself adequate to all. He was thoroughly master of himself, and could keep a cheerful face while his mind was oppressed with the heaviest weight of business. He could never have stood the incessant strain and demand upon him but for this natural light-heartedness, which enabled him rapidly to recover calmness and vivacity. He was, indeed, a rare man, as great and as attractive in the intimacy of private life as in his public career." [1]

It must be admitted that M. Thiers was often mistaken in his views of foreign policy ; that he was too

---

[1] " Le Gouvernement de M. Thiers," vol. ii. p. 241.

averse to the great reforms which were needful for restoring a country that had been so despoiled ; that he was too faithful to the system of protection in the matter of imposts, and too much attached to the old organisation of the army. In fact, he was unwilling for any change in this direction, especially in the law for recruiting the army.

But what are his errors in comparison to the vast services he rendered to the nation? Nor was it on account of those errors that he was overthrown on the 24th of May, for they were shared by most of his adversaries. That which they could not forgive him was his ever-increasingly hearty recognition of the Republic, on which he had thrown great *éclat* by his Presidential message of November, 1872. That day his fall was decided. His enemies only waited till the liberation of the territory should be complete.

The very day after the Assembly had voted that M. Thiers had deserved well of his country, the coalition was inaugurated which led to the famous and scandalous transactions of the 24th of May. History has not on record a more flagrant act of ingratitude. Its results strangely balked the hopes of its authors, for they had the effect of giving to the Republican party, the cohesion and caution to which it owed its success three years later. Never had M. Thiers risen to such a height of eloquence as in the proud speech which preceded the final vote. Two days later some friends came to bring him the expression of their admiration and sympathy in that Presidential palace of Versailles, all solitary and deserted, from which the liberator of the territory of France, the saviour of the country, was being driven out, as it were, by the impatient hatred of those enemies of the Republic whose impotence would bring its own Nemesis.

Thiers was even greater in retirement than in power. He remained the respected leader of the Republican party. It was to him men looked for the decisive word in critical moments. Even from the grave his voice made itself heard in his electoral manifesto against the coalition of the 16th of May, published after his death. He worked up to the last hour of life. He fell at his post on the battle-field, spending his last breath for his beloved country.

France showed the extent of her gratitude at the funeral of the great citizen. Thousands of men with tearful faces gathered around his bier, and repressed their indignation under unworthy provocations, in order to do honour to his memory by a last act of patriotic self-restraint.

There is something almost overwhelming in the retrospect of M. Thiers' indefatigable activity through his long life, and of all that has resulted from it. No one understood better how to make good use of time. He rose every day at five. When he was in power, he would take the morning hours, when he was sure not to be disturbed, for the preparation of his speeches, or for the more important affairs of home or foreign policy. He gave audiences at the most unlikely hours.

After his return to private life, he devoted himself uninterruptedly till noon, to his labours as a writer. In the afternoon he went to the Chamber, and regularly took a *siesta* from six to eight in the evening. After dinner with his guests, he would hold a reception till midnight, always standing, always animated, sparkling with wit, affable and unassuming. Gracious and kindly to all, he was particularly affectionate to his friends, and never forgot an act of friendship or devotion to himself or to his cause. He bore no malice against his enemies; he now and then gave a witty thrust at them, more or less cutting, but he knew how to forget the gravest wrongs. At the time of the nomination of the seventy-five irremovable senators to the National Assembly, there was an understanding between the Left and the Extreme Right which detested the Orleanists even more than the Republicans. One of the senators of this party had distinguished himself by his abusive speeches against M. Thiers. " Thiers will never give *me* his vote," he said to one of his friends. Thiers sent word to him that he might count upon his vote. " The next day," said the old President of the Republic, " I saw this same senator coming to me with a smile which was almost as affectionate as an embrace."

"Well, yes," I said to him, "I will vote for you; you see I am capable of anything." This fine irony was all his revenge.

One cannot sufficiently admire the energy displayed by this old man, in appearance so frail. His features had nothing remarkable in themselves, but his sensitive, intellectual face became irresistibly attractive in conversation.

He will live in history as the Thiers of the great days of blood and anguish, those days when he stood forth as the saviour of his country in distress. This is the Thiers whom we have represented with rare power in the admirable portrait by Bonnat. This is the Thiers who was named with acclamation by the majority of the Chamber of Deputies in the month of June, 1877, when one of the most maladroit Ministers of the 16th of May had the impertinence to pay homage to the Monarchists of the National Assembly, for the liberation of the territory. More than three hundred deputies sprang to their feet as one man, and pointing to the illustrious old patriot, exclaimed: "There sits the liberator of France!" No one could look on dry-eyed at such a scene. Thiers himself shed tears. Such an hour outweighs much calumny.

One of M. Thiers' last labours was the great philosophical work on which he had been long engaged. He constantly spoke of it in conversation. His aim was to oppose with all his energy the school of materialistic transformation, which banishes God alike from nature and history. It was to refute this, which appeared to him the most noxious error, that he entered on an extensive study of the natural sciences, gathering around him their most eminent representatives. He did not himself rise above deism. Full of respect for the religion of Christ, he yet did not cross the barrier which divides theism from supernatural religion. But his faith in God was full and strong, and in his preparations for its defence, he showed what importance he attached to it. There is something grand in this absorption of the mind of the great statesman, at the close of life, in such a theme.

The memory of Thiers remains dear and sacred to all who had the happiness and honour of his friendship. His name is inscribed in letters of gold on the annals of his country—that country which he so passionately loved, so courageously warned of its danger, so faithfully served and so gloriously saved.

THE ANTECEDENTS OF THE VATICAN COUNCIL.

THE ANTECEDENTS OF THE VATICAN COUNCIL.

THE signal triumph achieved by Ultramontanism at the Vatican Council was no sudden success. It was the *dénoument* of a cunningly contrived policy which had been at work from the beginning of the century. Of the importance of the end attained there can be no doubt; and we shall find much of interest in tracing the steps which led up to it.

Cardinal Consalvi said one day to Niebuhr, referring to the designs of the Roman Curia, " The desired result is not to be reached directly by way of the *Corso ;* it can only be arrived at by oblique paths." The able counsellor of Pius VII. characterised in these words the proceedings of the Curia up to the time of Pius IX. During the last twenty years, it has been able to cast aside concealment and *finesse*, and to advance boldly by the *Corso*, as by a new Appian way. Recent documents throw a clear light upon these tactics of the leaders of the Ultramontane party in both phases—first that of intrigue, and next of bold and triumphant advance. The excellent book published by M. Friedrich, of

Munich, the eminent disciple of Döllinger, on the history of the preparation of the Council, places within our reach abundant and reliable sources of information, by means of which we may trace the progress of one of the most astonishing enterprises of the papacy, one which has succeeded in transforming, in less than a century, the spirit and the institutions of a Church distinguished above all others for its Conservatism.[1]

This is the climax of the drama of the age, for the close of the century will be occupied with conflicts between the Church and the State, arising out of this dangerous triumph. The death of Pius IX., after he had accomplished this great work, was but an unimportant incident. It is of great moment for the representatives of modern society to know the adversary they have to contend with. No power has understood better than the Roman Curia how to bend to the necessities of the time, without renouncing its principle, and how to make itself all things to all men, while remaining really unchanged. At one time it appears as the avowed ally of the *ancien regime*, the moving genius of the Holy Alliance; at

---

[1] "Geschichte des Vatikanischen Konzils," by J. Friedrich. See also "L'État Moderne et l'Église Catholique en Allemagne," by Ernest Stroehlin; also M. Geffcken's able work, "Staat und Kirche in ihrem Verhältniss entwickelt." I have made use of many other works referring to the Council, which I need not enumerate.

another it apparently espouses democracy, adopts its methods and maxims, and learns to assail the Revolution with its own weapons. Now the Roman party is humble, pliant—*serpit humi;* it twines round its foe rather than strikes at it, because it feels itself suspected and detested; again it commands, threatens, inflames popular passion, or lets itself be borne along by the strong waves of an insensate reaction. *Patiens quia æturnus.* If its webs break away from one point, it immediately gathers up the broken threads and fastens them elsewhere. The State is far less wary; after resisting vehemently the encroachments of the Church, it allows itself to be diverted and surprised. Its adversary never slumbers or sleeps; it takes advantage of an unguarded moment on the part of a Minister, to slip into the nomination papers of a bishop, an equivocal clause infringing the civil rights. The reader needs to have before his eyes a comprehensive picture, or a powerful *resumé* of all the proceedings of the ecclesiastical policy, in order to form any idea of the subtlety with which all has been contrived to ensure success.

I.

At the close of the eighteenth century, the Catholic Church was in great part freed from Ultramontane influences. In the principal countries of Europe the civil power had offered a steady opposition to it, and one Pope had even gone so far as to condemn the Society of Jesus. That society had found itself compelled to quit France, though it had endeavoured to bend before the storm. There were even a certain number of its members who, hoping to save their order, gave their adherence to the declaration of 1682. It is said that the unhappy signataries affected not to read the document which was presented to them, and asked with an air of indifference, "if there was anything more to sign." "Yes," was the answer, "there is still the Koran, but we have not a copy at hand." Nothing could show more clearly how thoroughly humiliated were these defenders to the death of the Holy See. Expelled from France and Spain, their system was completely broken up in Austria and in Italy by Joseph II., who established not only the independence but the autocracy of the State in religious matters. The old French clergy, on emerging from the vortex of the Revolution, had not become Ultramontane, though they had nobly resisted the schism organised by the civil constitution of the clergy. They remained, for the most part, attached to that modified Gallicanism which gave them a peculiar character, since its close connection with the old royal family and the old *noblesse* was not compatible with the abandonment of the maxims of Old France. We have all known representatives and descendants of this distinguished body of the clergy, whom misfortune and persecution had only purified and ennobled.

There was about them an air of priestly gravity, and of dignity without arrogance, which marked them out from all their brethren. They bore no resemblance to the new generation, so degraded by servitude that they do not shrink from sullying with sacrilegious fingers the sacred memory of Bossuet. We have clear proof of the predominance of Gallican ideas in the Catholic Church forty years ago, in the language used in 1829 by the Vicars Apostolic of Great Britain, before the great Parliamentary Commission charged with preparing the abolition of the laws restricting their liberties. They affirmed upon oath "that the infallibility of the Pope is not an article of faith."[1] The doctrine of infallibility was, indeed, positively denied in the catechisms and theological manuals in use at that time.

It is, then, a fact capable of proof, that the prevailing doctrine of European Catholicism at the commencement of the century, was not Ultramontanism. We remember the resistance offered to it by the Government of the Restoration, in spite of the dangerous favours lavished by that Government on the Church. Half a century has barely passed away, and all is changed; the preponderating influence is everywhere in the hands of the Roman party. It is important for us to understand how this change has been effected, and to see by what a series of efforts,

---

[1] "The Vatican Decrees," &c., by W. E. Gladstone, p. 36.

and by what pressure on public opinion, the Roman Curia has attained its ends.

We have to observe, first of all, that it found facilities not hitherto enjoyed, in the state of men's minds at the close of the French Revolution. By the mere fact that the civil power had not only renounced its *rôle* of protector of the Church, but had also lifted up its arm against it in violent and unjust persecutions, the Church was led to seek the support of the Holy See. It had no longer to deal with an orthodox royalty which was always ready to defend it, and to bestow endless favours in return for its submission. Now that the old institutions had fallen, all their abuses were forgotten; a veil of poetry was thrown over their ruins. The soul, wearied with so many shocks, and with the tears and blood of the days of the Revolution, turned with relief to the past, and idealised it. Thus arose that romantic school, enamoured of everything mediæval, which made the fortune of the *Génie du Christianisme*, and which under Schlegel and Görres founded the Munich School, which exercised a great influence over an emasculated generation, and created a strong reaction against the liberal idea of the modern State.

The Roman Curia was not satisfied with these general influences favourable to its views. It had a definite plan, and its skill was exercised in bringing every influence to bear upon it. It knew how to take advantage of circumstances, and how to call them forth. Its action was twofold—by turns political and moral; sometimes the Roman Curia would negotiate with the powers; sometimes it would endeavour to create an opinion favourable to itself.

The Concordats which have been concluded in our time between the Holy See and the various Governments, have almost always been used by the papacy to secure great and important advantages; for, as they were negotiated generally with powers having but a slight acquaintance with ecclesiastical affairs, and averse, either from pride or from jealousy of their own authority, from consulting the national episcopate, the papacy took large advantage of their ignorance. This statement may perhaps seem surprising, at a time when the Concordat is regarded in France as the great bulwark against the encroachments of the clergy; but the explanation of this is that the Concordat is generally confounded with the legislation of Germinal Year X., which the First Consul drew up entirely by himself, without having consulted the Holy Father on this *postscriptum*, in which he embodied all his own views, with very little regard to the spiritual independence. To this he put his signature. The Pope had only consented to the Concordat, and the few concessions which he had made touching the unity of religion and the temporalities of the Church, were largely counterbalanced by the right he had obtained for the first time, of dismissing bishops—a right altogether at variance with the ancient constitution of the Church, which was based upon the Divine institution of the episcopate. It was the First Consul who had urged him to reduce the number of the dioceses. He showed himself by this act a strange disciple of Bossuet, whose name was perpetually on his lips. "It was the author of the Concordat," said Lamennais in 1819, "who made the Pope the supreme head of the pastoral order, and the source of the jurisdiction of the Church." The Concordat concluded with the King of Prussia in 1812, secured enormous advantages to the Court of Rome; the Concordats signed in 1865 by the Grand Duke of Baden and the King of Würtemburg went so far in this direction that they were met with invincible opposition in the parliaments of the two countries.

The Roman Curia has had to treat not only with princes, but with that modern democracy which can but excite its antipathy. Its great art has been to derive advantage from it even while condemning it, by turning to its own account the liberal institutions which had triumphed in spite of papal resistance.

The papacy formally anathematised these institutions in principle, as when Gregory XVI. condemned, in the Encyclical of 1833, the doctrines of "L'Avenir" as presented by Lamennais, their fervid apostle; but it deemed it well afterwards to observe a prudent silence, in order that its champions might secure to themselves again, under the broad shield of liberty, immunities which they could no longer hold as privileges. It was quite willing that its partisans should assume for a time the garb of sincere Liberals, since this gave more potency to their claims. Ultramontanism, under their advocacy, appeared shorn of all that could be antipathetic to the modern mind, and was represented as the guarantee of religious liberty, in opposition to the injurious pretensions of the State. We know with what noble eloquence and courageous loyality, Lacordaire and Montalembert played their part, the former in his white Dominican robe at Notre Dame, the latter from the tribune of the Chamber of Peers. The result of this brilliant campaign was the too famous law of 1851, giving liberty of teaching, which introduced the episcopate into the Superior Council of Public Instruction, handed over in great part primary education to the religious bodies, and practically removed the barriers to the re-establishment of the religious orders, foremost among whom came the Jesuits.

After the establishment of the Second Empire all was changed. The Ultramontane party, which until then had appeared united in its Liberal demonstrations, suddenly broke up into two factions at deadly warfare with each other. On the one hand were the Ultramontane Liberals, who continued to seek to reconcile Catholicism with modern liberties; on the other hand was a phalanx of Ultramontanes, the sworn enemies of all liberties except their own.

These, after hailing with acclamation the Dictatorship of December 2nd, shook off the dust of their feet against the whole social system created by the Revolution. For a long time Liberal Catholicism remained in the ascendant. It had in its favour the services it had rendered, and the patriotic attitude it had assumed towards the personal power. It was none the less doomed to defeat; for by exalting the authority of the Pope it had sealed its own sentence. When Montalembert ventured to vindicate religious liberty at the Congress of Malines, as a principle, and not merely as a concession to the exigencies of the times, the Encyclical of 1864 and the Syllabus were brought to bear upon him and upon his school, with all their crushing weight.

Ultramontanism had its reckoning with the Liberals of its party, after making use of them for its own purposes. Montalembert and Lacordaire both died, bitterly lamenting that all the devotion, zeal and talent they had expended in the cause of religion, had only ended in the destruction of liberty. They had been made tools of by a hand stronger than their own.

We know with what consummate art the Belgian Ultramontanes contrived to use liberty as a means of securing to themselves all the posts of power, till the time came when they could turn round and say: "The house is ours; it is for you to begone."

They were powerfully aided in their work by the

sincere Liberals among them who represented the school of "L'Avenir." Nowhere have these tactics been more successfully employed than in Germany. Wise and moderate views had gained a great ascendancy there at the commencement of the century, owing to the remarkable development of true scientific culture in some of the universities, beyond the narrow precincts of the seminaries. Bishops like Dalberg of Mayence and Wissemberg of Constance, there represented the tradition of the great Gallican Councils. Thoughtful statesmen imbued with the modern spirit, like Count Montgelas, the able Bavarian Minister, had firmly maintained the rights of the State. It had been difficult to assail their position in ordinary times; the formidable agitation which broke out in 1848 presented a more favourable opportunity for successfully urging the claims of Ultramontanism. The heads of the party did not hesitate a moment to throw themselves into the democratic movement which led to the Frankfort Parliament. There they made common cause with the advanced Left, asking, as the people's representatives, the entire separation of the Church from the State, and endeavouring to place the liberties which alone they had at heart, under the shelter of the general liberties claimed by the democrats. They hoped thus to checkmate the State, and to secure the interests of religion. "Let the civil power," said the Archbishop of Cologne to his clergy, " still lend us its support, but not fetter us any further in the fulfilment of our mission. Let us have no more *placets*, no more appeals against abuses, no more nominations to benefices, no more lay schools." A petition, to which were affixed more than 300,000 signatures, besought the Frankfort Parliament to put the Church again under the common law. The orators of the party got themselves applauded by the most advanced members, and secured by a large majority the all but absolute liberty of the Church, as one of the fundamental articles of the constitution of the Empire. It is true that they could not prevent the Parliament from secularising the schools and rendering civil marriage obligatory; hence the Roman party faced round with incredible rapidity; and while claiming to keep what they had gained, took advantage of the reaction that had set in in Bavaria, to demand from the Congress of Würzburg the recension of the few clauses favourable to the civil power, that had been passed at Frankfort. The Roman party has never ceased from that time to play the same double game in every one of the German States.

In vain at an assembly convoked at Durlach, in the Grand Duchy of Baden, to resist these encroachments, did the celebrated Hausser, a man equally distinguished as a historian and a politician, denounce the Ultramontane proceedings in the following words: "I know too well that the liberty of the Church is the illusive watchword beneath which lies the daring determination to drag back the

State, if possible, into its former state of servitude. Ultramontane liberty is not liberty for the State, but the subordination of the State to the Church." In spite of all this, the extreme party continued its noisy, hypocritical demonstrations in favour of democracy. In the very same Duchy of Baden, in 1869, it gave its hand to the most advanced democrats, and clamoured with them for immediate universal suffrage, as the inalienable right of the people. "The needs of the age," said Canon Lasker, "are in accordance with the designs of Providence." "Society will never be saved," exclaims another fanatic of the same party, "but by the alliance of Christianity with democracy."

The same tactics were pursued in Würtemburg, with this difference—that, at the very moment when the Ultramontanes were making a compact with the Republicans, they were also practising secretly with the opposite party. All their sympathies were really in this direction, for while they flattered the democracy, they hated it at heart, and utterly repudiated its essential principle, which is that sovereignty is conferred by the people, instead of having its seat on the cloudy heights of a divine right.

The proceedings of the Ultramontanes in Switzerland in 1848 form one of the most curious episodes of this crusade. They had chosen the canton of Lucerne as their battle-field; their chief aim was to obtain from the Great Council the reintegration of the

Jesuits, in order that the instruction of the people might be handed over to them. The task was a difficult one, for they had not only to contend with local obstacles, but also to enter into conflict with most of the confederated cantons. In relation to the incidents of this struggle, we have documentary authority which cannot be disputed, namely, the report of the ecclesiastical condition of Switzerland presented by Bishop Luchet, the Pope's envoy extraordinary. From this we learn that Ultramontane fanaticism would not bow even to the sovereignty of the Holy Father, when it received from Rome counsels of prudence and moderation. It was by unscrupulously stirring up the popular passions that the friends of the Jesuits, headed by Councillor Leu (who was afterwards assassinated), obtained a favourable vote from the Great Council, with this modifying clause—that the State reserved to itself the right of inspecting the schools ; a condition nullified at the same time that it was given by a secret clause, in which the reverend fathers declared that they could not in any way infringe the rules of their order. The ratification of the people was secured by means of a succession of open-air meetings, at which the new leaguers gave impassioned harangues, blending threats of hell with inflammatory appeals to the populace. The episcopate had not power to resist, and was forced to yield to the pressure of misguided popular opinion. The attitude of the Protestant cantons presaged a fearful civil war. The venerable Metternich counselled adjournment; the Nuncios of Lucerne and of Paris gave the same advice, which was confirmed by the Court of Rome. The Ultramontane agitators ventured to intercept the warnings of the Holy Father. The Nuncio of Lucerne could not restrain his indignation when he heard Father Roth, the superior of the Jesuits in the canton, declare that civil war did not terrify him. "What!" exclaimed the Roman prelate. "The Church bids us ask in its prayers to be delivered from famine, from pestilence, and from war, and here is a priest who clamours for war!" War did, in fact, break out—that impious war which pitted against each other Protestant and Catholic Switzerland. If it was promptly brought to an end, thanks to the clever manœuvres of an able and humane general, it was nevertheless a great crime, for which those fanatics are responsible who made the crucifix a firebrand to kindle civil disorder.

The war of the Sunderbund showed to what lengths this blending of fanaticism with democracy might lead, creating a new order of Jacobins, who could don the *bonnet rouge* without doffing the frock.

II.

The Ultramontane school was not content with turning the general liberties to the account of its own policy. When it failed to wring from the modern governments the concessions it desired, it made use of the democratic element in another way. It borrowed democratic methods of propagandism, when it no longer thought it necessary to swell the ravings of militant radicalism. In old Europe the Ultramontane school endeavoured to win over the minds of men, by learned or subtle dissertations; it flung dusty folios at the heads of its adversaries, and only the erudite could take part in the discussion. But in our day, doctrines the most hostile to modern society, are defended with the lightest weapons by daring innovators. The dust of the school is shaken off; and St. Thomas, broken up into small portions and presented in the form of popular pamphlets, is made singularly light reading. While heartily abusing the liberty of the press—which in *ex-cathedrâ* parlance is called a pest—the Ultramontanes nevertheless make large use of this powerful lever of public opinion. Ultramontanism has its irritating, sardonic press, ever ready to propagate scandal, seasoning its very theological treatises with the coarsest allusions, and endeavouring to crush its adversaries by the pitiless ridicule poured upon them. These proceedings have called forth earnest protests on the part of thoughtful men, who deem that religious discussion should be carried on seriously, and at the very least honestly. Bishops, and the learned and eloquent guardians of the traditions of the dignity and high culture of the Church, have attempted to stem the torrent, but in vain; they have only had to retreat, bespattered with foam, and having drawn down upon themselves the displeasure of Rome. Lacordaire wrote to Madame Swetchine : "I am willing to take my place at the feet of the successors of the apostles, but not at the feet of a band of scoffers, who bring everything to the tribunal of their satirical talent." Alas! the Ultramontane press rendered greater services to the school which sought to bring all into a common bondage, than did a noble spirit like Lacordaire, of whom Lambruschini once said : "He is another Lamennais." All possible encouragement from high quarters was given to this rabid journalism, of which all noble minds among the Catholics were heartily ashamed, and which was a disgrace to our common humanity. Words of approbation were followed by papal briefs. The *Civiltà Cattolica*, the organ of the Society of Jesus, was formally recognised in a Roman congregation. An agency for Catholic journals was founded in Rome, and more than two hundred daily and weekly papers were employed to disseminate sound doctrine and to dictate to the dioceses. Ultramontane journalism has created a sort of third order of a new kind. Laymen in short frocks, and with their sleeves tucked up, are seen entering like pugilists into ecclesiastical discussions, and laying down the law for the bishops, whose remonstrances receive no reply. Mgr. Dupanloup wasted his eloquence on this subject. The tribunes of the altar carried the day against the prelates, for they used all the means which current polemics put within their reach, to overthrow those whom they could not convince. It must not be forgotten that the programme of the last Council was prepared in the offices of the *Civiltà Cattolica*, and propagated by the Ultramontane press, which exerted an irresistible influence over public opinion.

One of the great engines of democratic propagandism is association, which is practised on a large scale, and fostered by noisy meetings. Congresses of all sorts have been much facilitated by the multiplication of rapid modes of communication. The school which is most averse to modern progress has not disdained to use these inventions of the devil, and has utilised them to its own advantage, perhaps more largely than any other party. There is no more effectual means of producing an agitation, and of overcoming inconvenient objections, especially those which are based on science or conscience, than these irregular gatherings, in which the voting is not determined by any fixed rule. It is quite easy to work up assemblies like these to a white heat, to an almost delirious fanaticism, and then to make use of them to bring pressure to bear on the regular authorities of the Church. This was attempted by the Ultramontane party in Switzerland and in Germany. The famous Association, known as the "Pius Verein," founded at Mayence, and recognised by Pius IX. in 1849, without any previous sanction from the German episcopate, at once raised the standard of the Ultramontane crusade. Under the direction of laymen, as fanatic as they were ignorant, and without any competence to resolve questions of dogma or of discipline, it yet exerted a widespread and fatal influence. Assembling at regular periods in the great Catholic centres of Germany, it was not inactive in the interval; and by its local associations for works of charity, for teaching, for the cultivation of religious art, and the dissemination through the press of right views, it cast around the Church a network so close, that it was impossible to break it. The intimidated bishops were obliged, though often reluctantly, to submit to its will, and thus it created an irresistible current of opinion in support of its favourite doctrines. Enlightened and wise men, like Hirscher, remonstrated in vain against these irregular, incompetent assemblies, which set at nought all constituted authorities in their gross adulation of the papacy, and were enemies alike of science and of true piety. Was it not their avowed design to form an international federation, which should cast at the feet of the Holy See the Churches of all countries, confounding them in one common servility? The voice of the great publicist was wasted on the desert air. The great jubilee of Boniface, which was celebrated with extraordinary pomp at Mayence, on the 14th December, 1854, raised the agitation to a climax. Switzerland, in its turn, had its "Pius Verein." At the same time

France was preparing to found Theological Committees, and to multiply their congresses, which have become, as we know, an important feature in the Ultramontane organisation.

The Catholic Working Men's Clubs, the object of which is more political than religious, are a powerful weapon in the hands of the same party for attacking modern society, which it would fain (to use the language of one of its lay leaders) conduct to a civil burial.

III.

Hitherto we have been looking only at the volunteers of Ultramontanism, its irregular forces which have succeeded in leading on the regular army. It is time now that we turned to the authorised heads of the Ultramontane school, who are no other than the heads of the Catholic hierarchy itself in its own metropolis. These were impatient to be no longer a school of disputed authority, but to become the Church itself, and so advance their pretensions as irrefragable claims. Hence their one object was to secure the proclamation of the dogma of infallibility. Until this was done their edifice lacked its keystone. In reality, that which they aimed at was the abolition of all liberty, of every right and privilege which could counterbalance or control the central power. For this purpose it was necessary to sacrifice all secondary authority for the benefit of the papacy, to destroy the last vestiges of national Churches, and especially to reduce the episcopate to an entirely subordinate position.

There could be no better way of doing this than a return to the old, sure method of despots who understood their business—the method which the Cæsars had so cunningly used in Rome, in sacrificing the patricians to the plebs. Modern Ultramontanism closely followed their example, not scorning to have recourse to the low but effective policy described in the famous words: "*Panem et circenses.*" We would be very careful not to seem to say anything against the bread of charity; that is sacred, if only it be broken to all the hungry, and not made the price for which they are to sell their consciences. As to the *circenses*—the great representations which appeal to the eye—have they not been lavishly provided for the Catholic masses, in those pilgrimages to miraculous caves, in which the fervour of the devotees is fed by fanatic hymns, and by feverish legends of virgins who see visions and utter infantile oracles? The character thus impressed during the last few years on popular devotion has done much to develop Ultramontane fanaticism. There would almost seem to arise from the lips of this fanatic host, the materialistic prayer of ancient Israel to Moses: "Make us gods to go before us." The tangible divinity thus sought has been given in the form of the infallible Pope. But a mere popular movement would not suffice for his deification. It was needful that the old institutions should be abolished, in order that an all-absorbing centralisation should be set up. Until our day, Catholicism, while preserving its unity, had still granted a certain latitude to national Churches. They had their general assemblies or Councils, their liturgy, and an episcopate which reconciled subordination to the papacy, with a measure of independence and an authority that made itself felt and respected. Now all this is changed.

We cannot follow out in detail the steps taken by the Roman policy to reach this important result, which is equivalent to nothing less than a revolution in the institutions of the Church. The Curia contrived to substitute in all the countries of Europe, mere provincial Councils for the old national Councils which have everywhere fallen into disuse. It was very easy to over-rule these provincial Councils and to lead them to vote in the desired direction, all the more that a special congregation was constituted at Rome for the purpose, which took upon itself to arrange the business of these Councils, and even to modify their resolutions, so that they were made, without their own consent, to acquiesce in the opinion of the infallible pontiff. It is easy to arrive at an understanding in a dialogue, in which the interlocutor and the respondent are one and the same. The Roman Curia was equally successful on the question of liturgies. This was of the utmost importance to it, for it would be impossible to exaggerate the influence of liturgies, which give to piety its popular form, surrounding it with a moral atmosphere which it is unable to resist. In France the Roman Curia was ably served by the celebrated Dom Guéranger, to whom we owe the restoration of the Benedictine order. Pius IX. devoted his Encyclical of 1853 to this cause, which he rightly had at heart, and the Curia has recently succeeded, in spite of prolonged resistance, in substituting everywhere the Roman liturgy for the beautiful liturgy of the Church of France, which was not defaced by the ridiculous fables of Italian bigotry. Lacordaire said bitterly of this daring attempt, even before it had succeeded : " It is a cruel insult to a Church which has never severed itself from the general community."

After gaining a complete ascendancy over the episcopal assemblies, it was not difficult to bring the bishops separately into submission. This was quickly done. The Roman party exalted to the clouds the prelates who boldly resisted the civil power, even when their conduct was most reckless and ill advised. When their extravagancies drew down the just vengeance of the State, they were proclaimed martyrs. The famous Archbishop of Cologne, Mgr. Von Droste-Vischering, who compelled the Prussian Government to deviate from its long course of toleration, by his unjustifiable resistance to every measure of conciliation in the case of mixed marriages, and by his irritating demeanour, was placed on a par with the first Christian confessors of the faith. Archbishop

Vicari, of Fribourg, was declared in his lifetime worthy of canonisation, for having disturbed the Grand Duchy of Baden by his imprudent proceedings. To violate the laws of the State is a merit in the eyes of the Roman party. Woe to the bishop who does not bend under the yoke, and who dares to offer any opposition to the *fiat* of the Curia. The illustrious Wissemberg knew something of this in his diocese of Constance, where he had secured universal respect by his toleration, his piety, his learning, and his noble liberality. His nomination as bishop was not confirmed; he died after having had the sorrow of seeing his diocese broken up, in order that Catholic Switzerland might be freed from an influence so much dreaded as his. Subsequently the liberal and learned school of Munich was loaded with outrages. Cardinal Andrea, for having desired to prolong his stay there, was severely condemned in a pontifical brief, which declared that the Pope had the power of governing directly all the dioceses. The Archbishop of Paris, Mgr. Darboy, complained to Rome of the denunciations to which he was subjected by his subordinates; he was even obliged in one case to adopt a measure of very mild discipline. The Holy See openly censured him, thus humbling him before all his clergy. The Bishops of Marseilles and of Chalon were severely blamed for showing some Gallican proclivities. The papacy made it evident on every opportunity, that it intended to have at the head of the dioceses, not bishops, but mere ecclesiastical prefects, whose office was simply to transmit the papal behests.

The Ultramontane party looks with suspicion on men of science. It never rested till it had thrown discredit on the teaching of theology in the German Universities. What it required was the hotbed of a seminary closed against general culture, and it had no confidence in any colleges which were not under its own special supervision. Hence every effort was made to induce young men preparing for the clerical office, to attend the famous Roman College, which it supplemented by the Germanic College, in which the same doctrines were instilled. "Distrust learned men," said one of the leaders of Ultramontanism. Nor was it deemed enough to seek to inspire distrust; scholars were condemned when, without going beyond the bounds of orthodoxy, they manifested some independence of spirit, like Dr. Hermes at Cologne, and Dr. Döllinger at Munich. All that was foreign to the scholarship of mediæval times, all that revealed some development of the philosophic spirit, though it might be in the service of accepted truths, was regarded as dangerous. Ignorance became increasingly a title to favour, and to the old theological virtues was added a new virtue, which consisted in ignorance of theology. How many fine intellects may have groaned and suffered under this cruel pressure! How many noble hearts may have bled in secret, as they saw the babblings of ignorance accepted as the wisdom of God, and all original development of religious thought, in an age of research like this, repressed by a petty and jealous authority! The true martyrs of our time are not the imprudent agitators who, under a government so moderate as that of Germany before its Prussian unification, were punished for having disturbed civil order by their fanaticism; they are such men as Gratry, Lacordaire, Döllinger, Hæfel, all misunderstood by the Church to which they were devoted, all regarded with suspicion, if not treated with severity, because they would not cringe with the ignorant multitude, or with the men of servile soul in high positions who only rise by flattery. Theirs was a very poignant suffering, more than once involuntarily betrayed.

It was not enough to depreciate the science of the day; it was needful also to efface from the documents of the past, everything that was at variance with the new doctrine, the triumph of which the papal party was bent on securing. The scribes of the Curia had always shown singular audacity in forging documents in support of their favourite theories. The False Decretals had shown how far they would venture in this sort of historic fraud. Much was said at the time of the Council, of their manipulations of the Roman Breviary, in the attempt to efface from the original text the name of Pope Honorius, who was there distinctly described as a heretic. It was on this occasion that Father

Gratry denounced, with such eloquent indignation, this interpolating and mendacious school, exclaiming, "*Indiget Deus mendacio vestro!* This habit of using a dishonest apology, is one of the causes of our decadence in modern times. So soon as mankind perceives in an apostle the faintest trace of cunning or duplicity, it turns away disgusted. Is not the time then come, in this age of publicity, in which everything is known and spread abroad, to reject with scorn the frauds, interpolations, and mutilations, which liars and falsifiers of documents—our most cruel enemies —have introduced into the archives of the Church? I have been long before I could bring myself to believe in the existence among us, of this apology of ignorance, of blindness, of dubious or even of bad faith, which seeks an end in the goodness and truth of which it believes, but in order to reach it has recourse to fraud and to the fabrication of false documents."[1] We shall be told that Father Gratry made his submission to the Council. We admit it; but has he therefore retracted his severe diatribe against the school of interpolation and historic falsehood? He never thought that the infallibility of the Holy Father implied the impeccability of Roman scribes. Friederich gives overwhelming evidence of the manipulations to which they have subjected, not only the old writers, whom the congregation of the Index assumed the

---

[1] Letter to the Bishop of Mechlin, by Father Gratry, p. 160.

right to correct, but also catechisms and theological manuals long in use, even those which bore the authors' names, like that of Bailly. No scruple has been shown in substituting for declarations of a decided Gallican character, some of the most daring formularies of Ultramontanism.

The attempt at interpolation and falsification is, however, a very futile one; there still remain too large a number of passages which cannot be so manipulated. Nor is it possible to efface the general tradition of the Church, and all the imperishable monuments of its glorious past. The great book of history cannot be completely falsified. If we adhere to the old notion of dogmatic authority, as formulated by Vincent de Lérins, according to which a doctrine is only to be regarded as true if it has been believed always, everywhere, and by every one in the Church—*ab omnibus, ubique et semper*—then the favourite doctrines of the Roman party are doomed, for not one of them can claim universal assent. Further, if all depends on the verification of tradition, the Councils assume very grave importance, since they alone are capable of verifying it by means of the bishops, who are, as it were, the witnesses of the universal Church, to declare that which has been the object of its constant faith. The Roman system crumbles to its base, if we admit the theory of tradition now under discussion; but this was unquestionably the *raison d'être* of general Councils in the past. Hence the Roman party has endeavoured, with consummate art and with extraordinary subtlety, to remove this idea. Two French Ultramontane theologians—Donnet and Gousset—had already prepared the way for the new theory, by placing on a par with tradition, as a criterion of the truth of a doctrine, the unanimity of the bishops of the day. This unanimity is all the more easy to secure since the silence of the episcopate is taken for consent, and every brief which is not protested is regarded as accepted. It was the Jesuit Perrone, the classic theologian of the present Curia, who had the honour of inventing a formula destined to be so useful. According to him, we must be on our guard against supposing that tradition is only to be found in the positive texts of Scripture, or of the Fathers; it may also be implicitly contained therein. A few vague indications suffice to denote it, especially if we do not neglect the spontaneous manifestations of religious feeling in the worship, the liturgy, and the literature of asceticism. An isolated contradiction proves nothing, for it is to the general sentiment of the Church that our appeal must be made. And where does this general sentiment express itself more forcibly than in the unanimous testimony of the living Church? Under the influence of the Divine Spirit it raises from obscurity some doctrine which had lain, as it were, buried in the tradition. By bringing it to light, the living Church proves at the same time its antiquity, so that we are saved from all the difficulties that a critical examination of the text might present. Thus is fulfilled the desire of Cardinal Manning, that the Council should shake off the trammels of history. It may indeed be said that history is cast aside by this new definition of tradition, which gives *carte blanche* to all the wildest innovations, provided they secure the assent of a servile episcopate. In truth, this theory of tradition was the most revolutionary system imaginable, for it gave unlimited scope to an arbitrary dogmatism. This assent of the bench of bishops was nothing else than universal suffrage without independence, carried on in the dark by an absolute power, intoxicated with the incense of idolatry. Thus the vaulting ambition of the hierarchy has overleaped itself, and it has become the mere stepping-stone of an autocracy.

IV.

Throughout the whole skilful policy of the Roman Curia, we recognise the influence of that famous school which, for three centuries, has contrived to combine the most rigid principles of absolute authority, with the utmost suppleness in the adaptation of means to ends. The Jesuit has governed the Church for more than half a century. He would not, however, left to himself, have so rapidly attained his end, but he had the good fortune to find the very Pope he needed to strike the great blow; and from that time it has been no longer necessary for him to advance, as Consalvi said, by oblique paths. He can march boldly, with head erect, along the Corso.

We would speak with the utmost respect of the old Pope who played the principal part in this triumphant campaign of Ultramontanism. Fully convinced of his mission, he believed himself called to be the instrument of God to assure the triumph of His cause, by consecrating, in his own person, papal infallibility. Rising above all narrow and petty ambition, animated by an enthusiasm which recognised no obstacle and could brook no delay, he regarded his own elevation as a duty, and treated as impious rebellion all resistance to his deification. That which in another would have been fanatic pride, was in him the fervour of piety. Ignorant of theology, he was not stumbled by any historic difficulties derived from the tradition of the early Church. The prudence which calculates the perils of an immediate decision would have seemed to him the abandonment of his faith in God—that is, in himself; for he never ceased to regard himself as the organ of absolute truth. His virtues, worthy of all respect, the majesty of his language rising sometimes almost to an inspired tone, his noble countenance beneath snowy locks—all these things combined to increase his ascendancy. Pius IX. was all the more ardent in his opposition to modern ideas, because at the commencement of his reign he had given them some encouragement. It seemed as if in him the liberal Catholicism of Lacordaire and Montalembert had received the tiara, and men thought that the reconciliation between the Church and the laity would soon be accomplished. But from the time of his exile in Gaëta, Pius IX. belonged unreservedly to the extreme party, and the Jesuits whom he had expelled were henceforth his counsellors and guides. He became more and more convinced of his Divine mission. The *Civiltà Cattolica* recalled complacently the predictions uttered with regard to him by Anna Maria Taigi, a holy woman universally revered in Rome, who declared before her death that he would be the Pope chosen to restore the Church. The Virgin of La Salette, whose apparition was declared at Rome to be genuine, proclaimed the new dogma. The growing idolatry of which Pius IX. was the object, made him believe that he could venture anything. Had not his name been put in the place of the name of God in a hymn, to the great indignation of Mgr. Dupanloup? A French Cardinal had called him "the incarnation of the authority of Christ." The *Civiltà Cattolica* went so far as to declare that the Word thought through him. He heard himself proclaimed Divine till he believed it, and did not fear to be identified with Christ. *La tradition c'est moi*, he said to those who had the indiscretion to appeal to history. In such a state of mind, he could not hesitate to employ decisive means to arrive at the definition of the new dogma. His long reign enabled him to remodel almost entirely the College of Cardinals and the Bench of Bishops, by nominating only declared adherents of the Ultramontane school. His briefs and sermons were powerful weapons against his opponents, who were intimidated by his *prestige* and authority. The Encyclical and the Syllabus of 1864 were the manifesto of triumphant Ultramontanism. It had already won one decisive victory in the great episcopal Assembly of 1854, which issued the proclamation of the Immaculate Conception. If M. Thiers could say after the review of Satory in January, 1851, *L'Empire est fait*, it might be said with equal truth, after this important act of the Council, that infallibility had gained the day. What was wanting to the elevation of the Holy Father above all Councils, when once he had been able without a Council, by a simple consultation with the bishops, to create a new dogma? This new dogma had done more than deify the Virgin; it had made a God upon earth. The Ultramontane party took advantage of this unexampled innovation, and deduced from the thing done, the right to do it. The great assembly of bishops convoked at Rome in 1864, hailed the Holy Father in language of such ardent adoration, that it lacked nothing but the precision of a formulary. In 1860, at the time of the celebration of the centenary of the martyrdom of St. Peter and St. Paul, the bishops responded in still larger numbers to the appeal of the Holy Father, who, after thanking them for having shown by their presence in Rome their filial subordination to the Holy See, announced to them the approaching Council. The address, which was drawn up in their name, and which passed without protestation, because it was imagined to be a matter of no consequence, since the address was not a doctrinal one, was dictated by devotees of the papacy, and contained homage, barely disguised under oratorical paraphrases, of the infallible Pope.

Even before they quitted Rome the bull convoking the Council was issued. The Roman Curia was careful to choose as advisers, only theologians, already pledged to extreme Ultramontane views, and for the most part obscure individuals. It refused the titulary bishops the right of being represented in Council, while it opened the doors to a thousand bishops of the Propaganda who had no dioceses. These docile creatures of the papacy assured it beforehand of a majority.

One is amazed, after such preliminaries, at the illusions by which the opponents of the new dogma still calmed their apprehensions. Those who had the good fortune to be at Rome in 1869, will never forget the extraordinary agitation of mind prevailing on the eve of the Vatican Council; it was more like the excitement in one of our political clubs at the opening of a critical session of parliament. The *salons* in which Ultramontane principles did not hold undisputed sway, re-echoed with animated discussions and passionate protestations against the extreme party, which they hoped yet to be able to restrain. We well remember the boldness of certain declarations, which would now greatly astonish those who then made them, and who have since done all in their power to obliterate them. "If the Council turns out badly, we will agitate for another," said a distinguished representative of the Catholic aristocracy, one evening in a large company. The women were not the least ardent supporters of the Left, in this Vatican Assembly, which had all the semblance of a real ecclesiastical parliament. The opposition had on its side men of science and distinction, who had rendered incomparable service to the Church, the very *élite* of the episcopate throughout the world. Its manifesto was contained in the last charge of the Bishop of Orleans, and in the resolution of the German bishops assembled at Fulda, to enter a prudent protest against the proclamation of the new dogma. The leading men among the German bishops appeared in the Roman *salons*. There was seen the noble face of Cardinal Schwartzenberg, who, having concluded the Austrian Concordat, had vowed never to do anything of the kind again. The Hungarian bishops, distinguished for their courage and eloquence, excited much curious interest. Catholic England had only sent extreme Ultramontanes to sit in the Council. It had, however, in Rome one of the most generous representatives of liberal Catholicism—Lord Acton—whom Mr. Gladstone had just raised to the peerage. He displayed great activity in the service of his cause, and was very hopeful, if not of securing its triumph, at least of averting a decisive defeat. All these hopes were vain; the whole opposition was to fail miserably, without having succeeded in coming even to a serious encounter; for, as the Jesuit Perrone has said very candidly, "All was ready, and nothing was wanting but the solemn proclamation of July 18, 1870."

Must we suppose that the proclamation of the new dogma will really be accepted by Catholicism as a final solution? We think not. We know that beneath the unreal appearance of unity, there are many consciences suffering and protesting in silence. There have been submissions, which have cost the lives of the noble thinkers who bowed beneath the arm of authority, because they were not ripe for the final decision which would have severed them from their Church. We are not building the smallest hope of a religious renovation upon the new Pope. He may be more moderate than Pius IX. in the form of his language and in his political attitude; but he cannot repudiate the heritage which has been transmitted to him. The fall of the temporal power will also have for a long time, the immediate effect of exalting Ultramontanism, as the destruction of the temple at Jerusalem enflamed Jewish fanaticism, which clung all the more closely to its religious idea, as that, in a manner, lost ground. If the extreme school should continue its development among the Catholics of to-day, it will in the end so isolate itself from modern society, that it will become a mere sect, considerable indeed in numbers, but cut off from the general life of modern humanity, resembling rather the Brahminism of India, which lives on solitary and irate, in view of a country renovated by civilisation. We believe, however, that in time the loss of the temporal power will have the effect of making it easier for hidden differences to manifest themselves, and thus in the end will hasten on the religious crisis which is brooding in silence to-day.

May governments not forget that they could not more surely strengthen Ultramontanism than by applying its own principles for its persecution. Every step beyond the legitimate defence of the rights of the State, will only involve the civil power in an interminable struggle, in which it must always fight at a disadvantage. Prussia and Switzerland know something of this. Let us keep the Catholic Church strictly within its own domain. Left to itself, it cannot escape that internal conflict which will either end in its transformation, or in the application of the extreme principles of Ultramontanism to modern society. Having reached this point, it will inevitably fall a prey to the avenging spirit of error born of its excesses, the unfailing Nemesis which tracks mankind upon its devious way.

STRAUSS AND VOLTAIRE.

STRAUSS AND VOLTAIRE.

A COMPARISON.

GERMANY has for the last few years devoted much attention to Voltaire. At the close of the eighteenth century its preference was for Rousseau, whose sentimental deism was thoroughly in harmony with the tendencies of German thought at the time, as expressed in the noble poetry of Schiller. At the present day Voltaire is in the ascendant. Goethe is known to have regarded him as representing the true type of the French mind. Dubois, Raymond, Grimm, Rosenkranz, have all recently offered criticisms of his literary and scientific work under various aspects. And lastly, the great master of the critical school, Strauss, has reared a monument to his memory, in the six lectures dedicated to the Princess Alice—a work in which he has displayed all his analytical talent and polemical acumen. It is at once obvious that Strauss did not intend this to be a mere literary study. This biography of Voltaire was a valuable weapon for him in the war to the death, which he had declared against the old ideas of religion and philosophy. He found that there was still much use to be made of his glorious predecessor. It seems to us very interesting to examine this judgment of Voltaire pronounced by Strauss, and to show how far the two writers differ from each other, while both appearing to serve the same cause ; how much generosity is hidden under the keen raillery of the older writer, in contrast to the implacable bitterness of the author of the "Leben Jesu."

We are fortunate enough to possess the philosophical testament of Strauss in his book, "Der alte und der neue Glaube." Only a few months ago there appeared as an introduction to a complete edition of his works, his literary autobiography, in which he gives us his own account of the development of his views.

Lastly, the very comprehensive work on "Strauss and his Times,"[1] published by Hausrath, supplies us with many valuable documents. We are thus in a position to draw a parallel, which is not merely fanciful, between these two great controversialists, since the sources of information about Voltaire are ample. The work of M. Desnoiresterres, on the Life and Times of Voltaire, is almost exhaustive. We shall not attempt to decide the comparative merits of the great

---

[1] David Friedrich Strauss, gesammelte Schriften, &c. Bonn. D. F. Strauss und die Theologie seiner Zeit. Von Dr. A. Hausrath, Heidelberg. 1876.

works of two such prolific writers, but merely endeavour to arrive at the leading thought of each. This will supply the key to the difference of the times in which they lived, and will enable us to appreciate the change that has passed over religious and philosophical controversy during the last century.

We have already said that Strauss loves and lauds in Voltaire that which, in his view, forms the unity of his life and of his work, namely, his vehement hostility to the religion of the past. He delights to picture him polishing his weapons for the attack, immediately on quitting the Jesuit college, where he had learnt to use them skilfully, if not in the defence of the faith; next putting a still keener edge to his wit in the society of the "Temple;" then, in his exile in London (whither his first escapades had driven him), imbibing from contact with English philosophy, that sincere but superficial deism which ever afterwards characterised him; and finally, returning matured, but with his youthful ardour unchilled, to engage along the whole line in what he calls the good warfare. All means subserve his ends: poetry, simple or severe, the pamphlet or the ode, science or history, all are engaged in a great pantomime, in which the actors utter the thoughts of their author, and reflect his genius and passion. Through all his restless wanderings over Europe, to-day the guest in a castle, tomorrow in an inn; passing from Nancy to Potsdam, from Potsdam to Geneva, and finally to Ferney, which becomes the holy city of the encyclopædists, he does not cease for a day to obey his ruling passion. It might be said that zeal for his cause consumed him. He himself gives us the epitome of his whole literary life in these daring words: "I am weary of hearing it said that a dozen men sufficed to establish Christianity. I long to show that one man is enough to destroy it."

Voltaire is not satisfied with giving currency to his ideas by his writings, which circulate all the more rapidly because they are proscribed, and have thus the inimitable flavour of forbidden fruit. He perpetually fans the zeal of those whom he calls his brethren; and his vast correspondence travels all over Europe animating and directing the conflict. He wrote as many letters as Calvin, who was also a great army leader. Both lives display the same ardent, universal activity.

With Voltaire passion does not exclude policy, and if he covets the apostolate, it is for the power it bestows, not for the martyr's palm. "I am a warm friend of truth," he writes to D'Alembert, "but none at all of martyrdom." It is true that martyrdom was no metaphor in the eighteenth century, and that the Parliament which had the writings of the philosophers burnt in the Place de Grève, was armed with dangerous powers against their persons. Voltaire did all that he could to escape perils which were not imaginary; he knew the Bastille, for he had lived in it. He first entered on a course of clever coquetry with the great ones of the world. In spite of the fascination of his graceful wit, he had small success with Louis XV., who must have been a prey to incurable *ennui*, since even Voltaire could not laugh him out of it. His indolent egoism shrank instinctively from this great agitator of ideas, and he felt vaguely that under his influence, the deluge which was to sweep away the old world might be hastened on so as to come in his days, after which everything was indifferent to him. The incomparable flatterer was more successful with Madame de Pompadour, and he might have safely counted on her protection but for the demon of epigram, which he could not resist. This weakness of his was so well known that some one wittily said that, in signing a compact with Voltaire, there should always be a provisional clause, "save and excepting his vagaries." The precaution was especially necessary in those unwritten compacts on which social relations rest. If nothing came to disturb the friendship which he always showed for the great Catherine, it was because he was never brought into too close contact with his idol, and the delicate incense which he burned to her always rose clear into the air, from a safe distance. We know how stormy were his relations with Frederic II. Strauss, as a good subject of the German Empire, and observing his oath of fidelity even in historical retrospect, lays most of the blame on the French philosopher. Nothing could be more unjust. Undoubtedly Frederic was thoroughly enamoured of the spirit of Voltaire; but how tyrannical, and at times even cruel, this passion was! How we feel always, as his victim said, that even in his sportive moods, the claw of the leopard was ready to rend him. He wished to make Voltaire a brilliant plaything, the first buffoon of a literary court, heavily paid, and to be dismissed at pleasure. He forgot that the buffoon was a rational being, the intellectual monarch of his age, and that he also had his claws, which could leave ineffaceable scars. "He is a terrible interlocutor," said Voltaire again, "who commands hundreds of thousands of men." Doubtless Voltaire had his faults; he was somewhat of a marplot in delicate matters; he did not sufficiently consider the susceptibilities of his formidable host; he pierced his friends with his keenest darts. But Strauss forgets the actual treason of which Frederic was guilty, when in order to bind Voltaire to himself by an enforced exile, he communicated to the French authorities a compromising paper of Voltaire's, which had been entrusted to him under seal of secresy.

In relation to the affair at Frankfort, the German writer also shows shameless partiality. The odious prosecution was, according to Strauss, a mere blunder chargeable to the stupidity of underlings. But he cannot erase those words of the Prussian Minister to the most brutal of these agents: "Fear nothing; all has been done by order of the king."

Nevertheless Frederic remains a great prince. His correspondence with Voltaire at the time of his most cruel reverses, when Voltaire asks him to intervene to make peace, redounds to the honour of both. They never ceased to have the liveliest relish for one another, while at the same time always on the verge of hatred. Let us admit, lastly, that Voltaire, in his correspondence with Frederic, understood how to keep up the dignity of a man of letters, and that his prudence had its limits. Strauss is fully in sympathy with him when he sees him displaying the craft of an old pupil of the Jesuits, in order to track his enemies. His grand device was perpetually to disavow the authorship of writings which were incontestably his own. "So soon as there is the slightest danger," he wrote to D'Alembert, "I implore you to warn me of it, that I may disavow the work in the public papers, with my accustomed candour and innocence."

When he was bent on forcing an entrance into the French Academy, he did not hesitate to take the following pledge: "If ever a page has been printed in my name, which could scandalise the priest of my parish, I am ready to tear it to pieces in his presence." Contemptible as this craft and disingenuousness seem to us, we must feel a still stronger indignation against that detestable system, which degraded thought by making it dangerous to give free expression to it.

We can make no allowance, however, for Voltaire's

spurious acts of devotion. When he cajoles the Holy Father into accepting the dedication of "Mahomet" to himself, this preliminary of infallibility only excites a laugh. But we feel very differently when we see the author of the "Dictionnaire Philosophique" partaking of the Communion. Strauss is very little shocked at this. He is, indeed, quite an advocate of mental reservations when they are useful. Before the brilliant success of his "Leben Jesu," when he was a country pastor, he quieted the scruples of his friend Moerklin, who found it somewhat embarrassing to clothe pantheism in Scripture phraseology, and to preach to the peasants of Wurtemburg the new faith under the name of the old Bible. One of Strauss' favourite heroes is Reimarius, whose biography he has written with his usual ability. This father of rationalism had given expression to his views in an anonymous manuscript which was only published after his death. In the meantime he appeared every Sunday with his white cravat, and in the costume of an ecclesiastical inspector, to listen with devout attention to orthodox sermons, at which he was laughing in his sleeve. Strauss is not at all offended at this excessive caution. His opinion is that "free-thinkers should avoid taking part in religious ceremonies, as far as they can do so without detriment to themselves and those who belong to them." This prudent morality reminds us of a famous saying about the angelic silence of the priest-philosophers who continue to perform mass.

One would hardly have expected to see the angels under such circumstances. To me it seems that the dignity of thought is much better represented by Pascal's saying : "Never have the saints been silent."

Strauss himself has been under no temptation to use such subterfuges. He has lived in a time of free thought and free speech, at least on all matters relating to metaphysics and criticism. This freedom is only restricted when politicians attempt to meddle with religion. The well-known caution given by the Lausanne magistrate to Voltaire, is still applicable in the middle of the nineteenth century. "It is a hundred times less dangerous," he said, "to attack the Holy Trinity than to criticise our authorities at Berne," or as we might say to-day, at Berlin and elsewhere. Strauss has observed this caution. Nothing could equal his theological radicalism except his political conservatism.

His "Leben Jesu" was allowed to circulate without interference, in spite of the grave attack it made upon the old beliefs ; for, as Edgar Quinet has shrewdly observed, Strauss, in this famous book, only acted the part of Anthony, drawing back Cæsar's robe to reveal all the thrusts that had been made upon him ; he only rent the veil beneath which, for more than half a century, German criticism had been striking at historic Christianity. For the first moment considerable excitement was created by the marvellous clearness of the exposition, and the art with which the writer brought into prominence the contradictions of the sacred narratives. At this time he was still fighting under the banner of Hegelian idealism; but gradually his thoughts emerged from this cloud which only veiled the great void. He ended by using to that God, who was a mere idea, the same language in which Voltaire had made Spinaye address his impersonal deity: "Between ourselves, I really believe you have no existence." The most absolute atheism is the issue of *the new faith*. After having formulated it, the old doctor intones his "*Nunc Dimittis.*" His version of Simeon's song may be given thus: "O great All! O vast Nature, from which I have driven out the Divine! Now mayest thou let thy servant depart in peace, for I have left nothing more to be destroyed." But he was mistaken. Positivism reproaches him, not without bitterness, for that chimera of the great All, which still has some semblance of the Absolute. This is a point very far beyond the deism of Voltaire.

It is true that the deism to which he always remained faithful will not hold as a system. It is very interesting to read Strauss' estimate of the Voltairean philosophy. He shows at once that it is full of contradiction. Voltaire has no definite opinion about moral freedom; he does not even express himself clearly about the immortality of the soul, though he always believed in it. With his pessimist views of history, which seemed to him a medley of errors, follies and misfortunes, he did not know what to make of the God whom he did retain. "The good Oromaze," he said, "who has done all, could not do better." The Almighty Author who had given to the world so faulty a performance would deserve rather to be hissed than worshipped.

Voltaire gave a true *resumé* of his metaphysics in these words: "For myself, I am sure of nothing. I believe that there is an intelligence, a creative power, a God. I express an opinion to-day; I doubt of it to-morrow; the day after I repudiate it. All honest philosophers have confessed to me, when they were warmed with wine, that the great Being has not given to them one particle more evidence than to me." It must be admitted that the mind of Voltaire, keen and supple as it was, was not capable of rising higher than the refinements of a brilliant society, and could not comprehend the grand poetry of the Bible, any more than he could comprehend Shakspeare. He could see nothing but lying or trickery in those great perturbations of the human conscience, out of which religion has been born. He lacked entirely the true spirit of criticism, which is not content with grasping the superficial and grotesque, but seeks to reach, through these, the underlying verities. In this feature of his mental habit, he was at the very antipodes of the nineteenth century, which has a magic wand to call up the past, whether from the recesses of the pyramids, or from the sacred books to whose hieroglyphics the science of our day has supplied the key.

How, then, are we to account for the fact that with so meagre a philosophy, Voltaire exerted an influence incomparably greater than that of the learned German doctor, and that in many directions that influence is felt even now? It is interesting to trace the causes of this superior power, as we follow out the parallel between him and his biographer.

It is needless to enlarge upon his inimitable style of writing. Strauss' style is also very remarkable, and so luminous is his exposition that on the most abstruse questions of criticism, he casts a flood of light. He understands the art of bookmaking—a rare accomplishment in Germany at the time when he began to write. We often feel a concentrated passion thrilling through his somewhat tame language. But there is no one, even on the other side the Rhine, who would dare to compare him to the French magician. The clearness of Voltaire's style reminds one of a rather low sky, which lights up every object without dazzling the eye. Now humorous, now eloquent, his vivacity never flags. Grimm said of him: " He makes arrows of every kind of wood, brilliant and rapid in their flight, but with a keen, unerring point. Under his sparkling pen, erudition ceases to be ponderous and becomes full of life. If he cannot sweep the grand chords of the lyre, he can strike on golden medals his favourite maxims, and is unapproachable in the lighter order of poetry. He is truly genius incarnate, but not the genius which sounds the depths of things ; rather that which rapidly seizes their contrasts, and brings them out in vivid colours. His power over his age was unequalled, and he swayed it by means of that light and charming sceptre, which was none the less a formidable weapon. Still acting *en bon prince*, he too often pandered to the taste of his subjects, by indulging in that literary libertinism, which was so much esteemed as a spice in the eighteenth century."

Never could it be more truly said than of Voltaire and Strauss, that the manner is the man. The sparkling vivacity of the former was the result of temperament. He was, as has been said, a creature of air and fire, the most nervous, the most mobile who ever lived ; in spite of his sardonic smile, his soul was all passion. His literary activity was prodigious. Wherever he was, travelling, or in a wretched inn, at the court of the King of Prussia, in the vortex of Paris, or in the quiet country, he could never restrain the demon of his inspiration or the fervour of the controversialist. "I have found Voltaire," said one of his visitors, "in bed, and in a high fever, but still writing, always just on the point of beginning or finishing either a tragedy or a pamphlet." His hatred was only equalled by his ardent friendship. While he would doom his enemies with pitiless severity to an immortality of ridicule, he was full of goodwill, generosity and tenderness to his friends. Often he would even take pity on the adversary whom he had almost annihilated, and would hold out to him a helping hand. His kindness to the descendant of Corneille was truly touching. One can but marvel at his patient forbearance with his intolerable niece, of whom Europe was disposed to say with Frederic: "Cease to weary me with her!" That which is most admirable in Voltaire is this humanity, ever responsive to any claim of suffering or wrong. His devotion to the family of Calas, to the Sirvens, to the Chevalier de la Barre, redounds to the eternal honour of his memory. He does not stop either to weigh or calculate; it is the simple love of justice that moves him. He would pretend to have the fever on each anniversary of St. Bartholomew. I do not know if his doctor ever felt his pulse on that day, but I do know that the great crimes of history always made him burn with the fever of a noble indignation.

This humanity is entirely wanting in Strauss, as is only too clear from his singular autobiography. He did not, indeed, fall into the same mistakes as Voltaire. Nothing could be more correct than his calm and studious career. His private life is worthy of all esteem. Only on two occasions did he emerge from his study, and the attempt was not successful. The first time it was to compose the libretto of an opera, which brought him into contact with the theatrical world. This libretto cost him very dear, by his own confession, for it brought him his wife, a brilliant singer, who could not bring herself to pass inglorious days by the fireside of her studious husband, and who at the end of two years left him with two children on his hands. The second time he was tempted out of his seclusion, was to attempt a short passage of political life. In the great fermentation which followed the Revolution of 1848, his countrymen sent him to sit in the Chamber of Würtemburg Deputies, imagining that the author of the "Leben Jesu," whose very name had occasioned a perfect tumult in the canton of Zurich, at the time of his nomination to a chair of theology, must be a Radical of the first water. This Radical went and took his seat at the extreme Right. The electors were hotly indignant. He hastened back into private life as fast as he could, vowing that nothing should tempt him again into the arena of political strife.

As we read his memoirs we can but be amazed at the narrowness of his spirit. No great cause of humanity excites his interest; what he is most concerned about is his reputation. He analyses his own talents with the most minute care. That he is a great critic, a great savant, *cela va de soi*, and he does not care to enlarge upon it. He goes much more into detail as to qualities, for which no one would have given him credit but himself. "I have extensive and profound learning," he says, "but have I also imagination, poetry in my nature? I cannot say that

I am a poet, and yet . . . ." Playing on his name, which signifies ostrich, he declares frankly that, like that powerful bird, if he has not the great flight of the wings of inspiration, he has the rudiments of wings, which make his progress rapid, and lift him above a prosaic vulgarity. The whole of this part of his autobiography is real comedy. He is far less amusing when, on the occasion of his famous correspondence with M. Rénan, at the time of the war of 1870, he shows himself concerned about nothing but the literary success of his odious apology for the enormities of the conquest. In the midst of this terrible drama of history, his main concern is to know whether the roar of the cannon will drown his voice, and he finds with unmixed satisfaction, that the sale of his pamphlet has not suffered very severely from the course of events. There is truly much of the Trissotin in this great scholar. He is wholly destitute of that order of sentiment which we designate by the name of humanity, and which Voltaire so largely possessed.

The contrast of thought between these two writers is still more marked than that of feeling. However incomplete, and therefore inconsistent, was the deism of Voltaire, it yet gave a place to the idea of justice, while the logical conclusion of the system of German criticism, especially in its later form, was the most daring negation of moral order. Let us be careful, however, not to lead to any misconception about Voltaire. This great iconoclast of religion remained in many respects a gentleman of the Chamber. He was little of a democrat who wrote these words: "I make no pretence to enlighten shoemakers and serving-maids; let us leave this task to the apostles."

The new earth is for *honnêtes gens*, and not for the rabble. It was enough for him that this new earth should be the paradise of persons of mind. His predilection was for a brilliant and tolerant social world, an age of Louis XIV., *minus* the Revocation of the Edict of Nantes. Here and there in his writings we can perceive some faint desires after social reforms, but nevertheless he was every inch an aristocrat, and had nothing but ridicule for the unfortunate apostles of democracy, who, like Rousseau, stood forward as the tribunes of the people, and urged them on to destroy that world of elegance and intellectual refinement, in which the author of the "Mondain" delighted. Hence his furious indignation at the article, "Sur l'inégalité des conditions." "That man," he said of Jean Jaques Rousseau, "tries to resemble Diogenes, and he does not resemble even Diogenes's dog."

It is, therefore, not without astonishment, that we see the French Revolution carrying to the Pantheon the coffin of so strange a forerunner. Yet the Revolution was right. Voltaire had, in fact, laid the axe to the root of the tree, of which he would fain have preserved the branches and the flowers. In attacking the religion of the old society, he wounded it at the heart, and thus rendered easy the task of those terrible destroyers, who learned their business by reading his books. We are bound, indeed, to admit that the religion which he pursued with such deadly hatred had miserably fallen, since it had been represented in France by a Church at once worldly and intolerant. It persecuted those who did not hold its creed, without itself really believing in it; and courtly abbés just emerged from the boudoirs of *grandes dames*, sold their subsidies to the king at each fresh assembly of the clergy, as the price of heavier restrictions to be laid on the Protestants and the philosophers. This was the scandal which Voltaire determined to put down. Unhappily he did not know how to distinguish religion itself from this odious perversion of it. In attempting to destroy everywhere the feeling of reverence, he did not root up only the parasitic plant of superstition: he carried away at the same time the very soil into which the moral and religious idea casts its roots. In this deplorable confusion, Voltaire laid profane hands upon everything, despoiling the past of all its grandeur, not sparing even the funeral pile of Joan of Arc. Too often he treated the human soul itself like another Maid of Orleans, delighting to humble it and to trample it in the mire.

> " En deux coups de sa griffe il dépouille tout nu
> De l'univers entier le monarque absolu ;
> Il vit que le grand roi lui cachait sous le linge
> Un corps faible monté sur des jambes de singe ! "

We must be careful, however, not to be unjust. It was in his very love to humanity that Voltaire degraded it. He longed to free it from all the tyrannies which are founded upon so-called divine rights. It is clear that a monkey can never be made a pope, and cannot assume airs of superiority towards other monkeys, his brethren. This was the fundamental idea of Voltaire, which we are bound to recognise through all the gratuitous libel and licentious buffoonery that overlies it. That against which he fought with all his eloquence and with all his power of satire, was intolerance; and it was this which rendered his arguments so effective against a perverted religion, which was associated with the worst iniquities of the past.

The toleration which Voltaire demanded was, indeed, a very incomplete thing; it had no analogy with true freedom of conscience or of worship, as is evident from these significant words: "The wise who do not recognise two powers are the best upholders of the royal authority." His conception of liberty was, nevertheless, very much higher than that of the State religion. And when any form of religion sinks below the general conscience of the age, it is very near its end. When man is superior to the gods who are held up to him, it may be safely predicted that the gods will soon disappear.

Things have greatly changed in our day. The great adversary of Christianity at the present time is, not Voltaire, but Strauss, and the ideal which he presents is not of a nature to commend itself to the conscience of the age.

All readers of his book, "Der alte und der neue Glaube," will feel that not many words are needed in order to prove this. It culminates in the materialistic doctrine of transformations, carried to its extreme issues, and boldly applied to human society. Strauss recognises in the world only matter and force. Society belongs to the strong; his system allows no place either for the right, for mind, or for liberty.

Tracing back the origin of universal life to one little cellule, he acknowledges no law of progress but that of a desperate struggle for existence. The strong to the front, the weak to the rear! this is his motto. When Strauss reaches the goal of his destructive work in philosophy and religion, he pauses before the only mystery which remains to him, namely, that of the sovereignty of royal races. There is no longer any good God, but there is a triumphant Cæsar.

Down on your knees, mortals! worship without understanding — you, especially, who are the conquered. Right is no more; might reigns. If some souls behind the age still urge, in opposition to the omnipotence of the State, the scruples of their religious conscience and its pretended independence, these must be severely dealt with. Strauss expresses on this subject a quite gratuitous anxiety, lest the

Imperial Chancellor should show too gentle a hand in the famous "Culturkampf," of which he is one of the warmest partisans. He says, in concluding, "Some may perhaps bring up in opposition to us the Sermon on the Mount, but this has only to be read *cum grano salis*, and we are prepared to agree with it."

The popular interpretation, which would derive from it protection for the weak and lessons of mercy, does very well for the ignorant. But here, also, with Strauss, might not only takes precedence of right, but does away with it. The General of the First Empire, who did not hesitate to turn his cannon upon his own wounded in order to carry a position, is a type of the new civilisation, the chariot of which advances, crushing all that has not strength to resist.

This philosophy of history is latent in Strauss' last book, and we have seen it unhesitatingly applied in some recent writings by men of his school. Our readers will understand, after this, how it is we prefer Voltaire to Strauss. Happily we are not reduced to either alternative.

The atheism of the nineteenth century declares itself more and more, as the implacable enemy of justice and liberty, at least in theory. For this reason it cannot exert the same influence as the philosophy of the eighteenth century, which was always generous and humane, even when it called in question the idea of God. It is not possible that democracy should hesitate in its choice, or that it should adopt doctrines which trample under foot all that is just and generous in its designs, by rejecting that spiritualism which is their true inspiration and sanction.

THE CULTURKAMPF IN GERMANY.

THE CULTURKAMPF IN GERMANY.

ITS PRINCIPLES AND RESULTS.

THE criticisms of a foreigner are always regarded with suspicion. It is therefore fortunate when the writer can call to his aid entirely impartial testimony. Such testimony we find in the work of M. Geffcken, to which our readers are referred.[1] We are glad, then, to avail ourselves of his light in the picture we desire to draw of the true state of the ecclesiastical controversy in Prussia.

The author, who is a man of influence in his own country, an eminent lawyer, well acquainted with the present position of European affairs (having been for a long time Minister of the Hanseatic towns in Paris and Berlin), has greatly enlarged on his original design, which was, undoubtedly, to impugn the reli-

---

[1] "Staat und Kirche in ihren Verhältnissen geschichtlich entwickelt." By L. Heinrich Geffcken. Berlin, 1875.

gious policy of Prince Bismarck. The part of the work devoted to this subject occupies but a few pages, which are almost lost in the midst of a long historical dissertation on the relations of Church and State. His book is, in truth, a tract for the times, with a preface, which is a treatise in itself. Possibly he said to himself, as did Louis Paul Courier: "It is dangerous, particularly in Prussia, to adventure oneself in a sheet or two which may be treated as a pamphlet; on the principle that a grain of morphia, which would be lost in a copper full of water, would be fatal in a spoonful." To this caution on the part of our author, we owe a very complete exposition of the actual relations between the two powers, temporal and spiritual, in Europe, which enables us, while devoting special attention to the facts affecting Germany, to determine also the conditions under which the ecclesiastical controversy must be carried on everywhere, if it is to have any decisive issue at all. That the struggle itself is inevitable and is gravely aggravated by existing circumstances, has been obvious for several years.

In the countries which are, as it were, the classic soil of religious liberty, the alarm has been given. The consequences of the late Council, as they have unfolded themselves, have startled and provoked the most decided adherents of State neutrality in matters of religion. Attention has been drawn to the manner in which the President of the United States has denounced the attempt made by the Ultramontanes, to change the unsectarian character of American schools, and to get into their own hands the management of popular instruction in the districts where they are most numerous. All remember Mr. Gladstone's emphatic statement of the incompatibility of Ultramontane orthodoxy with a sincere respect for the English Constitution. His powerful treatise produced a great impression upon public opinion at the time. The conclusions drawn by the great orator, though no doubt strictly logical, may be somewhat exaggerated in point of fact, since we must always make allowance for human inconsistency, which comes in to modify all merely theoretical calculations.

Upon the Continent of Europe, the irreconcilable opposition of the various schools threatens to assume a character of still greater acerbity, after the political changes which have lately taken place. We do not imagine that Italy is about to follow the example of Prussia. Well satisfied to have put an end to the temporal power of the papacy, and to have carried out, without disturbances, the great and difficult operation of adjusting ecclesiastical property, it is in no haste to leave the paths of moderation. The spirit of Cavour still governs it. Liberal Italy has quietly allowed the harmless thunders of the Vatican to roll over her head. She regards with amused indifference, the crowds of pilgrims passing through her towns from all parts of the world, well knowing that if they shake off against her the dust of their feet, they let fall some of their gold at the same time, and thus help to enrich the cities which their curses are powerless to harm. In France recently the whole aspect of affairs has changed. The Ultramontane party no longer holds in its hand that much-abused instrument—at once so convenient and so dangerous—a docile parliamentary majority.

The great antithesis between the modern State and Ultramontanism threatens to become a firebrand, scattering strife on every hand.

The surest way to escape this danger is to lay down clearly the liberal principles which ought to govern the whole debate, and to show, by contemporary history, what it has cost to deviate from them.

This is the twofold task to which M. Geffcken's book summons us, and we cannot do better than listen to him in his own cause; for, as an ardent patriot, and no friend to the Ultramontane "Centre," he follows only the leadings of reason and conscience.

I.

In order to form a fair judgment of the policy of the various governments of Europe, in the conflict between the Church and the State, we must revert to the fundamental idea of these two great institutions, for everything that is at variance with their true intention produces grave practical mistakes. The State is the representative of the law; it is the protector of all interests and all liberties, the venerable guardian of the peace of society, bound to favour every possible development of civil life and prosperity. The Church constitutes a higher society, destined to unite souls in the bond of a common faith, to uplift them and train them for a higher life beyond the limits of the earthly. These two organisations are both alike necessary, and are both based upon a divine institution; but, while neither can dispense with the other, they differ radically in their nature and mode of action. The State requires obedience to the civil law, while the Church would cease to be a spiritual and moral society, if it were to use coercion; its only authority is over its believing children. As the State is largely interested in the development of the religious influence, for the formation of good citizens, animated with the spirit of justice and of piety, the author deems that it is necessary for the State to enter into positive relations with the Church, and to encourage without controlling it, respecting its independence as the very condition of its influence. We leave to the German publicist, this chimera of the civil union of the two powers in mutual independence. History does not supply us with this philosopher's stone. Its uniform testimony is that in this union, which has neither reason nor moral affinity on its side, the power has always been on the side of the State, unless it was the Church itself which held the sword, as in the times when a triumphant theocracy made the civil power a sort of prince consort. With the exception of this error, which, after so many centuries of inextricable confusion of ideas, it is difficult to escape, the respective domains of Church and State are very clearly defined by M. Geffcken.

In his view three great spiritual revolutions have vindicated in theory this distinction, too often forgotten in fact. The first of these is Christianity, which put an end to the Jewish theocracy, and released from the old civic thraldom the domain of conscience and of the higher life, which paganism merged wholly in that of the community. The second spiritual power which, according to M. Geffcken, has helped to form the modern State with its constitutional principles, is the Reformation, which, in spite of many inconsistencies, successfully attacked the theocratic idea, and restored the rights of the State, perhaps in a somewhat exaggerated form. The third powerful influence which completed the demolition of the theocratic idea, is the philosophy of the eighteenth century, to which M. Geffcken does not attach sufficient importance. This proved a terribly destructive weapon to the established order of things, and none the less deadly because it was forged of bright and polished steel. It attacked every vestige of the middle ages with an energy of passion and satire, beneath which lay a genuine regard for liberty of conscience. It must be owned that this bold philosophy, in demanding liberty of conscience, had more regard for liberty than for conscience, and thus deprived the latter of its surest foundation; that it was content with toleration of ideas without seeking toleration of all forms of worship; that by showing more love than respect for man, and by ignoring his high origin, it failed to cast over his intellect and his soul, the sacred buckler of a truly divine right, which is the only sure defence against all aggression from without. A religious enthusiast like Milton will always be a firmer champion of freedom of conscience, than a great scoffer or sceptic. In spite of all its shortcomings, however, the eighteenth century gave the final blow to the theocratic idea, and triumphantly vindicated that conception of the lay State, which has taken too strong a hold of the modern mind ever to be again shaken off.

The part of M. Geffcken's book which is devoted to the French Revolution is of special interest, although many other works on the same subject give more exact information. We cannot too carefully study in our own day the lessons of this great era, in which the true and the false came into violent collision, like torrents of lava flowing from the rent sides of a volcano, which belches forth at once fire and mud. Hardly had liberty of conscience been formally recognised in the declaration of the rights of man, and confirmed by the repeated votes of the Contituent Assembly, after receiving the comment of Mirabeau, who gave it its noblest expression; hardly had it triumphed over its natural enemies of the Right, when it received a severe blow in the civil constitution of the clergy. The lay and modern State, but just freed from the fetters of theocracy, is at once hurried away in the eagerness of the conflict beyond its true domain. It ceases to be a lay institution when it tries to reform the Church by authority, and to turn the National Assembly into a Council. It does not impugn simply the factious proceedings of the old clergy—this would be within its competence —but it goes farther, and assails doctrines, ideas, beliefs; and when it seeks to put a constraint upon the religious conscience by the oath which it would exact from the priests, it arouses against itself the most unconquerable of all resisting forces. Having committed this great initial error, it was bound by the implacable logic of history, to fall into other and yet graver mistakes. Engaged in a hopeless conflict, in which it feels from the first it must be defeated, it soon passes on to open persecution, and makes itself gratuitously odious. But the hulks, the scaffold, proscription, all are in vain. Exasperated by the feeling of its own impotence, it only provokes a more dangerous reaction, driving the Catholic clergy to the feet of the papacy, depriving it of that feeling of nationality which gave it a measure of independence towards Rome, and thus paving the way for that brilliant triumph of Ultramontanism in the nineteenth century, which Napoleon was powerless either to stifle by kindness or to crush by violence, after his quarrel with Pius VII. It is the Revolution which is responsible for all that M. Geffcken describes as *Vaticanism*, because it fell into the mistake of trying to make Gallicanism compulsory — the sure way to discredit and to weaken it. With regard to religious beliefs, those who are protected by force are always in the end the conquered party, especially when the protection of the one side, implies the persecution of the other. To attack an idea is to strengthen it, to render it more sacred, more powerful, more invincible, even when the idea is associated with the most dangerous errors. This is the great lesson which the French Revolution has to teach us.

II.

Passing on to the controversies of our own day between the Church and the State, the author, before turning to his own country, shows us how, in spite of the decisions of the last Council, wise and liberal governments may maintain their rights without violating or suspending those of others, and still avoid great schisms.

Austria and Italy are held up to us rightly as models in this respect, while Switzerland has given us until quite recently, especially at Geneva and at Berne, the painful spectacle of demagogic radicalism trampling on liberty of conscience, and not shrinking from odious spoliations for the benefit of a State religion, which owed its origin to political bodies, the majority of whose members were either indifferentists or enemies to all religion. Happily a Liberal reaction has just set in, and we may hope that it will put an end to the era of persecution.

With regard to Prussia, M. Geffcken is equally severe on all that curtails religious liberty. He speaks with strong reprehension of the famous May laws of 1873, which not merely guaranteed the rights of the State, but impinged on so many points on those of the Church. That which it concerns us especially to learn from so impartial a witness, is the result of this Draconian legislation. M. Geffcken admits at once that it has shown the complete impotence of the persecuting State. This is made evident by the very severity of the laws designed to supplement the legislation of May, 1873. M. Geffcken protests with reason against the law which gives the Government the right to banish recalcitrant priests without a trial. "No penalty," he says, "except the penalty of death, is deemed heavier than that which exiles a man from his country, and sends him to wander through the world as a stranger. And to incur this a priest has simply to refuse to disobey the regulations of his Church, which he conscientiously deems incumbent upon him! Yet this is the law which has been voted by a parliament calling itself Liberal. The sequestration of ecclesiastical property, the prohibition of voluntary offerings, the imprisonment of several bishops, has had no effect. The Prussian State has only succeeded in arousing the opposition, not only of the clergy but of the laity, of the whole of that Catholic nation of several millions of souls, which backs up its priests and encourages their resistance. It is certain that in the silence even of the tribune, the conflict is being carried on unceasingly, and without any prospect of peaceful issue."

M. Geffcken adds : "A legislation which invades the proper domain of the Church misapprehends the nature of the struggle on which it has entered. The Liberalism, hostile to the Catholic Church, which is celebrating its so-called victories, regards that Church merely as a political adversary, whose dangerous organisation it must break up at all costs : it forgets that its strength lies in the religious influence which no law has power to cancel. The May laws are a return to the policy of Joseph II., who sought to make himself master of a domain which the State never could subdue. But where the avowed absolutism of the eighteenth century and the Convention failed, the modern State is not likely to succeed, in an age which boasts of liberty of the press, and of elections. Liberalism is mistaken as to the strength of the State when it thinks it can decide all questions by law. The only laws which have a guarantee of permanence are those which really fulfil their purpose. The Government may unquestionably go much further in measures of stern repression, but with no better success. In the heat of the conflict it has forgotten that if political passion is strong, religious passion is stronger still. From time to time the Government organs raise the cry of victory, and yet all they have obtained as yet has been the very opposite of what they sought. To the German episcopate, compromised as it no doubt was to some extent, by its submission to the Council, there has been given an opportunity of reasserting its moral dignity by steadfast resistance to oppression. It was hoped that the inferior clergy might be induced to sever from their leaders, but the contrary result has taken place. There was an attempt to emancipate the laity from the hierarchy, and the effect has been to unite the whole mass of the Catholics in one solid phalanx. It is not possible that the State should continue thus to make war on a third of the population, when it has no means of carrying the day.

"These deplorable conflicts have other consequences not less serious. They tend more and more to alienate from the Government the whole of the Conservative party; they bring dishonour on the National Liberal party, by making all its sounding declarations of justice and liberty nothing more than empty phrases; while the leaders of the Socialist party go on preparing for their impious war, loudly deriding all these inconsistencies, and availing themselves of all the popular elements which are not already enlisted in the Ultramontane cause. As Luther said: 'There is no fighting against opinions by the sword, and error is only overcome by truth.'"

Such testimony as that of M. Geffcken, coming from a faithful subject of the German Empire, who cannot be accused of sympathy with the foreigner, and who does not belong to the persecuted minority, deserves to be carefully weighed. It tells exactly what are the results of this famous "Culturkampf." The word itself carries the condemnation of that which it represents. The State, in declaring itself to be the defender of modern culture against Ultramontanism, shows that it is not content with defending the law, the public peace, the legislation and constitution of the country, but that it intends to enter into the conflict of doctrines and ideas, to attack principles, to oppose a certain mode of thought, to undertake, in short, a philosophic war, which is nothing else than a religious war. The State is the guardian of the high culture of the nation by its institutions for public instruction; and, above all, by the practice of a sincere and enlightened Liberalism, which alone permits national culture to develop itself freely in the open air, and not in a hot-house. We should pronounce the "Culturkampf," then, to be essentially a mistaken and dangerous enterprise, even if we did not know to what excesses and to what futile violence it leads on the Governments which allow themselves to be involved in it.

The demonstration of this given by M. Geffcken is as conclusive as it is opportune. It has been supplemented by the irrefutable evidence of facts. Have we not already seen the Prussian State ready to lay down its arms before the adversary whom it had thought to crush by an exceptional legislation? Whatever may have been the motives actuating it in this step, it is none the less a confession that it made a false move in its Culturkampf, and the price is a heavy one to pay for assuring a majority on the tariff question.

III.

We must hasten to a conclusion. Whatever liberal views might be entertained on questions of this order, it was impossible to doubt that a struggle between the modern State and the Ultramontane Church was inevitable in France. It is of the utmost importance, therefore, to determine what are the true conditions of the question, in order that the contest may not be embittered and rendered interminable. This we shall be most helped to do, by a careful observation of the experiments made elsewhere. To fail in the legitimate exercise of the protective power of the State, would be as dangerous as to be guilty of undue severity, for the weakness of one day might be followed by a violent reaction on the next. The duties of the State, as we understand them, consist in keeping up a vigorous defence against everything that menaces its safety, without having recourse to aggression, least of all in matters of opinion and belief, which are always intangible.

It cannot be denied that the Ultramontane party took large advantage of the favourable position it enjoyed in the last National Assembly, in its attempts to reconstruct the religion of the State for its own advantage. By observing the same wisdom which guided the Chamber of Deputies, in revising, with a studious regard to its principles, the law relating to the liberty of the higher education, it would be possible to correct, without danger, the legislative work of the National Assembly, and slowly but surely to restore the true idea of the modern State as a lay power. We hope, indeed, that recourse may be had to the surest, and at the same time the noblest, of all modes of defence, that which consists in extending the public liberties. The best rampart that can be raised against Ultramontane aggressions, is the full recognition of liberty of worship. At present, only those forms of worship are legal which have received the previous authorisation of the State. This has been simply a convenient way of stifling the free development of religious thought, since a partial administration was always sure to use it in subservience to the Ultramontane episcopate. What more excellent way can there be of combating the party of the Syllabus than by giving or extending general liberty, since it has no more deadly enemy than freedom of conscience, which it has ever loaded and honoured with its anathemas? We hope, then, that our assemblies will hear no more sophistical arguments about the liberty of fathers of families, which ought to be respected, as opposed to the principle which makes primary education compulsory; and that the law enforcing this will be voted all the more quickly, the more determined is the Ultramontane opposition to it. To make primary instruction by law universal, and thus to dissipate the ignorance of our country districts, would be the most effectual means of weakening the cause of Ultramontanism.

If from this defensive duty of the Legislature, we pass on to the measures to be taken against the positive aggressions made on the State, it is obvious to remark that the first obligation of the Government is to see that the administration is henceforth conducted on the strictest principles of religious equality. There is much to be done before this equality will be really restored, in the ordinary conduct of departmental affairs. Those open attacks upon the constitution of the country, which are too often associated with religious fanaticism, must be severely proscribed. It cannot be suffered that a holy war should be preached anywhere against the State, and against rights guaranteed by law, such as civil and religious liberty. The State must keep a watchful eye on all the great religious societies which have one powerful interest in common. Here, again, it is bound to exercise the strictest impartiality, and that which is forbidden in democratic gatherings, must not be tolerated in Catholic clubs. It has too often forgotten to use this vigilance and this even-handed severity.

But here it must stop. Let it be very careful not to interfere with any religious manifestations whatever, that do not trench on political ground. Let it allow pilgrimages to be multiplied till they wear themselves out; let it tolerate any manifestations of zeal, however eccentric, so long as they are not made the occasion for fanning political discontent. Let preaching have its full latitude; let it develop at will its theories of the latest Encyclical, and unfurl the banner of the Syllabus, provided only that it does not pass from theory to application, and does not incriminate any of the laws and institutions of the country. Under this reservation, let the State not trouble itself about the instruction given in the Seminaries, only claiming its right of inspection and control from a social point of view. For while France must be careful to avoid the errors into which Prussia has fallen, and not to make impossible conditions for the admission of her clergy to office, it is nevertheless her duty to keep a watchful eye over all the teaching given in the country, with the simple object of assuring herself that nothing is taught which is contrary to the laws and the Constitution.

It will be clear that such precautions as are here suggested, do not interfere at all with freedom of belief and opinion ; they are not calculated, therefore, to arouse determined opposition. The State does not enter upon a war of ideas ; it does not concern itself, either more or less, with orthodoxy, as in Prussia and Switzerland, where the civil authorities undertake to decide what is the true Catholic doctrine by proscribing the teaching of Ultramontanism. Thus, while still maintaining the right of the State to require reasonable submission to the civil power, as it is determined in the first article of the Declaration of 1682, we are not prepared to admit that it should require the official teaching of the three other articles, which imply the negation of the Ultramontane doctrine, the triumph of which was unhappily assured by the late Council. This would be to fight against ideas and doctrines, a conflict in which victory is always impossible. We plead for the prudent and moderate application of the Concordat, so long as that bastard system continues, which it is equally difficult either to improve or to replace.

All the prudence in the world must fail, however, if there is not on both sides the exercise of forbearance and discretion. It is not possible to take precautions against the freaks of insanity. But we ask: Is there not culpable audacity in defying the public conscience, as many of the representatives of Ultramontanism do, by their vindication of the maxims of religious absolutism? It might be said, in the eloquent words of one of the most illustrious Catholics of our age, that they treat the Church like one of the wild beasts which are carried about in menageries. "Look at it well," they seem to say, "and understand what is its true nature. To-day it is in a cage, made tame and spiritless by its condition; it has no power at present to harm you; but see what claws it has, and what tusks, and if ever it gets free you will see what it will do." Is not this a true version of all the rabid declamations of the defenders of the Syllabus, who, instead of leaving it in the safe obscurity of the sanctuary, drag it into prominence, swear by nothing else, and are eager to reorganise society according to its principles, the first result of which would be the suppression of all liberties, and first of all of liberty of conscience.

These senseless extravagances are fruitful sources of danger, for they give pretexts to the ultra-Radicals, who have already openly demanded the subordination of the Church. If the days of desperate and deadly struggle between the two powers should ever come again, much of the responsibility would rest on the numerous devotees of Ultramontanism. How can we forget that those who raise the cry that they are martyrs, before even a threat has been breathed against them, are the first to declare that were they only themselves in power, they would soon make martyrs? It is not enough for the moderate children of the Church, those who have not been carried away by the furious torrent of this new league, to groan in secret over these excesses of speech and of zeal. At all costs they must restrain them, even if they have to bear the supreme indignity of being called Liberal Catholics. But whether they do their duty or not, ours remains clear: it is to be consistent Liberals, even towards the worst enemies of liberty, respecting error which is merely doctrinal, while never tolerating any direct attack upon the State, and adhering strictly to law. This is at once the surest and the noblest path to victory, while violent measures only frustrate themselves by giving to the dangerous doctrines at which they are aimed, the advantage of being unjustly persecuted. Against such a course let the example of Prussia be a sufficient warning to us.

ARNAUD DE L'ARIÈGE.

ARNAUD DE L'ARIÈGE.

NONE of our contemporaries in public life will leave behind a memory more stainless and more justly esteemed, than Arnaud de l'Ariège. He was a man of rare courage, a bold and indomitable defender of our public liberties, ready in the cause of freedom to brave personal danger, to endure exile, and that which is more bitter still, isolation and inaction, while oppression was triumphant. But he was more than this. He represented a class of generous souls whose dream it had been to bring democracy into harmony with the religion of the past, strangely transformed by them into their own image, and whom the failure of this hope filled with an abiding sadness. Like the Rebecca of the Bible, of whom it is said that she bare within her womb two nations, the noble school to which Arnaud de l'Ariège belonged, embraced two brothers, or rather two worlds, which it strove to reconcile. To this impossible task he devoted himself with an energy and zeal which nothing could daunt, and the conflict, which found its counterpart also in his own soul, cost him the keenest anguish. His mental suffering was sufficiently indicated by the premature whitening of his hair, and by the fixed expression of melancholy on his fine features. Any one who watched him as he sat silent in his place on the left of the National Assembly, must have felt that he was one of those political anchorites who pursue their own ideal visions through all the hot strife of parties. It is said that when Lamartine entered the Chambers he replied to those who asked him whether he would sit on the right or the left, *Au plafond* (on the ceiling). Probably it was a ministerial of the day who originated this story of the great poet. Nor could it be applied without grave injustice to Arnaud de l'Ariège, for, however high might be his ideal, he never hesitated, in the great crises of national history, to take his place boldly on the side of liberty and the right. The Republican Liberal party has had no more honest representative, none more exempt from personal ambition, or more firm in the days of peril. His convictions were so deep that they produced a calm serenity, and no bitter or passionate word was ever known to escape his lips. He would make no compromises on a point of conscience, and his verdict was very severe on those who had no pity on France in her struggle to recover herself. His kindness was at the same time unbounded, but it never degenerated into weakness. He who is a real friend to truth and to mankind, carries his attachment to his cause to such a height of disinterestedness, that the mere fluctuations of passion have no power to move him, and the strength of his convictions gives stability to his character.

Such a man was Arnaud de l'Ariège in his stern endeavour to unite his religious with his democratic faith. Must it be said that he failed in this noble enterprise because, during the later years of his life, he saw the desired reconciliation ever receding before him? Broadly regarding the question, we think not. In the first place, he saved the honour of religion, by showing himself a great citizen in difficult times, when religion was dishonoured by its most prominent representatives, who gave their benediction and adoration to triumphant force. We know nothing more beautiful or more touching than the conduct of Arnaud de l'Ariège at the time of the December *coup d'état*. He was not content with showing his sentiments by associating himself with every attempt made at an organised resistance; but impressed with the feeling that it became the highest dignitary of the diocese to take up the cause of outraged liberty, he implored the Archbishop to remonstrate with the Emperor in the name of Christian conscience. It was in vain that he exposed his heroic wife and her new-born child to the perils of crossing the barricades, the only way by which the proscribed deputy could place his petition in the hands of the Archbishop. In spite of all his efforts, the *Te Deum* was chanted in Notre Dame the following Sunday.

Yet further disillusionising awaited Arnaud de l'Ariège. He had the sorrow of seeing the little band of Liberal Catholics dwindling day by day. In truth, he had been always in advance of them in the boldness and generosity of his views. Lacordaire was not allowed to preach again from the pulpits of the capital, after his impassioned denunciation of the *coup d'état* in his sermon at Saint-Roch. Ozanam died before his time, consumed by the fire of indignation in his soul. In the universal repression, nothing was heard but the outrages which the Ultramontanes, who had rallied around the Emperor, heaped on their former friends, who would not acquiesce in saving the Church at the cost of her honour. After the Italian war the Roman question presented itself in all its gravity, and yet further divided the few remaining Liberal Catholics. Arnaud de l'Ariège pronounced unhesitatingly against the temporal sovereignty of the Pope. He maintained, by argument and from history, that the Church had everything to lose in becoming a political power of the *ancien régime.*

He wrote two important books on this subject: " L'indépendance du Pape et les droit des Peuples," and " La Papauté Temporelle et la Nationalité Italienne." It is almost needless to say that Arnaud de l'Ariège was one of the defeated party in the Vatican Council. He had thrown himself heart and soul into the opposition made to the new dogma by his former friends, among whom he had the joy of seeing Montalembert. Happily this great man was spared the pain of surviving the defeat of his most cherished convictions.

The bitterest pang for Arnaud de l'Ariège was in witnessing the total demolition of Liberal Catholicism in France. Huet, the brave disciple of Bordas-Desmoulin, was led by his indignation at the results of the Council to abjure Christianity altogether. Silent acquiescence enwrapped like a shroud all that generous and ardent phalanx which had rallied around Lacordaire. Arnaud de l'Ariège remained what he had always been—a Christian and a Liberal; but he felt more than ever isolated, irritated and indignant at the excesses of triumphant Ultramontanism. He could only take refuge in the utterance of the dying Pascal: *Ad tribunal tuum, Jesus Christe, appello.*

He did not retract any of his early opinions. These have found their most complete expression in his book, "La Révolution et lÉ'glise," a book which breathes throughout the spirit of Bordas-Desmoulin, and which is dedicated to the great cause of the reconciliation of religion and liberty. The French Revolution is there represented as the legitimate offspring of Christianity, which reached its highest realisation in the great and lasting reforms then achieved. It is true that Arnaud de l'Ariège disengages from the terrible struggles of the Revolution, the new and fruitful principle, which in the dust and heat of the conflict was often lost sight of, and which has been strangely misconceived by many who have professed to carry on the same work. This principle, as he understood it, was the entire and absolute separateness of the civil power and religion. Pagan society was based upon the opposite principle. It recognised no right of the individual conscience beyond the control of the State. Primitive Christianity vindicated this liberty of conscience, and the Church, when it again placed religion under State control, returned to the principle of paganism. Hence the French Revolution showed itself more Christian than the Church of the old *régime*. Arnaud de l'Ariège carried these principles to their furthest issues. He remained always a declared and decided advocate of the separation of Church and State, though he never attempted to press the solution of this difficult problem prematurely, nor to lay so heavy a burden on the shoulders of our young Republic. He went so far in the direction of non-interference that there appeared an admirable letter in the *Temps* from him, earnest Christian as he was, protesting against the vote for public prayers in the National Assembly. He could not bear to see spiritual things, which are purely matters of conscience, put to the vote in parliament. When, immediately after the 24th of May, a fanatic majority approved the unqualified decree of the Prefect of Lyons, denouncing civil burials, Arnaud de l'Ariège made repeated efforts to gain a hearing; but he was not allowed to finish his eager remonstrance in behalf of that liberty of conscience which formed so important an article in his religious faith.

Arnaud de l'Ariège only made, to our knowledge, two great speeches in parliament, both in reference to the law for liberty of teaching: the first in the Legislative Assembly, on the 14th of February, 1850; the other in the National Assembly, on the 14th of June, 1875. Though thus divided by an interval of a quarter of a century, we find in both speeches the same doctrines, deeply Christian and daringly Liberal. Both express the same conviction of the necessity of keeping the domain of the State distinct from that of religion. There is the same elevation of view, the same perception of what will be the most glorious triumph of the future.

"It is the part of Christian democracy," said the young Deputy of 1850, "however unworthy may be its organ here, to define clearly and decidedly its view on this question, and to rise above prejudice of every kind—revolutionary prejudice no less than that of the old Conservative parties. The most distinctive and essential feature of the Revolution, is the limitation it has placed to the domain of the State. The sovereign to-day has no longer the same rights as before 1789. In the ancient community all the rights of the *man* were comprehended in those of the *citizen*. When Christianity had wrought its revolution, the freedom of man was asserted in matters of faith and of religion. It is this freedom which is vindicated in the principle of the separation of the two powers in religious matters."

From this principle the speaker argued the incompetence of the State to make any philosophical or religious teaching obligatory, so that he could turn round to the Church and say: " The State recognises the equal rights of all citizens; there is no Church with which it can treat as one power with another. All religions are free, as are all philosophical opinions. You, members of the Church, are, in the eye of the law, citizens on a par with other citizens; but in the name of the Church you have no rights. I do not acknowledge you. I declare you to be a usurping power. When the Church intervenes to lend its aid to the State in fulfilling its duty as a government, and in seeking to give education to the people, I declare that it goes beyond its rights, and is acting in opposition to the principle which is at the basis of our democratic system."

The Deputy of 1875, matured by the trials of life, and by the terrible catastrophes that had befallen his country (in connection with which he rendered eminent service as mayor of one *arrondissement* of Paris during the siege), used the same language, when the Right, having formed a fresh coalition, endeavoured to restore and extend the fatal law of 1850 for public instruction. On one point only he speaks somewhat less positively. While still maintaining the incompetence of the State in matters of philosophy and religion, he admits that there exists, apart from the various creeds and philosophic systems, a certain common stock of moral ideas which form a sufficient basis for government education. He recognises also the exclusive right of the civil power to confer degrees which entitle to the holding of public offices ; but he has not swerved at all from his essential convictions, as may be seen from the following extracts :

" Whoever argues, whether in the name of the nation or of the Church, that there is such a thing as a State doctrine, ignores two great facts in the world's history—first, the great Christian emancipation, and then the great French Revolution, which was the renovation of society. This great emancipation was radical and decisive, just because it gave freedom to the conscience. You men of little faith, whether Christians or Rationalists, if you were really influenced on the one hand by the spirit of the gospel, which is the spirit of liberty and justice, and on the other hand by the spirit of the Revolution, which is the very same, would cease to stand in dread one of the other. We must be careful not to mistake the movements of some excited minds, for anti-religious demonstrations. People are apt to think that the antipathy (often very strong) of the youth of France to the clergy indicates an irreconcilable hostility to the Church.

" Let me ask you to listen to a remarkable piece of

evidence supplied by contemporary history on this point. In 1840, in the great hall of the Sorbonne, an eminent priest, a professor of sacred elocution, uttered some words which aroused the indignant protestations of his hearers. Was it hatred to the priest that stirred their youthful blood? You shall judge for yourselves. A short time after, the same elocucutionary course was taken up by a new professor in the same great amphitheatre of the Sorbonne, before the same youthful auditory; and the new professor was received with enthusiastic applause. Why this contrast? Why did the one arouse a tempest of indignation, and the other restore peace and confidence in his hearers? Both were priests, both eloquent, both illustrious. Because the one—Abbé Dupanloup—had attacked our modern liberties, and the other—M. Cœur—had hailed these noble conquests in the domain of freedom, with the heart of a true patriot. It is this spirit of liberty which must be cherished in the youth of France, if we would elevate, purify, and strengthen the fibre of the nation. It is not by vilifying our newly-acquired liberties and signing protests against them, that you will maintain your widespread and powerful influence."

These words remain as the parliamentary testament of this noble and generous soul. And it shall not be unfulfilled. The religious forms under which he saw in vision the union of the Church with modern liberties, may undergo many changes in the future. What matter, if all that was eternally true, Christian, and liberal in his policy is assured of final victory? No truth can ever perish; and we know no higher truth in relation to social life than that complete enfranchisement of the conscience which Arnaud de l'Ariège proclaimed to be at once the first consequence of Christianity, and the essential idea of the French Revolution. This principle will survive all the calculations of parties. Its final triumph is certain, both in religion and politics, and it will then be seen that visionaries like Arnaud de l'Ariège were the really practical men of the future. He has not to wait, however, the vindication of history. Universal respect, blended with sincere affection, on the part of all those who knew him in his public and private life, is the tribute tendered to his memory to-day.

Arnaud de l'Ariège fought much and suffered much for his convictions in hard and troublous times, without being ever betrayed into personal animosity, and without ever having to retract his position. It was a beautiful life, and in our view not unsuccessful, though he died without having seen the triumph of his cause.

DUPANLOUP, BISHOP OF ORLEANS.

DUPANLOUP,
BISHOP OF ORLEANS.

IN November, 1878, the Church of France lost the most eminent of her bishops. The long career of Mgr. Dupanloup is a sort of epitome of the history of French Catholicism. Born in Savoy in 1802, he early attracted attention by his intelligence and energy, and by the fervour which he carried into all that he undertook. Distinguished as a catechist, and as a pulpit orator, though he never rose to the rank of such men as Lacordaire and Ravignan, he was chiefly remarkable as a teacher of the higher Catholic doctrine. As a leader, he had among his followers eminent and even royal personages, who contributed not a little to extend his influence. He had the honour of reconciling Talleyrand to the Church on his deathbed. His first appearance in public affairs was on the occasion of the famous law for liberty o teaching, which was voted in 1850 by the Legislative Assembly, by means of the coalition of the Catholics with the old supporters of the Orleanist monarchy— two parties who, as Montalembert said, were "cast by a common shipwreck upon the same raft." Unhappily, the liberty thus inaugurated was not the true liberty, which belongs equally to all citizens, but only the liberty of the holy Catholic Church, which had assumed a preponderating share in the direction of the University, and had contrived to get the popular teaching made over in great part to its religious bodies. Mgr. Dupanloup, who was their Abbé, took an important part in the Commission which framed that too famous law, the fruitful parent of so much evil to France.

We remember meeting him at this time in one of the tribunes of the Legislative Assembly. It was on the day when M. Thiers had given his support to the clerical party, of which till then he had been such a decided opponent. "This is a great and decisive day for that man," said Mgr. Dupanloup. He little thought that at the close of his career he would be the leader of Thiers' most determined enemies, fighting against that statesman's liberal and truly patriotic policy.

Abbé Dupanloup was raised soon after this to the see of Orleans. There he revived, as far as he could, the traditions of Joan of Arc, seeking on all occasions to combine Catholicism with patriotism. He was made in a short time a member of the French Academy, in recognition of his numerous writings on education, the style of which was impassioned rather than brilliant, as, indeed, were all the productions of his pen. He now entered into his first controversy with the Ultramontane party, who had attempted to proscribe the Greek and Latin classics, on the pretext that their entirely pagan influence was dangerous. Dupanloup, as a member of the Academy, vigorously opposed this new invasion of barbarism in the field of literature. He belonged at this time altogether to the school of Liberal Catholics, like Montalembert and Lacordaire, men whose great aim was to reconcile the doctrine of the Church with modern society. Into this endeavour he entered, like them, with very sincere religious enthusiasm. It has been recently reported that in the chapel of the Castle of Montalembert, in Burgundy, the Bishop of Orleans celebrated at this time a solemn mass, which was a sort of vigil of the champions of Liberal Catholicism, on the eve of the conflict. A tablet bearing their names, with the inscription, "*Pro religione et libertate*," is still to be seen in the chapel.

At this very time the Ultramontane party was letting loose all its fury against Liberal Catholicism, under the leadership of Louis Veuillot, the great scoffer of the age. He found a formidable antagonist in the Bishop of Orleans, who replied to the violent articles of the *Univers*, by charges which were admirable for their freshness and vigour. He was unquestionably most successful in these fugitive productions. On one point, however, he agreed with his Ultramontane opponents. He was always a defender of the temporal power of the Holy Father, and when he saw this menaced by the policy of Napoleon III., he threw all his energy into the contest. With this exception, he spoke and wrote as a Liberal. Great, then, was the astonishment created when, after the appearance of the Encyclical in 1864, which compelled him to abandon all that he had previously held most dear, he published an apology for the Syllabus. The surprise would have been greater still if it had been known that M. Dupanloup had done all in his power in Rome, to prevent the publication of this same Syllabus, which he afterwards endeavoured to justify by a softening and modifying interpretation. We have it on the authority of M. Guizot, who was closely allied with Bishop Dupanloup, that the latter spent his utmost strength in unavailing efforts to prevent the Roman Curia from taking so imprudent a step.

Our perplexity at contradictions like these will be lessened, if we consider how difficult is thorough honesty under a religion of absolute authority, which allows its faithful followers no alternative but feigned or unfeigned submission. From this time M. Dupanloup was far less liberal. Instead of being satisfied with refuting the false doctrines of materialism, he denounced them passionately to the political bodies then in power, and succeeded by his influence in closing the Academy against M. Littré.

When, several years later, the author of the great "Dictionnaire de la Langue Française" was admitted on the ground of his brilliant literary achievements

Mgr. Dupanloup sent in his resignation, which was never either accepted or withdrawn.

In spite of the Syllabus, and of his famous commentary on it, he was still a Gallican, and watched with displeasure the preparations for proclaiming the dogma of papal infallibility. On the eve of the Council he was among the foremost objectors. In 1869 he made himself the very leader of the opposition, to the great indignation of the Ultramontanes. His Catholic apologists of to-day draw a veil of prudent silence over this period of his life. It has not been forgotten, however, at Rome, for in resisting the policy of the Society of Jesus, he committed the sin for which there is no forgiveness either in this world or the next. Thus, in spite of his submission, and of the numberless services rendered by him since 1870 to the Catholic cause, he never obtained the cardinal's hat, which has adorned the heads of the most mediocre men of the French episcopate. Do what he might, he was still a suspected man, and was treated as such by the papal Nuncios in Paris.

The Nuncio even went so far as to deplore the fall of the Republican Ministry on the 24th of May, because he feared that the direction of ecclesiastical affairs in France would pass to Bishop Dupanloup. And yet, from the time the Bishop took his seat in the National Assembly, he never lost an occasion to serve those who so repelled him. He was the spokesman in the famous crusade of the bishops in 1871, in favour of the temporal power. He took the leading part in the discussion of the laws on public instruction; especially in that which constituted the new Catholic universities, and gave them the right to confer degrees. He did not cease to denounce severely all false doctrines, without being over-careful about the correctness of his quotations. His vehement opposition to the celebration of the Voltaire centenary is in the memory of all. In this instance, as in many others, his zeal carried him beyond all bounds, and made him blind to any but the evil aspects of that extraordinary genius. He had not the fairness either to recognise Voltaire's attempts to secure toleration, or to admit that Christianity was presented to him only under the hideous mask of a persecuting religion, which might well provoke his mockery and scorn. The Bishop of Orleans died on the eve of fresh conflicts for the advancement of the Church. It is but just to him to say that he never gave his approval to the superstitious vagaries of Ultramontane pietism.

Mgr. Dupanloup is a fair representative of this troubled period of French Catholicism. He was tormented by self-contradictions, which he never succeeded in reconciling; and it is this which gives him sometimes an appearance of insincerity. In reality he does not deserve the imputation; it was his position that was false, not himself. We must remember, moreover, what a passionate nature his was. Passion was expressed in the high colour of his countenance, in his eager gesture, in his speech, impetuous rather than eloquent, and weighted somewhat with the laboured rhetoric of the schools. Even as an old man he would walk bareheaded to cool the fever in his veins : age itself could not bring him serenity. It cannot be denied that, during his later years, he gravely compromised the cause he held dear by his controversial rancour and vehemence. The journal which breathed his spirit, *La Défense Religieuse*, was one of the worst organs of the clerical reaction. There can be no doubt that it helped to bring about the crisis of the 24th of May, for in our day prophecies so accurate and exact only come from behind the scenes.

But, in spite of all his errors, Mgr. Dupanloup remains a character well deserving our interest, and perhaps our pity. There can be no doubt that he suffered much in the sharp mental conflict between his early liberal convictions and the directly contrary conclusions of the Vatican Council. In the dignity and purity of his private life, Mgr. Dupanloup merits all respect, and during the war he showed admirable courage in his diocese of Orleans, which suffered terribly from the invaders.

He liked to invite to the representations of Greek tragedies, which were given in his little Seminary, the friends of high classic literature, and sometimes among them men who he knew had very little sympathy with clerical education. His *ménage* was simple almost to austerity, his manners frank and cordial. It was easy to talk with him on subjects of literary interest, or on the higher themes of patriotism and Christian spirituality.

The Catholic journals extol Dupanloup as a great defender of religious liberty. This encomium he merits less than any, for he never defended any but the " liberty of the right." He was the declared enemy of every legal measure that proposed to give liberty of worship. He even went so far as to describe the honest application of this measure to non-Catholics, as subversive of society.

The Bishop of Orleans was the brilliant representative of Catholic Liberalism, both in its earlier phase of imprudent generosity, and in its later period of retractation and submission. He showed by his example, how great a sacrifice is exacted from its worshippers by the idol of the Vatican. They cannot satisfy it by anything short of an apostasy from Liberalism. The great high priests of Ultramontanism are not content even with this apostasy; they have no forgiveness even for those who repent. This was very evident in the strange funeral oration pronounced by M. Veuillot upon Mgr. Dupanloup. In truth, the one body, the Church, is divided against itself, and the fictitious veil of absolute unity fails to conceal the fact.

ADOLPHE MONOD.

ADOLPHE MONOD.

THE influence of ideas on the drama of history is in no way circumscribed by the smallness of the theatre in which they are first produced. In truth, they rather prepare the drama than appear themselves as the actors in it. Without falling into the fatalistic and pantheistic idealism of Hegel, we are free to recognise that the movements of thought, or rather of the human soul, are reproduced in the domain of outward fact, and that this inner history is not governed by the strict laws of logic, but is enacted with the same freedom as that of the world without. Sometimes it is in an upper chamber, as at Jerusalem, sometimes in a monkish cell, as at Wittemberg, that a new era in the history of the human mind takes its rise, like a great river which has its hidden source in some remote mountain region.

Nothing could well appear more insignificant than the French Protestantism of our day, when compared with the Catholicism of the age, so ardent, sometimes so defiant, always so skilful in swaying the masses of the people. And yet this insignificant minority, so long ignored, has enjoyed in this century a very intense and fruitful religious life. The ideas which it has ventilated and helped to put into circulation in the intellectual atmosphere of the nineteenth century, are of the highest importance in the present religious crisis, and are such as, when fully developed, must exercise a weighty influence on the mind of the age.

It must be remembered, moreover, that French Protestantism is a branch of that great moral and intellectual development called the Reformation. This left its impress upon a great portion of Europe and of the world; it is one of the most powerful factors in the history of modern times. Everything relating to Protestantism must, then, be of the highest interest to all who rise above the prejudice—shall we call it Catholic or Chinese?—that nothing exists beyond their own intellectual boundaries. I may add that Protestantism does not take away from the French mind, those peculiar gifts of clearness and precision which make it so powerful an instrument in the diffusion of ideas; often, indeed, it has rather the contrary effect—stimulating to the highest and purest exercise of all the mental powers. Thus the various tendencies which in the present century have agitated the Churches of the Reformation throughout Europe, have acquired in France a degree of definiteness which has accelerated their development, either progressive or retrogressive. The history of French

Protestantism has told upon the history of Protestantism generally, and hence on the whole history of the age, as we shall presently show.

If we attempt to characterise the Protestant crisis of the nineteenth century, we shall find that the issues raised are twofold — theological and ecclesiastical. The faith of the Reformation had everywhere felt the influence of the eighteenth century. The stormy wind of negation had swept even over the desert, to which the heroic army of the French Reformation had fled, broken and proscribed. The eighteenth century had scarcely sunk below the horizon in a bed of clouds crimsoned with blood, when, aroused by such a series of tragic events in the history of the nations, religious feeling re-awoke in a state of strong excitement. This re-awakening produced important effects in the Catholic Church, and Protestantism felt its influence in an equal degree. The revival of religion is the characteristic feature of the commencement of this century. In Germany it became blended with speculation and mysticism; in England it drew yet closer the bonds of the narrow orthodoxy of the seventeenth century, but it introduced at the same time a devotional fervour and missionary zeal which gave it a marvellous power of dissemination. When peace re-opened the Continent to the influence of England, Protestantism in the French-speaking countries received the impress of the religious revival in Great Britain. It lost nothing in its transmission across the Channel, of either its fervent zeal or its intolerant dogmatism. When it had rallied around its banner an important section of the Protestants, a struggle was inevitable between its converts and the still remaining adherents of a vague and meagre supernaturalism, who, having suffered so much persecution themselves, made tolerance the prime article of their creed. The controversy which thus arose was at once religious and ecclesiastical. It was not enough to establish the just claims of orthodoxy; it was needful also to vindicate its rights in the Church. This attempt brought to light all the complications of the ecclesiastical problem.

It is not my intention to retrace the history of French Protestantism in the nineteenth century. I shall only attempt to show, through some of its noblest representatives, the principal phases of the religious revival of our age. After the first days of rapturous fervour, we shall find the earnest spirits of the French revival entering on a path of development, in which they keep pace more or less closely with the evangelical and liberal school beyond the Rhine. Their first advances in this direction are made with timid steps, in fear lest they should wound sensitive consciences, or do injustice to the absorbing claims of missionary activity.

Adolphe Monod represents the early phase of the religious revival, with a happy blending of holy austerity and brilliant natural endowments. The remarkable feature in his life is that he at first espoused, heart and soul, the theology of the religious awakening of the commencement of the century, without, however, falling into its theoretical or practical extravagances. Against these his high moral and intellectual qualities always proved a sufficient safeguard. A change, however, soon became apparent in his theological opinions. This change was as decided as it was moderate, and to the very close of his life we find him becoming more and more liberal and large-hearted. It is interesting to trace his growing aspirations after a broader and more enlightened theology, blended as they are always with the most profound and earnest piety. In the great heart of Adolphe Monod strict orthodoxy was forced to expand under the strong pressure of Christian feeling, as the mould which becomes too strait for it, is broken by the precious metal in a state of fusion.

In the case of Verny and of Robertson, the crisis by which their doctrinal views were transformed, was more severe and more painful in its character, so that it becomes a study of pathetic interest. In the case of Vinet, it was a gradual process of fuller development, and his faith flowed on in a quiet and even channel, like a stream no longer shut in between banks too narrow for it.

We have thus in these three men — all leading spirits—three epochs or phases of the history of the religious revival, which will not have accomplished its full work in France, till the Church has been made absolutely free by it, both in its doctrine and institutions. Not till then will Christianity be able truly to fulfil its mission in a democratic society which feels the want of adequate spiritual guidance.

I shall attempt nothing more than a sketch of Adolphe Monod, as of Vinet and Verny. We hope that Monod's family, who have already done so much for the publication of his works, will give us the complete biography so much desired by his admirers.

The materials of this biographical study are derived chiefly from Adolphe Monod's own writings. I have also drawn largely on my personal recollections, for I had the privilege of knowing Adolphe Monod from my childhood, and of being, in later days, honoured with his friendship. I have constantly before me, in memory, his earnest, expressive face. How vividly can I recall him in the intimacy of the home circle, beaming with love, but somewhat reserved and silent ; in the pulpit, with the flashes of his brilliant eloquence lighting up his whole face ; or in the professor's chair, with the calm patience of the master, gravely solicitous for his pupils' good. Last of all, upon his deathbed, when suffering had set its crowning seal upon his pallid brow. In the case of such a preacher, such an apostle, his words give us the man himself, so truly do they express the purity and earnestness of his moral life. The writings he has left enable us to trace his thought, from its very first inspiration, through all its various stages of development, to catch, as it were, the prayer for light that rises from the seeker after truth. Some publications that have long been out of print, such as the addresses delivered by him on his admission to the theological faculty of Montauban, and some occasional pamphlets, have supplied us with valuable information.

Adolphe Monod had not an imposing presence. He was of middle height and his features were irregular; but they bore the impress of high moral qualities, enhanced by the pervading melancholy peculiar to great minds. His smile, however, illuminated his whole face, and when he was speaking, his eloquence seemed to transfigure him as it does all great masters of the art. His gesture was perfect; and I have heard no other voice but Berryer's of so harmonious and penetrating a tone.

Adolphe Monod remains one of the noblest names on the roll of French Protestantism, surpassed by none in the disinterestedness and largeness of heart and mind with which he served the cause of Christ. So high has he been raised by the admiration and gratitude of Christendom, that he may be said to belong to the whole Evangelical Church of our day. If Catholic or free-thinking France had been animated by a more liberal spirit, it would not have been satisfied with the vague echo of an illustrious name coming to it across the Atlantic; it would have itself bestowed upon him literary honours. But these were matters of indifference to him; his ambition took a higher range.

I.

Adolphe Monod was born at Copenhagen, January 21, 1802. His father, a native of the Canton de Vaud, was pastor of the French church formed by the Protestant refugees after the revocation of the Edict of Nantes. A man of the utmost integrity, as well as a facile and eloquent orator, M. Monod, the father, was held in most affectionate esteem both in Copenhagen and in Paris, and exercised a wide popular influence. He held the opinions current in the Protestant Church of his time both in Geneva and in France. His was a warm and sentient piety, tender and benevolent in spite of its theological rigour, and more adapted to sustain than to enkindle religious life in the soul. He was always tolerant. He did much honour to Protestantism in the great Reformed Church of Paris, in which he exercised a long and valued ministry soon after the establishment of the Reformed religion by the First Consul. Nothing could be more beautiful than the family life of this patriarch of noble and venerable appearance, surrounded by his twelve children, all strongly attached to each other. Madame Monod (*née* De Coninck) was, as her name indicates, a Dane. She was the very type of a Christian wife and mother, and the light and joy of her family circle.

Adolphe Monod thus grew up in an atmosphere of purity, of affection, and of truly classic intellectual culture. He learned from his father to speak that correct and luminous language of the best French school, which he was afterwards to turn to such good account. At Geneva, whither he went to enter on his studies in the university, preparatory to the ministry of the gospel, he adopted the theology current at the time, at least in countries where the French tongue was spoken, a theology without depth, and amounting to little more than a vague supernaturalism. It was indefinite alike in its negations and affirmations. The divinity of Christ was ignored rather than denied. It would have been dangerous in France formally to repudiate this article of faith. Creeds still existed in the letter but not in the spirit—like the ark without the tables of the covenant. That which had especially dropped out of the religious teaching and piety of the day, was that deep conviction of the the misery and impotence of man, which brings sinners to the foot of the cross, there to receive forgiveness and new life from the sovereign grace of God. Justification by faith had been more than the central doctrine of the Reformation; it had been its great moral and religious lever. That lever had now ceased to act. Men thought themselves set right with God by the mere practice of human virtue, combined with certain exact observances of piety and a sincere veneration for historic Protestantism.

Adolphe Monod himself subsequently described this attitude of the Reformed Church of France, painting it perhaps in somewhat too strong colours.

"The doctrine of works," he said, "took possession of our academies, our pulpits, our pastors, our flocks. Our confession of faith was forgotten, our discipline set aside. The voice of the Synods was silent. The spirit of the age, the philosophy of the day, took the place of the spirit of the Bible. Faith was eclipsed, and knowledge hid its face. Since the Bible was to be less consulted than the spirit of the age, what inducement was there to study deeply the meaning of the Bible, when slight and superficial studies sufficed to give an initiation into the current philosophy? Science went out of vogue among our clergy. Instead of preachers like Dumoulin, Dubose, Bailli and Claude, our pulpits were filled with men of no enlightenment of mind. Hence the Reformed Church of France lost all consideration as a Church. As a social, industrial, political, moral body, it was still respected, but as a Church it forfeited all claim to regard. Hence arose among the Catholics, the false notion that the Protestant Church does not believe in Jesus Christ, and unbelieving Catholics were known to wish themselves Protestants, that they might be deists."[1]

---

[1] "La Destitution d'Adolphe Monod," p. 100.

At Geneva, Adolphe Monod was a conscientious student. He carried into his studies the natural vigour of his mind. He traces to this period the commencement of that religious crisis which was to end in his conversion. This result, however, as we shall presently see, was not reached till he went to Naples. His brother Frederic had a considerable share in this great spiritual and intellectual transformation. Three distinguished men exerted a decided influence upon him, as he himself tells us in a letter written during his last illness. We quote this as the most reliable source of information on this interesting subject.

"There are three friends whose names I love to associate, because they were all three at different times greatly helpful to me in my conversion. I wish to testify my gratitude to them to-day, when I am expecting so soon to leave this world and go to the Father, and when all my consolation is derived from the faith they taught me. These three friends are Louis Gaussen, Charles Scholl,[1] and Thomas Erskine.

"The first produced a gradual impression upon my mind by his benevolent life, by his preaching, and by his devout conversation. The second, with whom I had less prolonged intercourse, presented the gospel to me in a practical aspect so attractive, and at the same time so wise and true, that he won my heart to it.

---

[1] Charles Scholl was pastor of the French Church in London, and subsequently of the Free Church at Lausanne.

The third, at Geneva, removed my intellectual prejudices by showing me the harmony between the gospel and sacred philosophy; and afterwards, at Naples, he put the finishing touch to the work, in so far as man's influence was concerned, by the example of his perfect peace and tender love towards all men. I shall never forget our walks on the Capo di Monte, nor the tone in which, as we watched the sun going down over the magnificent Bay of Naples, he exclaimed, 'Truly the light is sweet; and a pleasant thing it is for the eyes to behold the sun!'

"These three friends, to whom I address these lines, were called by God to exercise over me a joint influence, in which each unwittingly supplied what was lacking in the others.

"I render first all glory to God, and then I say to them, that my heart glows with love for them, and that I pray God to enrich them with His choicest blessings in life and in death, and to spare them, if it may be so, the furnace of suffering through which His mercy has called me to pass.

"At the same time I commend myself to their prayers, that they may crown all the good they have already done me, by asking for me grace so that my patience may not fail, but that I may glorify God to the very end, though my sufferings abound more and more." [1]

---

[1] This letter has appeared in Erskine's "Correspondence," published in Edinburgh.

Erskine, the gentle and profound mystic, of broad and enlightened views, exercised a most beneficial influence over the Christians of his generation. His teaching produced a deep impression upon the Duchesse de Broglie, who knew him at this time. He soared far above the rigid orthodoxy of the day, into the pure heights of heaven, opened by the Apostle John to the Christian soul. He tempered the somewhat too severe dogmatism of M. Gaussen, the eminent pastor and professor, especially in reference to the inspiration of the Scriptures. Adolphe Monod doubtless owed to him his escape from the irksome fetters of narrow English Evangelicalism. It is clear, however, that it was the experience of his ministry at Naples which led to the decisive changes in his life. He became in 1826 the first pastor of a French colony in that city, and it was when he was called for the first time to fulfil the serious duty of instructing men in religious truth, that he was startled to discover how inadequate were his own convictions. He then passed through the great crisis of his spiritual life. He does not appear to have been diverted for a moment from his earnest quest of truth, by the magical beauty of the land in which his lot was cast, where ancient art lives again in the immortal youth of Italian nature, and under the smile of its unrivalled sky. Like Paul at Athens, he heeded not, the enchantment of the outward and visible things in the passionate eagerness of his search after the invisible, and to him as yet almost unknown God, whom he would fain declare to men. He found Him after an agonizing spiritual conflict. There was indescribable bitterness to him in the discovery that all which he had hitherto taken for piety was really worthless in the sight of God. Trembling beneath those thunders of a broken law, under which in after days he so often made his hearers quail, he took his place with the publican and the woman who was a sinner at the feet of Jesus. Faith in a crucified Saviour alone calmed and uplifted him. There is no moral revolution more wonderful than that which is effected when a sincere Pharisee takes his place by the side of the lying publican, smiting, like him, on his breast, and crying, "God be merciful to me a sinner!" It was a crisis like this which transformed the disciple of Gamaliel into the apostle of a free salvation.

Adolphe Monod has left no other record of this phase of his life than that which we find in his preaching. Although he never indulges in personal allusions, we find abundant traces of that spiritual tempest which first plunged him into the depths of despair, and then cast him, trembling with joy, upon the Rock.

In his early discourses on the misery of man and the mercy of God, there is no word about himself; and yet how clearly they reveal that the writer had been passing, like Pascal, through one of those soul-vigils, one of those wrestlings all the night, which leave the combatant, to use Monod's own words, *vainqueur, mais tout meurtri ; tout meurtri, mais vainqueur.*

Can we not catch an echo of the bitterness of soul through which he himself had passed, in this concluding passage of his first sermon?

"O God! who humblest only that Thou mayest lift up, who troublest only to calm, who dost shake only to stablish and settle, we bow to the sentence which condemns us. We accept it with penitence and tears. Hide nothing from us of our misery. Shed abroad in our souls Thy pure and searching light, that we may see ourselves as we truly are! And at such a sight let there rise at once from this whole congregation, a cry of surprise and anguish which shall rend the atmosphere of indifference around us, which shall reach Thy ear and move Thy fatherly compassion towards us, so that, renouncing henceforward all our self-esteem, humbled with a deep humility, believing with a simple faith, we may yield ourselves unreservedly to Thy love, to be raised out of the depth of our misery by the depth of Thy mercy."[1]

Where has the writer found those sombre colours in which he depicts the self-condemnation of the sinner, if not in the sacred terrors of conscience? It might have been said of him still more than of the great Florentine poet, that he had gone down into the lower world, so thrillingly does he describe the ever-deepening horrors awaiting the unconverted, like those enormous cavities sometimes found in a vast abyss, whose gloomy profundities go down into the very bowels of the earth.[2] He confesses to the

---

[1] Sermon by Adolphe Monod, p. 42. Paris Edit. 1818.
[2] Sermons, vol. i. p. 377.

ardent desire he felt for a long time to escape from this doctrine of perdition. He could only bring himself to submit to it, he says, "with bowed head and laying his hand upon his mouth."

This is not the place for us to inquire whether he did not, in the ardour of his new conversion, go beyond the teaching of the gospel on this important point. We are now only describing the psychological crisis which made a new man of him. We find the same tone of deep experience in his early writings on the work of redemption.

"The marble of my heart has been broken!" he exclaims. "O my God! what love, what love! And yet I see only its utmost edge. It is an abyss into the depths of which I cannot look. But even in that which I do behold, I discern a love that passes knowledge ; and in those depths which as yet are hidden from me, my soul foreshadows a love which baffles thought, which confounds and absorbs my whole being. Redeemed at such a price I am no more my own, and to Him I give all my heart!"

Are we not reminded by words like these of the sublime utterance of Pascal in his hour of holy rapture: "God of Abraham, of Isaac, and of Jacob! . . . Not of the philosophers and learned men. . . . Assurance, assurance, love, joy, peace! . . . God of Jesus Christ! . . ."

II.

Still thrilling with the emotion of this great spiritual conflict, and glowing with his first love and zeal, Adolphe Monod, at hardly twenty-five years of age, was called in 1828 to the pastorate of the great Reformed Church of Lyons. A conflict was inevitable. Beneath an austere demeanour he carried a soul of fire, an indomitable spirit; and his youth lent both to his convictions and words a tone of somewhat undue positiveness and exaltation. This was only strengthened by the opposition which he encountered, though he never allowed a touch of spleen, or of wounded self-love to give added vehemence to his convictions.

It may be said that throughout this long controversy Adolphe Monod had no thought of himself; that his sole concern was for what he believed to be the cause of truth and sound doctrine. The crisis was hastened and rendered more formidable by his remarkable power as an orator, which made indifference impossible.

His eloquence was not only the forcible expression of his holiest convictions, but reflected all the passionate ardour of his soul. The incompatibility between the young preacher and his new church was radical and complete. We have no wish to rekindle the smouldering embers of old quarrels; and we would not forget that the historical events which profoundly affected French Protestantism generally at the beginning of the century, pressed with peculiar weight upon the Church of Lyons. M. Martin-Paschoud, the pastor who took the most prominent part in these stormy controversies, has left a memory which we ourselves cherish with well-deserved respect and affection. However widely we may have differed on points of doctrine and ecclesiastical policy, we always found him full of ready and right-minded sympathy on all questions affecting the public welfare. His generosity of heart and mind endeared him to a circle far wider than that of Protestantism.

We will not dwell on the painful incidents of the internal history of the Church of Lyons, at this already remote period, except so far as is absolutely necessary in order to explain the position taken by Adolphe Monod. It may suffice to say that nowhere was the eclipse of the old reformed faith at this time more complete than among the Protestants of this great city. They were distinguished, like all their co-religionists, for probity and morality; they belonged to the higher class of the *bourgoisie*, and were regarded everywhere with all the consideration due to their character and to their high commercial *status*. They were accustomed to the most moderate religious teaching, of the order of the Savoyard vicar rather than of Calvin. A correct worldliness had at this time free play. Never had these good folks heard such a thing mentioned as the necessity of repentance, and the worthlessness in God's sight of their good works, which they associated with their almsgivings in the category of virtue. We can easily understand the indignant astonishment with which they heard the first sermons of their new pastor. This young man, with the pale brow and the thrilling voice, made a direct assault on all their received ideas, and shook all their prejudices. He began by proclaiming plainly that the virtuous themselves have need of pardon, and he threatened them with the judgments of God no less than the people of evil life on whom they looked down with scorn. He drove their human pride from one hiding-place to another, till at length he denounced it at that very intellectual and moral height at which it felt itself safe, and secure of all the rewards of heaven. The new preacher thus raised very urgent personal questions in an audience accustomed to be left unmolested in its calm repose. Thus in his sermon, "Can you die happy?" his powerful arguments disturbed the most easy-going consciences. To these wavering minds, satisfied with a religion of sentiment, which was often nothing more than theism disguised under a traditional outward observance, the earnest disciple of the religious awakening preached the necessity of a clear and definite belief, in his sermon on "Sanctification by the truth." The offence was aggravated by the unquestionable power and ability of the new preacher, which made it impossible to remain unmoved and lukewarm under his teaching. The opposition was at first vague; then it took positive shape, and a majority of the Church and of the Consistory decided to request the removal of the obnoxious innovator. We will not go into all the details of this obstinate controversy, in which the meekest of men appeared the most intractable, because he felt it a matter of conscience to resist.[1]

He was unquestionably right in his refusal to yield to the solicitations made to him to alter or modify his preaching. To do so would have been to belie his convictions. He was perfectly justified in appealing to the ancient constitution of the Reformed Church to prove that he was no innovator, that he was, in fact, simply recalling the Church to her old traditions as still embodied in her liturgies. He was invincible so long as he kept to this position. His speeches in his own defence in the Consistory are models of eloquent argument. Never did a witness of the truth appeal more forcibly to the sacred obligation of confessing the whole truth as he himself believed it. In the Session of the Consistory held April 24, 1827, he said :

"As a doctor does not choose the remedies most agreeable to his patients, but those most needful, which are also often to the taste the most unpleasant, so I do not choose that which may please my hearers, who are my patients, but that which may do them good. I am willing to consult the taste of the majority on all points where conscience is not involved, as in my mode of living, in my manner, in my forms of speech, but I cannot be guided in the choice of my principles by the plurality of votes. In matters of principle I have no right of choice at all ; I do not make the truth, for I am not God; I receive it complete from Him."[2]

---

[1] See "La Destitution d'Adolphe Monod." Paris, 1864.
[2] Ibid. p. 12.

We feel that he was right when he indignantly refused the assistance of a suffragan, who held opinions different from his own, and whom the Consistory tried to press upon him, on the excuse that his feeble health rendered additional help necessary. On this occasion he writes: "I owe it to myself to say that I have not given any of you occasion to esteem me so lightly, as to think I do not believe in my private life that which in public I profess to believe; that I could give up for any earthly consideration the deep convictions which you know I entertain; and that I would not rather die at my post than call to my aid a man who would oppose, or who would at the least not seek to cherish in the souls committed to me by God, the principles which I believe, and which I know to be indispensable to their happiness in this world and in that which is to come."

It was in vain that the Consistory tried various plans to compass its ends. It sent a deputation to Monod to complain that he was propagating principles dangerous to the morality and peace of the Church. In one of its regular sessions it exhorted him to modify his preaching and his manner of life. He has only one reply to make to all these demands, and we give it in his own noble words:

"I count neither my glory, my honour, my health, my life dear to me, save as the gifts of God. I am conscious how easy it would be for one so young as I am, and with a naturally warm temper, to feel personal resentment at the opposition offered to me. But I have constantly sought, and I believe, by the grace of God, I have been able to overcome this temptation. I long to assure you that the deep grief you have caused me, is wholly free from the slightest admixture of bitterness towards any one of you, and that I would willingly devote all that remains to me of health already impaired, if by this sacrifice I could make one of you a partaker of that Divine felicity, the contagion of which you dread! The Bible has taught me that the life of man has two parts, the one transitory and the other eternal; and that the importance of the former is lost in that of the latter, as the finite is absorbed by the infinite. It has taught me that the only way to a happy eternity is faith in Jesus Christ. It has taught me further what this faith in Jesus Christ is, as a conviction, as a state of soul, as a life. It has taught me yet again that it is the will of God that certain men should devote themselves to the work of leading souls into the faith. I am one of those men, and I thank God for it; for, next to the privilege of being a Christian, I know none more to be desired than that of being a Christian pastor. Henceforth, all my time, all my power, all that I have, all that I am, belong to the service of God in the gospel; and it is my constant prayer that I may do nothing which shall not tend to confirm in the faith those who do believe, and to bring into it those who do not."

The firm tone thus maintained by Monod, with all the dignity becoming a faithful witness of the truth, only had the effect of irritating the opposition, which became also numerically stronger and stronger. We can gauge the hopeless distance which separated Monod from his ecclesiastical adversaries, by the petition put in circulation by them in the Church to obtain his removal. It certainly was not wanting in *naïveté*. The petitioners complained that a young theologian had come among them, if not to destroy, at least greatly to disturb, the *divine calm* which had been enjoyed at Lyons, by exhuming old doctrines, which the good sense and sound reason of man (more advanced now than in the age of the Reformation) had wisely buried in oblivion. It was useless, they went on, to go back to such pernicious teachings, which were contrary alike to the majesty and goodness of God and to that religion—the most difficult and the noblest of all—the religion of good works. The petitioners therefore asked that the competent authorities would take efficient measures against a religion which renders virtue useless, unless it is associated with a romantic and indefinable gracious disposition, which is an offence to human reason, the offspring of the Divine.

The signataries bitterly reproached the evangelical pastor with the determination shown by him to make proselytes, especially among the Catholics. *Each one for himself and God for all*, is the universal motto of sceptical latitudinarianism.

The complaints made bore relation not merely to the substance of Adolphe Monod's preaching, but also to its captivating form, and to the vehemence of his oratory. It is beyond question that he was guilty every Sunday of flagrant offence on the score of eloquence, and might well thus perturb the souls of the lovers of the *divine calm*. They would only too gladly, as in the days of deacon Paris, have placarded above his pulpit a Consistorial decree to the effect "*that it was forbidden by God* to work miracles in this place;" and that he must confine himself to utterances as dull and cold as their own spirits. We can hardly keep back a smile when we see Adolphe Monod attempting to justify his oratorical offences, and half promising to restrain their impetuous ardour by committing his thoughts to paper. He only made this concession, by which it was simply impossible that he or any other born orator could be bound, to show that the one point on which he could not yield a hair's breadth, was the substance of his teaching.

The Consistory took into consideration the petition against Monod on the 22nd of December, 1829. It made the complaints urged by the petitioners the pretext for asking the obnoxious pastor to resign. This he refused to do. The Consistory dared not yet go so far as to dismiss him, and a sort of truce was concluded without any concession on M. Monod's part. The situation remained none the less intolerable, and the Consistory tried by all means in its power to show its ill-will, refusing in the report of proceedings to insert his own words, and depriving him of the right of regular religious instruction.

So far the wrong is entirely on the side of the ecclesiastical authorities. It cannot be denied, however, that from the year 1831 Adolphe Monod, being pressed beyond endurance, hastened the final rupture by proceedings which would have rendered his continuance impossible, even under the best disposed Government.

The interesting report which he gave at the commencement of the year, of the state of the Church at Lyons, probably brought matters to a crisis. He rose altogether above local circumstances, and described with great power the close conflict between Rationalism and the religious Revival then going on throughout France and Switzerland. It is in this masterly paper that we discover what is the weak point of Adolphe Monod's position. He completely confounds the attitude of a State Church composed of heterogeneous elements, with that of a Church of professing Christians, governing itself by principles which it has freely accepted. This confusion is very apparent in the following passage:

"The Reformed Church of France," said Monod, in a session of the Consistory, "may be regarded in a twofold aspect: from a religious point of view, as a Christian Church, founded by God and under pledge to God; and from a civil point of view, as a State Church, under the protection of the Government. From the religious point of view, it is a union of men who believe the principles contained in Holy Scripture. As a State Church, it has a rule to which it is bound by its constitution. That rule is the confession of La Rochelle."

The preacher concluded from these considerations that he was the sole representative at Lyons of the true Church, and that the State was bound by the confession of faith to uphold him. This was clearly a misconception of the character of the modern State, which is essentially a lay institution, and cannot enter into doctrinal discussions. It takes simply a historical view of the Churches associated with it. It is quite incompetent to interfere in any differences that may arise on points of dogma. Besides, a Church composed of a promiscuous multitude cannot be bound by the letter of its creed, especially when, as was the case with the Reformed Church of France, after the laws of Germinal, it has no ultimate and competent authority on matters of faith. In cases where, as in the Church at Lyons, the majority have become estranged from the old religion, there is no means of compelling them to come back to it. It is very grievous that the faith should be thus abandoned, and a vague historic tradition substituted for it ; but it is impossible to reimpose by force a creed which no longer commands belief. An evangelical preacher confronted with a State Church like that of Lyons has only one alternative ; he must either work on patiently till he can win back the majority to his own faith, or he must take up an entirely independent position and say, " Let who will follow me."

We do not blame Adolphe Monod for having failed to make these distinctions. Indeed, it would have been scarcely possible for him to make them at a period when the ecclesiastical problem was still undefined. Even half a century later we find the same confusion still prevailing, and involving in inextricable confusion the affairs of the Reformed Church of France, after the Synod of 1872. It is an error that can only be dissipated by stern and repeated lessons of experience, and it is far from having vanished, even in our own day. Adolphe Monod had, indeed, already perceived what was the true solution of the problem, for he did not hesitate, in one of his speeches in the Consistory, to express his sympathy with the Free Churches of North America.

He now felt himself impelled by conscience to a course of action which was, to say the least of it, imprudent.

On Sunday, March 20, 1831, the Sunday preceding the great Easter Communion, he was observed to be more pale than usual when he entered the pulpit, and evidently overcome with the feeling of his tremendous responsibility. The subject which he took up was felt by all to be a crucial one. The congregation was astonished to hear him read the words of the institution of the Lord's Supper, although no eucharistic table was spread. His object was, in fact, to guard against unworthy communicants by putting to his hearers this question, in its novelty very startling to them: "Who ought to communicate?" Never had his eloquence risen to such a height of power and holy passion. After recalling the sacred character of the eucharistic table and the barriers by which the discipline of the early Church had fenced it, in order to avoid a profanation which was an outrage to Christ, and brought swift condemnation on the head of the guilty communicant, he drew a terrible picture of the irregularities and scandals of the Church of the day and of his own Church. Then he exclaimed, in accents never forgotten by those who heard them :

"O Church of my Saviour, thou wast a church beloved of God, a plant of His own right hand planting, and cherished by His care. But the barriers have been thrown down. Those who called themselves by the name of Christ, but who were not of Christ, have sought to be received into Thy bosom, and they have entered in only to ravage and defile. All have become mixed together in hopeless confusion; and now, in the midst of this motley crowd, without faith and without law, but still calling itself the Church of Christ, there can only be found here and there a few children of God who can scarcely recognise each other, so scattered are they in the midst of the unbelievers and enemies of the Lord. And in regard especially to the Communion, this is what has happened. Every one who says 'I am a Christian,' all those who have been baptized, all who attend religious exercises, claim to be members of the Church, and to have a right to the Communion; as if Church membership meant nothing more than bearing the name of Christ, as if regeneration came by baptismal water and not by the Spirit; as if a human voice, a certain building, the walls, columns, arches, seats of a place of worship, could convert a sinner! O lamentable confusion! O desecrated body and blood of the Lord!

"And shall the table of my Master be always thus profaned? Shall the days of Communion always be to a faithful minister, days of lamentation, mourning and woe? For myself, I would rather lay the body of Christ upon a stone, and scatter His blood to the winds, than present them to unbelieving and profane lips. O my God! Thou knowest that I speak truth. Wilt Thou not arise and take away this scandal from Thy Church? This is no slight darkness, no trifling error, no small irregularity. It is dire disorder, gross darkness, utter infidelity—infidelity wearing the name of Christ."[1]

Adolphe Monod himself afterwards admitted that he had gone too far in this sermon. To us it appears

---

[1] Sermons, vol. i. pp. 271–282.

exaggerated only in manner; it is the exaggeration of a great orator, carried away by his impetuous eloquence and fired with a righteous indignation.

It will be readily understood, however, that a challenge like this gave terrible offence, though the intention of the author was only to make a strong appeal to conscience. To the vote of censure passed by the Consistory upon the sermon of the 20th of March, Adolphe Monod replied on the 14th of April by a formal proposition to restore in the Church of Lyons the ancient discipline of the Reformed Church of France. This was an implied acknowledgment that the ecclesiastical law of the past needed a fresh sanction on the part of the regular authorities.

This inconsistency did not strike him. The next day the Consistory replied to him by an order for his dismissal, which, however, could not take effect till it had received ministerial confirmation. Adolphe Monod rendered the confirmation inevitable, in spite of his eloquent written vindication of himself, by his startling proceeding the next Sunday (Whit-Sunday), when, after preaching, he left the pulpit in order not to preside at the communion of the day. It should be added that he had done everything in his power to provide a substitute for himself on this occasion. On the 19th of March, 1832, the royal confirmation was given to his dismissal from office. It must be admitted that no other course was open to the Minister of Public Worship.

We have dwelt at some length on this half-forgotten episode of the internal history of French Protestantism, because it is characteristic at once of the troublous times in which Monod lived, of his own courageous fidelity to the cause of what he believed to be true, and of the remarkable oratorical powers developed by him in these stormy controversies. As soon as he found himself dismissed from the pastorate, he gathered around him his adherents, united himself to a small evangelical Church which had been formed in Lyons, and began to conduct worship in a humble building, very inadequate to the exercise of such gifts as his, which could command the attention of multitudes.

There are few sacrifices more costly to a great orator than this; but Adolphe Monod accepted the changed conditions with touching humility. He did not wish to be regarded as the founder of a new Church. He objected to this for two reasons. First, he was fully convinced that the Reformed Church of France was by its constitution evangelical, and that therefore its sons ought not, by founding another Church side by side with it, to proclaim its fall, and to hand over to the Rationalistic school the heritage of their fathers. Second, it was his fixed opinion through life, that on matters of this sort it is wise to be as prudent and moderate, as on the side of evangelical truth it is incumbent to be bold and unflinching. His abiding convictions on this point are expressed briefly in his interesting appeal to the Christians of France and of other lands, on behalf of the Evangelical Church of Lyons. In that appeal he says : " I shall wait; I shall follow the Lord step by step, day by day, acting, as necessity arises, in what appears to me the path indicated by Providence. I shall mark out no fixed course beforehand. I shall go straight forward, guiding myself outside the sanctuary (since I have no longer a place within it) by the same principles which I have ever preached."

It was needful, however, to render habitable this tent, pitched opposite that house of God from which the preacher had been shut out. The Evangelical Church of Lyons was led on to establish, one after another, the institutions essential to a Church which would subsist and develop itself upon the basis of a living faith. The new ministry of Adolphe Monod, begun in poverty, and without any assured means of maintenance, soon became abundantly fruitful. The Evangelical Church of Lyons, for which he always cherished a tender affection, received from him the two special characteristics by which it has been so honourably distinguished, — a large-hearted Christianity which commended it to all believers, and a missionary zeal so active and intense that it brought in large numbers of converts from surrounding Catholicism. It had a succession of pastors all animated with the spirit of its founder. During this, the most straitened period of his pastoral career, Adolphe Monod found a true helpmeet in his wife, to whom he had been married in 1832; she entered with hearty sympathy into all the great purposes of his life, shared his activities, comforted him in his sorrows, and lightened by her hopeful spirit all his hours of depression. He found himself surrounded by a rapidly increasing family, to whom he was the tenderest of fathers, devoting himself specially to the moral education of his children. His home was a beautiful example of what a Christian household may be. I hold in grateful memory some of the Sunday evenings I myself spent there, when Monod gathered his young children around him and presented the gospel to them in its most winning and attractive form.

III.

In 1836 Adolphe Monod was called to fill the Chair of Morals in the theological faculty of Montauban. Here he found a new sphere of usefulness not less practical in its results, for we can trace the beneficial effects of his training in successive generations of pastors. His influence over the youthful mind was extraordinary. He was a true master, in the noblest sense of the word, kindling in young and eager souls the spark of a higher life, so that they looked up to him reverently as their spiritual father. He had not the transcendant inventive or creative genius which has distinguished some of the great professors of science and philosophy in our day. He has not left any strong impress on theological teaching; in truth, peculiarly adapted as was the study of morals to his habits of mind, he at this time only treated it slightly. He had not the leisure necessary to make his mark in Hebrew philology, and it was not till a later period of his life that he fully recognised the requirements of scientific criticism. He had hardly time to sketch out his exegetical course of the New Testament. His teaching was, however, so remarkable for its severe beauty of form, its clearness of exposition, and the spirit pervading it, that it exerted a very wholesome influence over his students. They could not but admire in him the man and the orator. This was the secret of his power over young men. He set before them so lofty a standard of Christian morality that he commanded their respect, and gave them a very high idea of the calling of a Christian and a pastor.

Though reserved and silent, his unvarying kindness rendered him always accessible to his students, and no master was ever more beloved and respected. His eloquence became constantly more impressive, and riveted his youthful hearers, who were never weary of listening to him. He in his turn devoted to them the noblest efforts of his genius, not only in consecutive homilies on Holy Scripture, such as his expositions of Paul's Epistles to the Ephesians, but also in lectures on sacred oratory and in the great sermons belonging to this period of his life, which were all delivered first at Montauban. He thus formed around him a sort of evangelical Port Royal, one of those quiet retreats open to all that is noble and pure, where the love of letters is elevated by the grandeur of the object pursued, where study is blended with prayer, and the consecration of soul lends a sacredness to all the work of preparation.

It was not my privilege to be one of Adolphe Monod's disciples, but a short stay at Montauban, in 1844, gave me a vivid impression of his extraordinary power as a Christian and as an orator. It was impossible not to be struck with his happy blending of fervour with soberness, of kindness with severity, of brilliant gifts with unfeigned humility, and by his complete absorption in his double work—the care of the Church and the watchful training of its future pastors. Virtue went forth from him, and it seemed as if all who came in contact with him felt its influence. He impressed on them, more or less, his own image. His memory is as living to-day as it was thirty years ago, in the hearts of his disciples. Montauban did not exhaust his activity. He never allowed himself to rest, and almost all his vacations were devoted to preaching tours, which carried the influence of his powerful words into the humblest villages as well as into the great towns of France. His health was, however, always feeble, and his naturally melancholy temperament, though it could not disturb the quiet depths of his faith, often made his work a weariness both to the flesh and the spirit.

Before passing on to a fresh stage in Monod's life, let us attempt to describe what he was as a theologian and an orator in this his first manner. His appearance in the Protestant pulpit was a marked event. No such eloquence had been heard since the days of Saurin. The desert had been a school of confessors rather than of orators. The preachers who came forth from it on the eve of the French Revolution had wellnigh lost the staunch convictions of their fathers. There was no inspiration in their colourless doctrine, and they borrowed from the First Empire the insipid eloquence of its official literature. There were, no doubt, exceptions to this prevailing mediocrity. A powerful thinker like Samuel Vincent was able to hold the eager attention of his hearers, though he lacked the gift of real eloquence. We have already alluded to the distinguished abilities of the elder Monod. M. Athanase Coquerel the elder, who had become his colleague a few years before the commencement of Adolphe Monod's work at Lyons, displayed during more than half a century a remarkable versatility of talent. He was distinguished for his inexhaustible *verve*, his rare faculty of giving freshness to his subject, though without any of the highest gifts either of thought or language. He was a ready and effective speaker, and a careful observer of classic forms. The marked success which attended him through the long career of his ministry is the incontrovertible proof of his powers as an orator. It was impossible, however, that the vague belief in the supernatural which prevailed from the beginning of the century, should give as powerful an impetus even to sacred oratory as an earnest evangelical faith. It recognised neither the terrors of condemnation nor the ecstatic joys of pardon. Its optimism made it glide over the surface of things, without discovering beneath the smooth and brittle ice, the abyss into which poor humanity had fallen. Nor did it catch a glimpse of that other abyss of infinite mercy which forms so glorious a contrast. The cross, in ceasing to be the mystery of redeeming love, loses all its supreme beauty. The emotions which appeal most strongly to the soul of man are thus withdrawn. Instead of paradise lost and regained, there remains only a moral idyll. We have a Gessner instead of a Milton. On the other hand, it is not enough to be possessed of an organ of rich and deep-toned harmonies; it is needful also to have one who can make the music. The beauty of the instrument is nothing without the skilful artist. In France, at least, until Adolphe Monod appeared, the Protestant Church had produced witnesses, sometimes truly apostolic men like Felix Neff, but no orators in the true sense of the word. Often it was a matter of principle with them to be careless of the forms of speech, either from an idea that time devoted to the cultivation of the beautiful would be so much taken from that earnest appeal to conscience which seemed their supreme work, or from some scruple about allowing the least part to the human element in the work of conversion—a sort of unconscious Manicheeism, which is the natural result of a narrow Puritanism. The rigorous orthodoxy with which they satisfied themselves, and which they readily confounded with eternal truth, was ill adapted in its rigid forms to a broad and living exposition. It is true that these defects were redeemed by the ardour and purity of missionary zeal, but they were none the less great obstacles to the exercise of pulpit oratory. Adolphe Monod possessed this gift in the very highest degree. He had, as we have already observed, the outward gifts of the orator—the sonorous voice, the expressive gesture, and, above all, a face which was the true reflection of his pure and ardent soul. His imagination was vivid, his mind clear and strong, and his utterance naturally ready, exact, and powerful. Above all, he had that indescribable faculty in a speaker, of arresting and holding the attention of his hearers, and of imparting to them his own enthusiasm.

At Geneva he had found a school of oratory on the academic model, which had largely cultivated a diffusive style of pulpit rhetoric. This was probably not without its uses for set preaching, but Monod soon cast off that which was artificial and declamatory in its method. His natural gifts received their highest impetus from his new convictions, which had shaken his being to its very centre. These gave him that concentration of thought and feeling which is the first condition of passion. One great element of his power was his intense earnestness, which his hearers could not but feel, and which gave energy to his every word and gesture. Christianity, as he understood it, revealed to him the tragic and sublime aspect of things human and divine, and the rich poetry of the Hebrew Scriptures supplied him with the glowing colours and images in which he delighted. His imagination revelled in the Bible; his heart and his head fed upon it. Lastly, his love for the immortal soul, his eager longing to rescue it from itself and from supreme peril, gave to his discourses that pointedness and directness which makes the words sharper than a two-edged sword.

His highest preparation for work was prayer. This is very evident from his manuscripts, in which we find the thread of thought often broken that his soul may cry out to God in utterances like the following: "O Christ, help me by the blood of Thy cross."

One of his sermons opens with this prayer, which was plainly the secret outpouring of his soul to God:

"O my God, give me by Thy Spirit to lay down at the foot of the cross of Thy Son, that searching of myself, and that disquietude which have overcome me for these three days, to the detriment of my sermon, of my faith, and of Thy glory, and to the scandal of my brethren. As for my sermon, help me to make it not such as I will, but as Thou wilt. Thou hast the secret of helping to do much in a little time. I give myself up to Thee, and begin my work without fear, my eyes being up unto Thee. Enlighten me for the love of Christ."

Theremin has written a book at once ingenious and true, under the title, "L'Eloquence est une vertu." In it he shows how much even natural eloquence owes to the qualities of the soul. The example of Adolphe Monod is a strong confirmation of his theory. He himself fully realised this co-operation of conscience, and he attached great importance to the moral condition in the preparation of his sermons, even from an artistic point of view; for in his case the mystical preparation was in no way incompatible with the other. He was an artist not by temperament only, but as a duty. Is it not a point of conscience to neglect nothing which may give to truth a form worthy of itself, and make it effective and impressive?

Surely the feeling of a sacred responsibility will be alone sufficient to prevent the use of declamation and mere meretricious oratory. A true love of souls must forbid the pandering to a false taste by ornate and florid speech, and thus the Christian orator will be saved from one of the worst faults of an age of literary decadence. Even manner, the most purely external adjunct of oratory, cannot escape the influence of the speaker's prevailing tone. On this point Adolphe Monod gave some words of wise counsel in an inaugural discourse of the faculty of Montauban. Addressing the future pastors, he said:

"Exercise yourselves without scruple, gentlemen, in the art of speaking and of style, but let it be in a Christian spirit. Let these be to you always simply a means, not an end. If you make oratory itself the end at which you aim, you are no longer preachers, you are not even orators, you are actors. If you cultivate speech as a means of glorifying God and of doing good to men, you fulfil a duty."[1]

After dwelling on what was purely technical in style, the professor took up its moral aspect. He said:

"The fundamental principle which forms the basis of all rules, is that oratory has its seat, not in the lips, but in the feeling and thought, and that it depends less on the voice than on the soul. It is the soul which must speak. This is the condition of all true eloquence. If the success of an actor like Talma depended, as he himself said, on the intensity of his meditation on the dramatic work which he was to render, how much more must this be true of the preacher? The more deeply he is impressed with the subject he is to advance, the better will he convey it, and the more natural and simple will his manner be. The best method for acquiring that ease and freedom of speech which is without stiffness, effort, or strain, is the heroic faith which leans upon God Himself, and in the greatness of the cause loses sight of the creature. Thus regarded, true elocution is itself a virtue."

Monod was never willing, however, to dispense with the inspiration that comes from the presence of a large assembly. Hence, after most careful preparation, he almost always preached extempore. He has himself told us that at Lyons it was his practice to preach from notes. The discourse in this, its first form, was afterwards subjected to a severe revision. Each of his sermons, especially during his stay at Montauban, was a complete oratorical treatise em-

---

[1] Discours de rentrée, Nov. 26, 1840.

bracing some one aspect of Christian doctrine, often clothed in the most brilliant forms, and having all the vivacity of unwritten speech. Hence his sermons were of extraordinary length, such as only his rare gifts could have made acceptable. It was, to use his own expression, preaching with a full orchestra. To us he seems to excel far more in this than in the homiletic style, which he also cultivated very carefully, as may be seen from his sermons on the temptation of Christ, and on the creation.

Adolphe Monod's preaching is not essentially either exegetical or psychological, although it contains both exegesis and psychology. It is primarily synthetic. Doctrinal exposition hurries on to practical application. *Festinat ad res.* He is fond of using striking, sometimes paradoxical expressions, as when he speaks of *virtuous sinners*, and is apt to conclude each portion of his discourse with an oratorical refrain too often repeated. When he takes up an ethical subject he always comes back to the great doctrine of justification by faith and of conversion. It is plain that his only aim is to show the impenitent sinner that he is in a position from which he cannot of himself escape. His logic is close and forcible; but sometimes it is carried to an extreme, and goes beyond the mark, as in the sermon on the fifth commandment, "Thou shalt not kill." The idea of murder carried to this length loses all exactness, and takes in every form of evil, since there is not one which is not deadly to the soul.

Imagination plays a great part in his preaching, but he mixes on the palette only sacred colours. History and nature are alike regarded through the medium of the Bible, of which Monod makes most skilful use, though he is sometimes too profuse in his allusions to texts less generally known than he supposes. The description of the murder of John the Baptist at the request of the dancing Herodias; of the anguish of the jailer at Philippi, and of his deliverance after his attempt at suicide; the touching delineations of the scenes of the passion, and the account of the first apostolic mission, all these remain among the masterpieces of the Christian oratory of our day. Monod does not quote either from the Fathers of the early Church nor from the Reformers, and scarcely ever makes an allusion either to contemporary history or literature. In this respect he presents a strong contrast to Lacordaire, who was, under his white Dominican robe, the most modern of French preachers. Adolphe Monod dwells by preference on those immortal themes of all Christian eloquence, which alone respond to the cravings of humanity—suffering, sin, death, the eternal hope, the Divine Fatherhood, the mercy of Christ. If, in his treatment of them, he lacks the originality and suggestiveness of Vinet, he handles them with majestic eloquence, with brilliant imagination, and fervid passion. He belongs rather to the school of Bossuet and of Saurin, than of Fénélon and Massillon.

His influence on the pulpit oratory of the day was great. It must be acknowledged, however, that his disciples have not always followed him without peril; for in their imitations they have often caught what was external merely in his great gifts—his striking oratorical modes of speech. In this way they have made grievous failures, like those Austrian generals who were never worse beaten than when they attempted to copy the tactics of Napoleon without understanding the secret of their use.

The early preaching of Adolphe Monod has an authoritative character derived from his views of theology. Both manner and matter were to be, to some extent, modified in the next period of his life. During the first years of his stay at Montauban he remained firmly attached to the orthodoxy of the revival, at least in its main outlines, for he was never one of those who went to the greatest lengths.[1]

While appealing to the ancient confessions of the Reformation era, in confutation of the innovations of Rationalism, he did not hold himself bound to the letter of creeds, which were, after all, of only human origin, and therefore inadequate, and bearing too distinctly the peculiar impress of the age which called them forth. Monod was not a strict Calvinist, nor a millenarian of the English school; but he had,

---

[1] The discourses of this early period form the first two volumes of the collection of sermons of Adolphe Monod, under the heading, "Naples—Lyons—Montauban." Paris, 1850-59.

nevertheless, accepted the leading principles of the orthodoxy of the age, which was in many respects more akin to the scholasticism of the seventeenth than to the theology of the sixteenth century. He held it in high estimation, because it was under this rigid form that the everlasting gospel had first reached his conscience, and he lent to it the warmth of his own ardent nature. This theology was based upon a wholly inadequate view of authority, very different from the broad and living view of the Reformers. Apparently the theologians of the revival were only carrying on the work of the Reformers in appealing as they did to the sovereignty of Scripture. But the seventeenth century had greatly modified their views on this important point, casting into the shade that which was to the Reformers the conclusive proof of the inspiration of the Bible, that *testimonium spiritus sancti*, which bases the authority of the book on the testimony of the conscience divinely enlightened, and clings to the person of Christ Himself as the great central fact of revelation. The theologians of the seventeenth century and those of the revival, following in their footsteps, based the authority of the book primarily upon the miraculous, proofs of which they sought now in the fulfilment of prophecy, now in the multiplication of signs and wonders. It was upon this letter of credit that Scripture and revelation were to be accepted, even before the soul had been brought into contact with the truth itself, and primarily with the living truth, which is Jesus Christ. The way was from the Scriptures to Christ, not from Christ to the Scriptures.

In such an apology there is not simply the error of isolating the internal from the external evidence, but also injustice is done to the latter, which has an indispensible historical value in the establishment of the credibility of the facts and documents of revelation. When it is thus appealed to as a final authority to cut short all inquiry, it becomes rather an obstacle to conviction than a means of producing it. The authority of Scripture is lowered, and made to appear of the same character as that claimed by the Catholic Church. We are not surprised, therefore, to find in Adolphe Monod's apologetic work, "Lucile," that the enlightened Catholic priest who is charged with the task of establishing the authority of Holy Scripture, does so by arguments almost identical with those which he employs in the second part of the book to vindicate the authority of his Church.

The same apologetic point of view is presented, with great force of thought and expression, in the sermon on "Belief and Unbelief." It is always by prophecy or miracle—that is, by the supernatural attestation of Divine power—that the preacher silences the doubter. He does, indeed, repeatedly break through the limitations of his system, as when, at the commencement of this very sermon, he tells his hearers that the best way to prove to them that the Bible is the sword of the Spirit is to pierce them through with it; but there can be no doubt that he was at this time a theologian of the authoritative school. With such views of the authority of Scripture, it was difficult to escape the doctrine of literal inspiration, though Adolphe Monod never gave his formal adherence to the theory of the infallibility of the sacred letter. In his sermon on the " Temptation of Christ," he attaches an exaggerated importance to the written word, to the mere letter of the text. The book is certainly made to play the part which belongs properly only to the truth which is in the book. The casket is made more of than the contents.

"This quotation," says the preacher, referring to the text cited by Christ, "stops the enemy at once." [1] The authority of the Bible thus regarded, gives it rather the character of a formulary or Divine *credo* than a history. The writing which contains the revelation becomes confounded with the revelation itself, and religion assumes an essentially dogmatic character. History has, no doubt, still a place in the system, but it is a subordinate place. Jesus Christ fills an important position, but He is not the very centre, life and substance of the whole. Purity of doctrine is scrupulously guarded, and a hedge of thorns is placed around it, as the ancient law was protected by the synagogue of old. Adolphe Monod never fell into these extremes; he always presented

---

Sermons, vol. ii. p. 177.

evangelical truth from a moral point of view; but it must be admitted that in his early teaching he gave too prominent a place to doctrine in the development of the religious life. This is very evident in his sermon on "Sanctification by the Truth," in which he argues that truth is necessarily the parent of good, and error, even though unwitting, must result in evil, just as in nature every seed, no matter how sown, produces after its kind.

"Wheat," he says, "sown with or without design, will always produce wheat; and tares, in like manner, will never bring forth anything but tares. Even so, a doctrine can only yield such fruits of good or evil as are germinally contained within it. Truth, whether acquired with or without moral effort, will always bear its happy fruit—sanctification; so that in order to express the moral condition of a soul, we have not to ascertain in what way truth or error has gained a lodgment within it, but which of the two reigns within."

Revelation is thus regarded too much in the light of a mathematical proposition, which appeals to the intellect alone. It would be unjust to press this conclusion too far in the case of Adolphe Monod, for the fervour of his genius constantly carried him beyond the narrow bounds of his system. At the close of the same sermon from which we have just quoted, we find the following glowing panegyric on the heroism of the modern missionary:

"I have seen the young missionary tear himself from the weeping embrace of a mother, and make the only sacrifice that could be greater than hers; I have seen the mother, bidding back her tears, sustain and encourage him when his heart seemed ready to fail in the prospect of the parting. And I have seen the same mother again, weeping over his death; but not at his grave. His grave—if he has one—is in the far East, and he has been borne to it, perhaps, by some faithful Hindoos, anxious to return to the lifeless body the same faithful care which he had bestowed upon their souls. His is the forgotten grave of an unknown martyr in a land of strangers, unwatered by a mother's tears; and the only sound which will break its stillness will be, perhaps, the tumult of some barbarous and bloody rite, to do away with which he gave his life."

This peroration is in itself the refutation of the general tenor of the sermon, for this martyr-missionary might have gone forth from the Roman College, instead of from one of the orthodox societies of Paris or Basle. Adolphe Monod would not have waited to know his creed before rendering tribute to his heroic self-devotion, thus showing that above orthodoxy there is the faith which moves in a higher sphere. This faith does not necessarily remove all intellectual doubts; these may still exist, but they affect only the form or formulary of truth, not its essence, which is a life, a person, to be apprehended by the heart and conscience, which is, in a word, Jesus Christ.

We need not dwell on Adolphe Monod's early view of the doctrine of redemption. This was entirely in harmony with the prevailing teaching of the Revival, and erred, as it appears to us, by exaggerating the judicial aspect of the question, regarding the cross as a sort of Divine retaliation, the actual condemnation of the Son by the Father.

Monod never changed his views on this point. They became firmly associated with his conception of the justice of God, while he failed, as we think, to recognise how mercy tempers justice. These two attributes became, in his treatment of them, conflicting hypostases, instead of blending in the unity of a holy love. Hence he was led to insist on the suffering of the cross as being really infinite, and exhausting all the moral agony of hell. Even this view, however, was inadequate, since the element of the endless duration of suffering was necessarily omitted. From the same premises Monod was led to accept the final and hopeless doom of those who die impenitent, —a doctrine affirmed with a certainty which is not justified either by the letter of Scripture or by the competence of the finite mind to judge of eternal issues.

Eternal punishment is a constantly recurring topic in Monod's early sermons, and he rises to even unwonted fervour when he touches on this awful theme, though he never attempts, by harrowing descriptions of the anguish of the doomed, to excite mere nervous terror. We are bound to respect his faithfulness to convictions which must have been intensely painful to his generous heart. "Those who heard him tremble still," said Michelet. He himself was the first to tremble—to tremble for the immortal souls whom he yearned to save from the abyss. It was to arouse them from their deathful sleep that he sounded again and again that awful alarm bell, at the tones of which the most indifferent cheeks grow pale. In truth, Monod made use of all the narrow dogmatisms of the Revival, to startle out of its crass indifference and worldliness a generation which had been lulled into a false security by the facile, sentimental Protestantism of the nineteenth century, crying "Peace! Peace!" when there was no peace.

To the doctrine of justifying faith Monod gave powerful affirmation, not pausing like Vinet to discover the synthesis which brings St. James into harmony with St. Paul, and shows how sanctification springs from justification, like the oak from the acorn. He always maintained a clear distinction between grace and free will, not trying to reconcile them lest he should weaken the force of either.

No preacher ever made more direct and telling appeals to man's power of choice. In a word, Adolphe Monod, in this his first period, is the faithful exponent of the current orthodoxy of the religious Revival, while avoiding the extravagancies which here and there defaced it.

In the fervid eloquence of his preaching, however, it is easy to trace, even at this period, the elements of a broader and fuller conception of Christian truth. It could not be otherwise in a heart and mind cast in so generous a mould. It would be easy to multiply passages from Monod's early sermons, which point to a greater freedom in dealing with Scripture, and a less exaggerated estimate of the importance of mere doctrinal beliefs, than is consistent with his systematic creed. But we must always bear in mind that a religious system is to be judged, not by its recognition of this or that isolated fact, but by its general tone and spirit, by that which Spinoza calls the *vinculum substanciæ*. Now it is indisputable that the prevailing tone and spirit of Adolphe Monod's teaching in the earlier part of his career was such as we have described. It is equally certain that in later years his theology underwent a very real change, though his faith remained the same. In tracing the causes, both external and internal, which contributed to this result, we shall have to go back to the history of his life.

IV.

We left Adolphe Monod commencing at Montauban that professorial career in which he was so useful. The sermons which he published in the early part of his course exhibit no change of opinion. His apologetic work, "Lucile," is, on the contrary, the fullest expression of his early views.

This book was written in 1840, in the form of letters. It was suggested by facts in real life, and we ourselves were personally acquainted with the characters represented. The substratum of fact was, however, soon transformed and enriched by the hand of the artist. No publication of Adolphe Monod's was more successful than this. The ease and animation of the letters and dialogues, the beauty of the language, the close and lucid reasoning, the high tone and simple, earnest piety which characterise it throughout, all combine to make "Lucile" a *chef d'œuvre*. It presents the grand arguments which never grow old, as well as those which were adapted only to a form of thought now passed away.

As an apologist, Adolphe Monod belongs to the English school. He not only ignores the great and immortal apology of the Alexandrine fathers, but he pays too little attention to Pascal, who in the seventeenth century restored the psychological, without derogating from the value of the historical evidence of Christianity.

In "Lucile" the whole weight of the demonstration is made to rest upon the authority of Scripture, as vindicated by outward signs, rather than by the witness of the Spirit of God. Much more stress is laid upon miracle and prophecies than upon the person of Jesus Christ. This is its weak point.

At the very time when "Lucile" appeared, Vinet was taking up and carrying on the work of the great thinker of Port Royal. The influence of Vinet's writings did more than anything else to enlarge Adolphe Monod's theological views. Monod was a diligent reader of the religious journal, "Le Semeur," though but rarely a contributor to it, and he could not but be struck with the wealth and depth of thought which characterised all the articles, literary and theological, of the Lausanne professor. Just as we can trace through every line of the Epistle of Peter the influence of Paul, his junior in the apostolate, so Adolphe Monod became, perhaps unconsciously to himself, deeply imbued in mature life with the spirit of Vinet.

He was no copyist, and in the writings of the two men we find scarcely two expressions in common; but the assimilation of thought was deep and real.

Adolphe Monod's duties as a theological professor became also a means of enlarging his views. It was not possible for him, with his keenness of insight and uprightness of conscience, to carry on a course of sacred criticism, without becoming conscious of many difficulties in the way of that theory of literal inspiration, which he had accepted without thorough investigation. If the whole edifice of Christian conviction is to be based upon the authority of the Scriptures as demonstrated by miracles, the verbal infallibility of the canon is an indispensable condition. Failing this, recourse must be had to some other criterion—to historical evidence, on the one hand, which guarantees only that which is indubitably authentic; and, on the other hand, to the witness of the Spirit, which testifies first to Christ Himself—the centre and soul of revelation—and through Him to the Book, of which He is the Alpha and Omega.

Literal inspiration, and an indisputable canon—these are the two pillars of the strict orthodoxy of the Revival, which on these two points differed widely from the Reformation of the sixteenth century. The question at issue between this orthodoxy and the liberal evangelical school is, whether the higher authority belongs to Jesus Christ or to the Book, provided always that the authenticity of the record be established by competent historical evidence. With however much of prudent reticence Adolphe Monod entered on his course of sacred criticism, it could not fail to modify—at first, perhaps, unconsciously to himself—his views of revelation. On his young hearers, less fettered than himself by a traditional faith, the effect was very manifest. There can be little doubt that they were somewhat unsettled by the critical problems which now presented themselves for the first time to their minds, and it was in all probability the desire to find some basis for their convictions which could never be shaken, that led Adolphe Monod to recast his apology, and with it, to some extent, his theology. It would be erroneous to suppose that there was anything like a violent rupture between the first and the second period of his intellectual life. The transition was a very gradual one, wrought without observation in the quiet domain of his own thoughts. The change must have been more marked if he had ever professed the Calvinism of the Scotch Churches, or the doctrine of plenary inspiration taught by the venerable Gaussen. But he had never gone to extremes; and it is only by a careful perusal of the sermons preached after his removal to Paris, that we discover how completely he had changed his standpoint.

He was called to be suffragan in the great Church at Paris in the year 1847. We shall presently speak of the important ministry he there accomplished. For the present we shall continue to trace the development of his theological views. From his very first sermon it was clear that these had undergone a change. He was most careful, however, not to put anything in a way which might be likely to cause a division among evangelical Protestants; hence he avoided giving anything like a polemical turn to the expression of his new convictions. The great purport of his preaching was, moreover, still the same. He proclaimed restoration for lost man by the redemption of Christ, justification by faith, a salvation full and free. His convictions of the holiness of God's law, of His claims, and of the desperate condition to which man was reduced by sin, were as strong as ever. This was the vital truth of the orthodoxy of the Revival, and this gave force to its reaction against the frivolous optimism which had crept into the Protestant Church. Adolphe Monod, so far from derogating at all from the holy austerity of the

Revival, gave most emphatic vindication to it in his later sermons. If he no longer dwelt so largely upon eternal punishment, if towards the close of his life he recognised the scriptural truth, that the secret things (of eternity) belong to the Lord our God, he did not therefore lower the standard of holy living. Thus in one of his latest sermons we find him exclaiming: "Far be it from us to preach a salvation in which the glory of God should be sacrificed. Let His holy law first be vindicated, and then, if it may be so, let my salvation be secured."[1]

In the following passage we trace the bond of union between the two phases of his faith: "O Cross! O blood of the Holy One shed for my sins! O bitter sacrifice of a spotless victim! O scene, which justifies alike the sinner in the eye of a holy law, and the God who can be just, and yet the Justifier! O thrice blessed cross, my whole soul flees to thee. It yearned for thee before it knew thee: with what ardour shall it not embrace thee, now thou art known!"

These closing words introduce us to the new world

---

[1] "Doctrine Chrétienne," Quatre Discours. Paris, 1869. "Discours sur l'Œuvre du Fils," p. 167. The works of Adolphe Monod dating from this period are, in addition to these doctrinal discourses: Vol. III. of his Sermons, Paris 1859, containing his sermon, "La Parole vivante;" "St. Paul;" Cinq Discours, 1862-63. Some single sermons of great value; among others, "Nathanael," "Les grandes âmes," " Explication de l'Epître aux Ephésiens." Paris, 1867.

in which for some years Adolphe Monod's thoughts had begun to move. He says that he was yearning for the cross before he knew it. What is this but an acknowledgment that the gospel, of which the cross is the foundation and the top-stone, appeals to the deepest instincts of the soul and conscience, and derives its highest title to our acceptance, not from miracle or prophecy, but from its response to our universal human needs?

This is the point on which he dwells with so much emphasis in the second period of his preaching. He delights to show the harmony existing between conscience and the gospel, and appeals constantly to Tertullian's *testimonium animæ naturaliter Christianæ*, and to the apologies of Clement of Alexandria, of Pascal, and of Vinet, in support of his views.

We should like to quote, just as they stand, his two admirable sermons upon Nathanael and "Les grandes âmes." The thoughts themselves are only new in his perception of them, but they come out with fresh brilliancy under his treatment, and show how his own mind had been expanding. In his sermon on Nathanael he says :

"All upright hearts belong to Jesus ; He claims them from the first, and disposes of them as of that which is His own, and which sooner or later must come to Him. The faithfulness of Nathanael to the light he had received, placed him in a position to receive the greater light, which as yet he lacked. It only needed that he should be brought into the presence of Christ to recognise in Him that which he sought. The true moral measure of every man is not the measure of light he possesses, but his faithfulness to that which he has. Between an upright heart and Christ there is, if I may so speak, such an affinity, such an attraction, that if they were as far apart as the ends of the earth, they would find some means of drawing near to each other, or if they could not find a way, they would make one. The parched earth has not more need of the rain from heaven, than the weary and heavy-laden sinner has need of Christ. This utter need makes him recognise, even afar off, the power that is coming to his aid. This was what he had been seeking, longing for, yearning after; and had he not found it, he must have invented it."[1]

The sermon on "Les grandes âmes," is even more daring in its use of the purely moral apology. In it Monod says:

"The more truly great a soul is, the more will it be prepared, all other things being equal, to receive Jesus Christ. There is no soul which has not in it the elements of greatness, since all were made by God, and made in His own image. It is only the petty in us that is against Jesus Christ; all that is great in us is on His side."[2]

Then, taking up one by one each separate faculty of man—the reason, the heart, the conscience, the imagination—he shows that in all these regions "the current that bears us away from Jesus Christ is superficial, troubled, polluted; while that which draws us to Him is deep, quiet and pure."

Christianity thus comes to us not so much in the form of a doctrine as of a person; it is embodied and personified in Jesus Christ. Revelation, therefore,

---

[1] Sermon on Nathanael.
[2] "Les grandes âmes," pp. 42, 43.

assumes a different aspect. Adolphe Monod, under the influence of his earlier convictions, was wont to present revelation as essentially a doctrine contained in a book, and his apology was directed to establishing against all opposition the authority of the Book. But from this time we find him giving the first place, not to the doctrine or the book which contains it, but to the person of Christ; and both doctrine and book, so far from being depreciated, become illuminated with a new and clearer light. The authority of the Book, being derived from the authority of Him who, as Luther says, is greater than the Book, is established on a stronger basis. It is in his sermon on the living Word that he gives fullest expression to these views. He begins by distinguishing between the written and the living Word, while recognising that historically we only arrive at the latter through the former. He unhesitatingly places the living above the written and spoken Word.

"The one explains the thought of God, the other reproduces God Himself. 'He who hath seen Christ hath seen God.' The life means the entire being, and the preacher of the living person of Jesus Christ, alone gives us the whole truth. No written language, not even the Word of God itself, can express all. There must always remain between the lines, gaps which mere words cannot supply, which the life alone can fill. The life means unity — the harmonious blending of even opposite elements. The preaching of the living person of Christ is the only means of satisfying all needs, even the most diverse, by virtue of the elasticity peculiar to life." [1]

---

[1] "La Parole vivante," pp. 9, 27.

It follows from this distinction between the living and the written Word, that the latter derives its dignity, its grandeur, and consequently the best proof of its Divine character, from Jesus Christ. *Incessu patuit Deus.* There is no need, then, to follow the devious course of the old apology, which led from the Book to Christ, laboriously demonstrating the authority of the Bible from miracles and prophecies, which the sceptical are always ready to call in question. We must reverse the process, and lead from Christ to the Book.

Adolphe Monod says, in a passage which shows how far his views had advanced since he wrote "Lucile :"

> "With reference to the Divine authority of Scripture, we may no doubt maintain it on the ground of those prophecies, miracles and facts which bring irresistible conviction to the upright mind ; but I would rather turn from all this, and appeal directly to Jesus Christ Himself. Did He not strengthen Himself by the written Word? Did He not recognise the inspiration of the prophets and guarantee that of the apostles? And was He not without error and without sin—those two immovable poles of the human conscience? Believe in Christ as His own witness. Bring your hearer into the presence of Christ, the Holy One. You have not to lead him from the Bible to Jesus ; rather try to lead him from Jesus to the Bible."[1]

From these premises Monod naturally derived an enlarged conception of inspiration, thought it appears to us that he did not go far enough in this direction.

---

[1] "La Parole vivante," pp. 30, 44.

We cannot agree with him when he says, as in the passage just given, that Christ, by His quotations from the Old Testament, solved the gravest problems of sacred criticism. Still more must we differ from him when he maintains that there was the very same transfusion of the human with the Divine in Holy Scripture as in the person of Christ. We cannot admit that the human element in the written Word had the same absolute perfection as in the living Word. Monod had himself completely abandoned the idea of the plenary inspiration of Scripture. He thought it a proof of littleness to attach importance to slight differences between the narratives of the sacred writers, or to the real or supposed historic impossibility of a figure or a date. He evidently admits that there may be such historical inaccuracies or slight deviations in the narrative, even though he adds that the inconsistency is, perhaps, only superficial. He thus abandons the theory of exact literal inspiration, which admits of no concession. "The devout soul rises above all these petty details, and will not make its faith dependent on the correctness of a copyist, or on the solution of some question of criticism; it comes straight into the presence of Christ Himself." In truth, the Book itself is not simply a book, a mere collection of inspired oracles; it is an organ instinct with the religious and moral life of the writers. This view is expressed with the greatest clearness and force in the sermons on

St. Paul. "Inspired words," says Monod, "break forth from the troubled soul of the apostle, like lightning from the heavily-charged thunder-cloud. Great agonisings of souls precede his sublimest revelations." He had himself been pierced through and through by the sword of the law; he had himself trembled beneath the thunder of Sinai, before he launched his thunderbolts against Pharisaism. Hence the importance attaching to the spiritual history of the great apostle, who was to be fitted by his own deep experience to become the living, personal organ of revelation. Adolphe Monod expresses his idea in the following striking words: "The organs of revelation are regarded by the vulgar as the spoilt children of inspiration, while in truth they are its martyrs. Blessed is the fire which comes from heaven; but woe to the cloud charged with its transmission to earth, whether it bears pent within its bosom the sacred burden, or rends itself that the celestial fire may break forth." [1]

Monod was so strongly impressed with the importance of his new views, that he did not hesitate to insist on them as opposed to the views of the narrower Evangelicals. Deep as was his respect for the religious Revival, he was bold to affirm that its piety was of too dogmatic a character in its teaching, and had dealt the much with the externals of religion;

---

[1] Sermon on St. Paul, p. 53.

that it had been too much a matter of creeds, while the secret springs of the life had too often remained untouched.

Adolphe Monod was quite conscious of the change that had come over his views since his first religious awakening. He looked upon it as a painful but necessary process through which not the individual Christian alone, but the Church of the future must be called to pass.

The task devolving upon that Church would be to give greater breadth to Christian doctrine, while still holding fast the divine folly of the cross ; and to develop gradually true catholicity by means of the Evangelical Alliance, of which he was one of the founders, and in which he rejoiced as one of the grandest facts of the Christianity of the day, and by giving the preponderance to the great central truth over all that was particular and subordinate, uniting all hearts in a common worship of the Christ of God. It was in order to build up this Church of the future, and to free it from the trammels by which it is at present fettered, that Adolphe Monod laboured to rally round the Living Truth a valiant and believing people of God, aspiring after this new land of promise, consumed with the desire to enter upon it, and preparing themselves for that holy warfare by which alone it could be won. Before this people of God he sets as a model the great conqueror of the apostolic age, St. Paul—that apostle of intrepid courage towards men, but of deep self-abasement before God. In St. Paul's tears of pity, of tenderness, and of humiliation, he finds the secret of his success. How far removed is all this from the rapid awakenings, easy conversions, sudden sanctifications, incessant congratulations by which many characterise the apostolic era. The alleluias rise out of the groanings which cannot be uttered: the soil out of which a new and glorious harvest is to grow, must be watered by nothing less than the tears of a St. Paul.

It is peculiarly interesting to watch the growth and progress of a soul so upright, a conscience so tender, as that of Adolphe Monod from the beginning of that religious revival of which he was one of the finest fruits. It seemed as if he, the great preacher, the eminent Christian, had only to lead the way in the course on which he had entered, in order to accomplish, under the most favourable conditions, a theological renovation which would satisfy the legitimate aspirations and meet the requirements of the most enlightened minds. Unhappily the ecclesiastical crisis intervened to hinder this happy consummation. It remains for us to see what part Adolphe Monod took in it during the remaining years of his life.

V.

Adolphe Monod had been hardly a year in Paris when the ecclesiastical controversy, which for a time had slumbered, broke forth with renewed vehemence. It is not our purpose here to enter at any length into the merits of the question. Let it suffice to say that the internal condition of French Protestantism had greatly changed since Adolphe Monod was dismissed from the Church at Lyons. Its organisation had not improved. The glorious institutions of its early days had no longer any existence except in its historical archives. The Councils of the Church were always self-elected, the members being taken from the list of the wealthy Protestants. There could scarcely be, I imagine, in any Church a mode of proceeding more contrary to the spirit of Christianity. It was the survival in the religious world of the famous list of notables of the First Empire, and altogether alien to the spirit of the Divine Founder of the religion of the poor.

Meanwhile true religion had been making rapid progress. The number of the Evangelicals was every day increasing. They had set on foot noble mission works at home and abroad, and their moral influence was spreading far and wide. The question of the separation of the Church from the State was forced upon men's minds by the foundation of the Free Church of Scotland, by a similar creation in French Switzerland, and by the powerful polemics of Vinet, sustained by the principal organ of Protestant thought, "Le Semeur." All these causes acting together had shaken the old prejudices in favour of national

Churches. An important section of the Evangelical party was tending, almost unconsciously to itself, towards the enfranchisement of the Church. It was logically led to this in its anxiety to restore synodical government and the unity of the faith. It was soon brought to perceive that this was utterly chimerical under the union of Church and State in the nineteenth century, because it was impossible for the State to swerve from the principle of absolute neutrality in matters of religion, and to espouse the cause of the Evangelical party.

At the head of this movement was one of the most respected and beloved pastors of the Reformed Church of Paris, the brother of Adolphe Monod, and the chief editor of the "Archives du christianisme." Frédéric Monod exerted a great influence over the French Protestantism of his day. United to his brother by the tenderest affection, he was yet of a very different temperament. One of the most generous, faithful, true-hearted of men, he had neither the oratorical nor the theological culture of Adolphe Monod. He remained inflexibly orthodox, but he had so much largeness of heart that he never fell into the narrowness and injustice too often associated with severe orthodoxy. His was a fresh and noble soul; his cheerfulness seemed the exuberance of moral health. A man of indefatigable activity and sound judgment, he took a prominent part in the direction of Christian effort. He was one of the leaders of the religious revival in Paris. He was to show subsequently how far he could carry the spirit of self-sacrifice at the call of what seemed to him duty. His memory is still held dear, and is venerated not only by those who, like ourselves, from our very cradle loved him as a father, but by all Evangelical Protestants.

Frédéric Monod had long been urging in his journal the necessity of reconstituting the Church upon its true basis, when after the Revolution of 1848, an unofficial synod was called in Paris to prepare a scheme of reorganisation, which was to be submitted to the government of the Republic. Frédéric Monod, supported by Count Agénor de Gasparin—whose name is associated with all that is most noble and chivalrous in our day—urged the synod to make a profession of evangelical faith the basis of the ecclesiastical constitution, since without this there could be no Church. The synod could not pass such a vote without creating schism, and splitting the Protestant body in two. It passed to the order of the day on the proposition of M. Monod and M. de Gasparin. These two brethren, who might have resigned themselves even to that which seemed to them the worst of disorders, when it arose out of the unhappy circumstances of the time, did not feel that they could accept the prolongation of doctrinal anarchy as ratified by the vote of the Church. MM. Monod and Gasparin and several of their colleagues sent in their resignation. Shortly after Frédéric Monod left his pulpit in the Oratoire, to commence a new ministry in a humble building, without any guarantee for his own support. He carried with him into this difficult and precarious position the esteem of all right-hearted people. The union of the independent Evangelical Churches was founded in consequence of his secession. Poor and despised, they have maintained since then a painful existence. Theirs will always be the honour of having led the way in the direction in which every Church which has a regard at once for evangelical truth and for its own dignity, is now tending, as one attempt after another at an adequate and equitable organisation in union with the State is found to fail. The synod of 1872 was the last effort in this direction.

Adolphe Monod did not see it his duty to follow his brother in his secession. He is equally entitled to our respect for a decision which was not in reality more easy to him. There was no contradiction between his decision of September, 1848, and his conduct in Lyons in 1832. Eighteen years earlier he had been equally averse to secession, and had allowed himself to be dismissed rather than quit his post in the Established Church. He held then, as in 1848, that it was not for the servant of the Church to take the initiative in a question of this kind. His motives are clearly explained in his pamphlet, "Pourquoi je reste dans l'église établie." He vindicates his preference for what he calls the path of spirituality over the path of secession. Spirituality in the ecclesiastical domain seems to him to consist in patient continuance in Christian activity in the midst of a defective organisation, till, by a simple process of growth, the chrysalis form should be cast aside and the new life spring into new developments. He did not feel it to be obligatory upon him, or in accordance with the will of God, to leave the Established Church, unless the authorities interfered with him in the performance of his pastoral duties. We cannot but respect his motives, for they were prompted by his deep Christian conscientiousness. We are fully convinced that Adolphe Monod, and those who shared his determination, contributed also in their way to prepare the Church of the future. Indeed, he always held fast the true principle of a Church, and with all his breadth and toleration, never accepted the system of a heterogeneous Church, having no bond of cohesion but the State budget, open to all comers, and guided, like a flock of sheep, by the crook of its spiritual leaders, who can never be, in the Protestant Church, other than a bastard priesthood. On the one hand, he showed himself entirely free from all ecclesiastical superstition. He even went so far as to declare not only that Jesus had never given His signature to any ecclesiastical organisation, but that He had not even formed a Church, strictly so called; that all He did was simply to unite

His disciples by a purely spiritual bond, by instilling into their hearts those principles of truth and holiness which He knew must win their way, and gradually renew the whole face of civil and religious society.[1] On the other hand, Monod accepted, almost in its integrity, the ecclesiastical theory of the secessionists, and the new Churches appeared to him to be hurrying on the separation of Church and State, which, as he frankly acknowledged, " would, in the existing state of society, be a blessing from God, if it came in God's time."[2]

It is in the definition of God's time that we differ from him. The pressure of outward circumstances is not the only sign by which we recognise the will of God. He has assigned a larger part than this to human liberty, and great reforms have been courageous attempts to break the old fetters, which will not give way at the mere groaning of the captives. Paul was obliged to snap with a strong hand the cable which bound the young Church to the shores of Judaism; and it was only when this had been done that the sails of the vessel filled with the wind which was to bear it onward. All the reforming zeal of the ardent controversialist, the courageous innovator of the first Christian century, is passed over in silence in the grand sermons devoted by Adolphe Monod to his life teaching. He also failed to do full justice to the

---

[1] " Pourquoi je demeure," &c., p. 75.   [2] Ibid. p. 8.

holy boldness of the Reformers. Spirituality must not be confounded with all-enduring patience, where the interests and order of the Church of Christ are involved. There is a yet higher spirituality, which consists in the courage to sacrifice immediate and visible success in religious matters, to a future which may seem uncertain.

We do not mean by these remarks to imply any blame to Adolphe Monod for the course on which he decided in the sight of God and for the benefit of His Church. His heart was not narrowed in its sympathies even by the controversies which sometimes grew sharp and hot. He never shared at all in that absurd bigotry which will only recognise the Reformed Church of France in one particular form of it, and which speaks sentimentally of the holy traditions of the Fathers when it is referring only to the laws of Germinal year X. The decision of Adolphe Monod cost him all the more, since it placed him in opposition to the brother whom he tenderly loved. He aptly expressed the feelings with which his heart was full, when he compared this passing difference to that which separated for a time Paul and Barnabas.

"At the very time," he says, "when Barnabas was embarking for the island of Cyprus, I see Paul going up to him, grasping him by the hand, and bidding him God-speed ; and by and by Barnabas stands on the deck of the ship, following in thought his beloved brother Paul as he goes again on foot through Syria visiting the Churches ; and as he asks that the grace of the Lord Jesus Christ may be with him, his eyes fill with tears at the recollection of their joint labours in the past. Yet a few years, and we find Paul and Barnabas together again, tenderly united in faith and works. Perhaps the present separation between us and our brothers who go out from us, may also be but for a time. Assuredly neither the Church in which we remain, nor the Church which is being founded side by side with ours, answers fully the conditions of that Church of the future to which we all look forward, and towards which we are all hastening. But who knows whether both the one and the other may not help to prepare its way." [1]

We share these aspirations. Whether our eyes may see it or not, the blessed day will come when the Reformed Church, having prepared itself for the beneficent reign of liberty, as it has already begun to do since it has ceased to seek to secure its ends by means of State intervention, will renew the most glorious traditions of its past history, and will realise that ideal of fidelity, of breadth and of independence, which is our standard, as it was that of Adolphe Monod.

VI.

In 1849 Adolphe Monod was appointed pastor, and he devoted himself unsparingly to a task which was soon to exhaust his strength. His was a grand ministry. His preaching exercised an ever-increasing influence, and he devoted more and more care to it. Perhaps it cost him a greater mental effort, after he had accepted the possibility of moulding a new theology,

---

[1] "Pourquoi je demeure," &c., p. 89.

within limits, however, which he never allowed himself to pass. He could not henceforth bring his influence to bear in one direction only; he saw more and more clearly that truth had two poles. His sermons at this period sometimes betray this new complication, which was, in truth, an expansion of his views. The plan of his preaching is less methodical, his language less positive, but the preacher has made great advances in the psychological and apologetic treatment of his subject. He is more real, more modern, more in harmony with the age. In passages, too, we find all his old fire and brilliancy, as in the sermons, " If any Man thirst ; " " Give Me thine Heart ; " " Mary Magdalen ; " " Too Late," and others.

In his sermon on " Exclusiveness " Monod compares the fervent faith, which cannot acquiesce in any violence done to the truth, to the real mother in the judgment of Solomon, whose mother's heart cries out against the sword lifted to divide her child, while the pretended mother, like the half-sceptical latitudinarianism of our day, stands by unmoved. The illustration is a very happy one. We have already drawn attention to the admirable course of sermons on St. Paul.

Pastoral duties occupied a large share of Adolphe Monod's time, especially the religious instruction of the young. He was resorted to by catechumens from all parts of France. This was one of his most important spheres of usefulness, and the results of the influence thus exerted are still felt in numbers of homes. The whole of evangelical Protestantism came to look to him more and more as its leader and model. His reputation spread far beyond his own country. He visited England more than once, and addressed large assemblies in English, with which he was thoroughly familiar. He occupied a place of honour in the first great Œcumenical Assembly of the Evangelical Alliance held in London in July, 1851. The object was one which called forth all the sympathies of his large and loving heart, and we heard him speak in Exeter Hall on this occasion in a way worthy of himself.

It was in 1854 that he felt the first germs of the malady which was rapidly to undermine his strength. He went on working, however, till he was utterly spent. After a long rest during the summer months, he resumed preaching; but the effort cost him such intense suffering that he could only continue it at irregular intervals. On Whit-Sunday, in the month of June, 1855, he preached for the last time. The sermon is still unpublished, but we have seen the notes of it. It is the song of the reaper binding up his sheaves. Never was his enfeebled voice more thrilling in its tones; never did his thought take a loftier range; never did his piety seem more deep and tender. The text he had chosen was that glorious promise of Christ, "If any man drink of this water, he shall thirst again: but whosoever shall drink of the water that I shall give him shall never thirst; but the water that I shall give him shall be in him a well of water springing up into everlasting life."[1] It is easy to imagine how the preacher would use the comparison between the fleeting and uncertain joys of the world, and that infinite, inexhaustible well of life which the Divine Spirit opens in the soul.

"Worldly happiness," he exclaimed, "the happiness that comes from a certain amount of wealth, and from no other; from a certain disposition of body and mind, and no other; from some one creature, and no other; at a certain time, and no other; from youth, not from age; from health, not from sickness; from fortune, not from poverty; from summer, not from winter; from sunshine, not from rain—let us hear no more of happiness like this. We have been in pursuit of this happiness long enough, and it has left us panting and disappointed, and all the more miserable the higher our hopes had been raised. But here is a source of happiness that can satisfy us always, perfectly, for ever. There is no craving so large that this is not enough for it, or so deep that this cannot fill it to overflowing; no aspiration after holiness so high that this does not rise above it, none so deep-seated that this does not go below it. It is God Himself giving Himself in the form of man to man."

In this sermon Adolphe Monod makes free use of that vein of mysticism which for many years had given graphic force to his words. It is touching to read the closing passage, in which he refers so calmly to himself and his sufferings.

"Happy people," he says, "to whom God has been pleased to give the kingdom, do not lose courage. Only believe, and you shall see the glory of God. In the Holy Spirit we have

---

[1] John iv. 13, 14.

infinite resources, and resources which may be made more abundant by the cutting off of every other supply. Yes, God the Holy Spirit within us can make us even more happy by the loss of earthly joy, more strong by the loss of our own strength, more holy by the ever-deepening sense of our low and lost estate. For myself, whom my failing health compels to bid you again farewell, perhaps for many months, I have much need to rest in this comforting doctrine. Broken down and enfeebled as I am, I yet believe that there remains a spiritual ministry for me to exercise, more fruitful, perhaps, than any that has preceded it, and for which God is preparing me by trial. Yes, my faithful friends in Christ, I have this confidence—that this sickness is for the glory of God, and that, whether I recover or not, it will enable me to do the will of God more perfectly. This will be the subject of my prayers during my painful absence from you, and it is this that I would have you ask in your prayers for me. Our very preaching needs to be renewed by the Holy Ghost. It is He who will enable us to pass from the preaching of the lip to the preaching of the life, from the word of teaching to the word of possession, from the word which sets forth the truth, to the word which makes us one with Him who is the truth and the life."

These were the *novissima verba* of the preacher.

We shall not dwell at any length on the last sufferings of Adolphe Monod. All are familiar with his own touching memorials of them. His "Adieux" form part of that treasury of Christian mysticism in which the afflicted seek holy examples and efficient consolation. They contain the last exhortations of the dying pastor, who every Sunday gathered around his bed a little circle of friends, among whom all denominations were represented, and partook with them of the Holy Communion, as a renewed proof of that evangelical catholicity of which he had been so faithful an apostle.

"When the Lord's Supper was distributed," we read in the Introduction to the "Adieux," "M. Monod would speak in accents of such quiet serenity, of such deep and tender love for those whom he was exhorting, sometimes even of such power and thrilling eloquence, as those who were used to hear him at other times can partly imagine, but only those who were present in those solemn hours of a closing life, can really understand. All such cherish the recollection as among the purest and holiest memories of their life. 'My life is my ministry,' he said, 'and I will exercise it till my latest breath.'"[1]

His face, pale and emaciated by suffering, was radiant with hope and immortality; the divine flame shone through the frail earthly tenement. In these last testamentary words the preacher summed up his teaching, and cast it sometimes into a more exact form than he had used for many years. He endeavoured to concentrate his belief in a few pregnant statements, without detracting anything from that mysticism which had of late characterised his preaching. The importance which he attaches to the Living Word is in no way abated, though he dwells more upon the written word. The exhortations which have been published in a connected form under the title, "Les Adieux d'un Mourant," are peculiarly touching. I extract from them the following sentences:

"O the unutterable sweetness of the rest that we find at the foot of the Cross! Let us grasp the Cross, preach the Cross, die clasping it in our arms, die proclaiming it to the world, and death will be the beginning of our life. Let none rest till he has found rest at the foot of the Cross of his Saviour God, though he

---

[1] "Adieux," p. 34.

may be driven to it by windy storms and tempests, and may sink rom mere exhaustion into that place which he will never wish to leave again."[1]

A very short time before his death he composed a hymn on the resurrection, which expresses with manly vigour the steadfastness of his hope. He was too purely an orator to be a poet in the special sense of that word, although his language was richly poetical, as is all eloquence worthy of the name. His hymn on Christian gratitude has become classic in our language. We quote one verse :

> " Que ne puis-je, ô mon Dieu, Dieu de ma délivrance,
> Remplir de ta louange et la terre et les cieux,
> Les prendre pour témoins de ma reconnaissance,
> Et dire au monde entier combien je suis heureux."

The hymn on the resurrection is a translation into verse of an admirable sermon, which we remember hearing Adolphe Monod preach at Easter 1844, in the Reformed Church of Marseilles. It had at the time all the character of an extempore address. The idea is very beautiful. The inhabitants of the spirit world, devils and angels, are represented bending over the open sepulchre of Christ, and expressing their feelings about His victory.

The humble Christian, groaning upon his bed of pain, echoes the anthems of the angels.

> " Ma faible voix s'unit à ce concert immense,
> Et tout en moi, Seigneur, t'adore et te bénit ;

---

[1] " Adieux," pp. 60–66.

Âme, esprit, cœur, vers toi tout mon être s'élance,
Et de joie et d'amour ma chair même frémit.

    ✻   ✻   ✻   ✻   ✻   ✻

Pour lutter dans les maux, dans les cris, dans les larmes,
Je ne suis que langueur, faiblesse et lâcheté ;
Mais lavé dans ton sang, et couvert de tes armes,
Je puis tout en Jésus, mort et ressuscité." [1]

The 30th of March was the last Sunday which Adolphe Monod passed upon earth. He had chosen for the subject of his address the love of God, and took as his text Psalm c.

"I have only strength enough left," he said, "to dwell upon the love of God. God has loved us : this is the whole doctrine of the gospel. Let us love God ; this is the whole of its morality. Hardly knowing if I can make you hear me, I gather up my little remaining strength, that we may call together upon the eternal and infinite love of God. O God, who art love, who hast done, art doing, wilt do nothing to us but in love, how can I thank Thee enough, as I see around me these brethren whom love has gathered here by my bed of sickness, of suffering, and of what else Thou alone canst know. I have rejoiced in their love. To whom was ever more love shown? Therefore, my God, I thank Thee, and I thank Thee still more, if it is possible, for Thy love which has so much afflicted but so much sustained me ; and I confess before these my friends that Thou hast never let me want for help, though I have often failed in faith and patience ; and that I am far from having yet attained to that perfect patience for which I long. But Thou, Thou hast been to me all goodness, and while life or strength remain I will never cease to praise Thee before my brethren."

---

[1] "Jésus-Christ ressuscitant des morts. Dec. 1855. Souvenir aux amis qui prient pour moi."—Sold for the benefit of the Evangelical Church of Lyons.

After enumerating with deep emotion the many tokens of that sovereign love which had been ever around him, his broken voice faltered out his last hymn of praise to Christ, his life, his all, " with whom," he said, " I am about to enter the everlasting mansions,

> " 'For this I can find,
> We two are so joined,
> He'll not be in glory and leave me behind.' "

In one last effort of brotherly love, he brings to the foot of the Cross, all the sufferings and sorrows of his brethren, bearing them with tender compassion on his heart. " I am suffering greatly," he said at last ; " my joy and my hymn of praise are much dulled by these sufferings, and by the constant exhaustion; but Thou, Lord, hast sustained me till now, and I have this confidence, that my prayers and those of my family will obtain for me patience to the end." His last utterance to his friends was praise and benediction ; "Grace and peace be with you all now and for ever."

I shall never forget the impression which this prayer of the dying man produced on one of the most eminent and excellent representatives of the highest culture of our day in France, M. de Rémusat, whom I induced to read it at a time when he was plunged in sudden and overwhelming sorrow. It struck him as one of the grandest utterances of that Christian faith which he respected, without being prepared to accept its mysteries.

The last week of Adolphe Monod's life was devoted to tender leave-takings with his own family. We will not lift the veil of this sacred sorrow, though to do so might show how exquisite is the blending of human affection with Christian devotion, and how far more heroic than stoicism.

On Saturday, April 6th, he fell asleep in Jesus, and the Tuesday following he was borne to the grave amid the tears of his flock and the deep sorrow of the whole Protestant Church, every section of which was represented at his funeral. No words could express the affection, respect, and gratitude testified by the survivors.

In his last sermon but one, preached in the church of the Oratoire, during the winter of 1855, when he was already so weakened by illness that he was doubtful whether he would be able to finish his sermon, Adolphe Monod had described, in powerful language, the poverty and lowness of our religious life. Then in a tone of intense earnestness, which seems to ring in my ears still, he said : " It must be known when I am gone that I was not satisfied with a Christianity like this, even when I was in the body." Thus he expressed the deep yearning of his soul after that Church of the future, which was ever increasingly the object of his desires and of his efforts. We find united in him a happy assurance of faith with a yearning so intense as to become almost an agony after the highest ideal of truth and holiness, or rather, after the fuller realisation of the type of perfectness given in Jesus Christ. We cannot but be struck with the same blending of ecstatic joy and unutterable sadness in St. Paul, in Pascal, and in all great Christian souls. Love, when it is true and deep, touches both extremes, supremely happy in the possession of its God, yet grieved not to apprehend Him more fully and to glorify Him more, and deeply wounded by the rebellion and perversity of sinners.

Such was the joy bequeathed to the Church by the Man of Sorrows—a joy tempered with the tears of love, but bright with its heavenly radiance. It was his Christ-likeness in this respect which made Adolphe Monod one of the grandest Christians of our generation, and one of the most powerful witnesses of the everlasting gospel.

ALEXANDRE VINET.

ALEXANDRE VINET.[1]

WE live in an age of restless, almost feverish activity, yet in an age which, by a sort of paradox, seems more disposed than any other to the contemplation of the phenomena of the inward and spiritual life. It abounds in biographies of this order. We are no longer amused, even in France, with memoirs which treat human life purely as a comedy, drawing back the curtain only to throw an ironical light on all the foibles and paltry disguises of the actors. This style, once so peculiarly French in its fascination and in its heartlessness, has almost passed away from our literature. Beside the great parliamentary memoirs, which hand down to posterity the eloquence of the tribune, and the authors of which studiously avoid all familiarity as unworthy the dignity of their subject, we have an abundance of private memoirs which, by means of correspondence and

---

[1] "Alexandre Vinet. Histoire de sa Vie et de ses Ouvrages," par E. Rambert.

autobiographic journals, give us an insight into the hidden life of our contemporaries. With their help we are enabled to penetrate to those soul-depths from which we are often told that eternal questions are in our day excluded, but which we find to be more profoundly exercised than ever before, over the solution of spiritual problems. "Les Lettres du Père Lacordaire à Madame Swetchine," "Les Récits d'une Sœur," the letters of the two Ampères; the later volumes of the "Correspondance de Lamartine," the "Biographie du Père Gratry," and (belonging to a different order) the "Autobiography of Stuart Mill"—all these remarkable works bring us into the very midst of what I may call the spiritual drama; the conflict perpetually renewed in our day, between liberal aspirations and positive dogmas, or, it may be, between the thesis of philosophy and the unsatisfied yearning of the heart and conscience.

The life of Vinet, which is before us now, forms a very important addition to this spiritual history of our age, bringing before us one of its most powerful minds, and allowing us to learn from himself how his genius was formed and developed. M. Rambert, the biographer of Vinet, simply gives us the connecting thread between the extracts from his correspondence or his private notes; his aim is to allow Vinet on all subjects to speak for himself. He has executed his task in a manner worthy of one of the most distinguished writers of French Switzerland, a land to which we are indebted for so many remarkable works. We recognise with hearty admiration the studious self-repression which has thrown all the light on to the great central figure of his picture. He has thus the rare merit of bringing before us a living likeness, in no respect overdrawn.

Sainte-Beuve was the first to call the attention of France to the genius of Vinet, for whom he never ceased to testify the highest admiration. M. Scherer also wrote a very warm and appreciative notice of Vinet, in which the keen sagacity of the critic was tempered by the affection and deferential sympathy of a personal friend. M. Astié, a French professor at Lausanne, published, under the title " Esprit de Vinet," a very admirable collection of his opinions on the various subjects which had come before him. Presented in this form, and apart from their proper surroundings, the ideas may seem somewhat overcrowded, the sheaf almost too heavy with the ripe golden grain. The collection is, nevertheless, a very valuable one, and it called forth several fresh studies of Vinet, notably that of M. Saint René Taillandier in the *Revue des Deux Mondes*.

M. Rambert's work appears to us exhaustive, so abundant were the sources of information open to him. It gives us the portrait of Vinet drawn by his own hand, without any thought of the public eye, in presence of which it is almost impossible not to attitudinise a little. Our endeavour will be to reproduce this noble spiritual presence by the aid of M. Rambert's book and of our own personal recollections, for it was our inestimable privilege to be for three years a diligent listener to Vinet, and to enjoy a close friendship with the Pascal of the Reformed Church.

This is the name that most fitly describes him, whether we consider the breadth of his religious sympathies, his character as a writer, his unflinching sincerity, or that trait of melancholy which is common to all great Christian souls. We may add that Vinet, like Pascal—of whom he was the most faithful interpreter—graduated in the stern school of sickness, and that it was while contending with an incurable bodily malady that he accomplished his vast intellectual labours. His whole spirit, soul, and body were tried and purified in the crucible of constant suffering. But Vinet was a son of the Reformation, not a timorous disciple of Port Royal. His glance was not more penetrating than that of Pascal, but his horizon was wider, his spirit more unfettered. He is thoroughly the man of his age, passing through its storm and tempest. His faith is controlled by a critical spirit: though fixed in its principle, it does not shrink from a testing examination, and cannot rest satisfied with an assurance based only on external authority, which it rejects as false and illusive. His intellect never laid upon itself any monkish fetters; it remained thoroughly and broadly human. In fine, Vinet was one of the grandest and truest

Liberals of our time, and religious liberty in its fullest expression has had no more determined and powerful defender. It may be asked, perhaps, why such a man was not better known in his generation? Sainte-Beuve excited a surprise not unmixed with irony, when he dedicated to Vinet one of his most beautiful literary sketches. He was accused of sacrificing to unknown gods. It is easy to explain the semi-obscurity in which Vinet has remained as regards France. In the first place, he preferred to be in the background; he was as studious in hiding himself from the public gaze as others are in courting it. This large-minded man was an ascetic, and this union of the most exalted liberalism, altogether free from any sectarian prejudice, with an austerity almost without parallel towards himself, is not the least of his idiosyncrasies. These significant words were found inscribed on the memorandum-book which contained his most private meditations: "The love of glory is the dangerous neighbour of the love of truth; the one loses all that the other gains." Vinet loved the truth, and not glory. Hence, his unfeigned contempt for everything which would have made him prominent, and his repeated refusal of positions in which he might have become a central luminary.

Distance from Paris is a very grave disadvantage in the eyes of the dispensers of fame. They are ready to say, like the Rabbis in the temple, "Can any good thing come out of Nazareth?" They look with contempt on all that transpires outside that centre of science and civilisation in which they reign as kings. Thus, however important the discussions that may arise in small and remote countries like Switzerland, they are regarded as insignificant by superficial minds because of the narrow limits of the arena in which they are first agitated. And yet the fire kindled by this tiny spark has sometimes spread through all Europe, and made an era in the destiny of nations.

The discussion of religious liberty raised the same questions in French Switzerland which Mirabeau had argued from the tribune of the Constituent Assembly, and which subsequently set all the four corners of Europe in a blaze. This must be borne in mind as we read the detailed account of those discussions in which Vinet took so large a part. That which seems at first sight a quarrel about trifles, will be found to involve really the issues of the great controversy between the authority of the State and liberty of conscience, which has come to a crisis in our own day. We must remember also that Vinet belonged to the religion of the minority, which is another reason for his being left in the shade. M. Guizot said one day, in his great voice, to a young Protestant writer : " Sir, you were born in a corner ; try to get out of it." This Vinet never attempted to do. But from that obscure corner of Switzerland, which Parisians regarded so slightingly, he exercised a deep and wide influence over the great Protestant nations which, in the nineteenth century, have carried their civilisation and culture to so high a point. Among these nations he is still recognised to-day as an intellectual king, and it will be the worse for France if she fails to pay homage to his just claims.

Balzac, in his famous quarrel with Sainte-Beuve, rallied the author of the "Portraits Littéraires" with a satirical laugh, on the tribute he had paid to so obscure a man as Vinet. The laugh may well be turned by posterity against himself, for ignoring a man of world-wide fame.

France is beginning to appreciate truly this great Christian Liberal. His teaching is destined to win its widening way, and to leave a deep furrow even in our light soil, for it responds to all the higher aspirations of the national life, political, religious and philosophical. France could find no better counsellor than Vinet in her efforts to conclude that great alliance between religion and liberty in the fullest sense, without which French democracy will fail to stand, and religion will lose its empire over the souls of free men.

We shall endeavour to reproduce, with the aid of M. Rambert's book, the leading features in the life and work of this remarkable man.

I.

Vinet was born at Ouchy, near Lausanne, in 1797, and died at Montreux in 1847, in the full maturity of his powerful faculties. His outward life was singularly uneventful. He travelled but rarely, and then only for the sake of health, and as rapidly as possible. "Not being able to travel in person," he wrote to a friend, "I allow my imagination to travel. The only true liberty is in a state of dependence frankly accepted." This is Vinet in his true character—the captive of duty, but with the free mind which spreads its wings in all the realms of thought. Though he scarcely ever left his study, his life was full of varied and lively interest. His unpretending little room reminds us of Rembrandt's picture in the Louvre, of the philosopher resting his tired head upon his hand, after a long day of mental toil. The bare walls are draped with the glory of the sunset, but the face of the old man kindles with a yet more unearthly brightness. We feel that these four walls enclose that which is mightiest upon earth; thoughts which can flood the world with renovating light. Within this humble dwelling a Descartes may utter his "*Cogito, ergo sum*," or a Pascal may open a new kingdom of thought to the wondering world. Here greater battles may be fought, and grander victories won, than any immortalised in history; for here those great principles may be evolved which shall afterwards be proclaimed from the forum, and embodied in the progress of nations. It matters little, then, that Vinet passed his days in almost unbroken obscurity. There were, nevertheless, marked eras in his intellectual and moral life, which have left their impress upon the religious history of the age.

Vinet was not cradled in luxury. On the contrary, the family were often in straitened circumstances. His father belonged to the petty *bourgeoisie* of French Switzerland, and could with difficulty provide bread for his household. He was a man of the old school, hard-working and incapable of self-indulgence, concealing a warm heart beneath a somewhat rigid and rough exterior. Vinet found in him a wise counsellor, who presented life to him under a rather stern aspect, but who always exhibited towards him, in his own way, the greatest affection. Like the father of Schleiermacher, the great founder of the German theology of the nineteenth century, the elder Vinet was uneasy at the first signs of intellectual independence in his son. Accustomed himself to adhere rigidly to rules, he could not understand any deviation in religion from the beaten track. The tenderness of Vinet's mother tempered this severity, which was doubtless, on the whole, salutary in its effect, for the best school of liberty is the stern discipline which teaches us to govern ourselves.

After a thorough course of literary and theological study at Lausanne, Vinet was called to the professorship of the French language at Basle. He had long shown a strong interest in French literature. It is said that at seventeen years of age he could not read the "Cid" aloud without bursting into tears.

He delighted in giving a poetical form to his impressions; they flowed at first in light and easy strains, like the amenities of youth, then in more powerful verses, which burst spontaneously from a heart deeply exercised with the mysteries of life. Vinet was never a poet in the sense of one who could only give true expressions to his thoughts in the form of rhythm; but he had, nevertheless, a deeply poetic soul. Not only did he keenly enjoy the masterpieces of poetry, but he had recourse to poetic forms in the supreme moments of his life. The deepest sorrows of his heart found expression in verse; and whatever these productions may lack of æsthetic beauty, they bear the unmistakable impress of deep and genuine feeling.

Vinet married early, and the union was one of rare congeniality and helpfulness. His home was early visited with domestic affliction. His son suffered in a way which painfully separated him from home ties; his daughter was cut off in the flower of her youth; he himself was the victim of a disease which rarely allowed him a day's respite. Death visited his home with repeated strokes. Yet all these trials only wrung from his wounded heart this cry of sublime acquiescence, uttered at the grave of his daughter:

> " Sous ton ciseau, divin sculpteur de l'âme,
> Que mon bonheur vole en éclats !
> * * * *
> Mourir c'est naître ;
> D'un nouvel être,
> C'est jour à jour se revêtir."

We should give a wrong impression if we led the reader to suppose that Vinet knew and understood only the sorrowful side of life. He had an intense appreciation of the joys of friendship and affection; he had an enthusiasm for the beautiful, whether in the world of letters or in the sublime and tender forms of nature. Still the prevailing tone of his mind was one of sadness. In truth, the sufferings of the outward life were slight compared with the poignant anguish often endured in the struggle with himself. From each renewed conflict he came forth, indeed, more victorious, his heart increasingly weaned from vanity and selfishness, and set upon the service of truth, justice, humanity, of every good cause which could commend the gospel to men. But he took too serious a view of life, and was too sincere in his dealings with himself, not to be more saddened by his failures than gladdened by the measure of success achieved. Leading himself a life of rare purity and nobleness, he was ever abased in the dust, because of the evil he saw in his own heart, and in the world around him. He wept tears, now of repentance, now of compassion. These were not tears wrung from him by the fear of punishment, for he believed firmly in the infinite love which comes to pardon and restore all. They expressed rather his unutterable yearning after perfection, and his deep compassion for all the hungry souls around him, and most of all for the souls that did not hunger, but were satisfied with the ashes of a low and miserable life. Firm, too, as was his faith, it had not been accepted on slight grounds. As he himself tells us, he reached it through a sea of speculation, often having to contend hard for the faith with those " insolent doubts" which would arise in his heart. From these struggles of soul and spirit, he came forth sore wounded, but victorious, to use the expression of one of his honoured brothers in arms— Adolphe Monod.

Protestantism, like Catholicism, has its facile adherents ; but we do not find upon this path of easy devotion the footprints of those great Christians, whose souls have apprehended the true ideal of the Christian life, and who refuse to be comforted because of the depth of human woe. These bear upon their hearts, not only their own sorrows, but the burden of an unhappy race ; and from the days of St. Paul to those of Pascal and Vinet, these men have been climbing the hill of sorrow, with their eyes ever fixed upon the cross which crowns its summit. They know that this is the symbol of the great victory ; hence their joy. But they know also through what bitter anguish the victory was won ; hence their sympathetic sorrow. Vinet wrote one day in his journal, when he was saddened by the discovery of a base deception : " This is evil ; but in another way it is very good. It is a thorn of the crown." The crown was on his brow, but it was a crown of thorns. Vinet's Christianity was altogether of this lofty type.

It was at Basle, in the year 1820, that he passed through the decisive crisis of his spiritual life. The Protestant Churches of the Continent began at that time to feel the reaction of what was called in England the great Revival. M. de Rémusat, in a very able article on Wesley, written with all his characteristic clearness of insight and breadth of view, brings out the significance of the movement which, at the close of the eighteenth century, profoundly stirred Great Britain, and startled it out of the state of religious lethargy and formalism into which it had sunk under the enervating influence of the age. Wesley and Whitfield spoke like the apostles of old—with tongues of fire. Like the first missionaries of the new faith, they went through the country from north to south and from east to west, gathering vast multitudes by the force and charm of their eloquence, and setting before them the living gospel instead of the cold and colourless deism to which they had become accustomed. These two extraordinary men as truly made the England of the nineteenth century, as the Roundheads made that of the seventeenth. The terrible ordeal of war through which the country was passing gave point and appropriateness to the stern message of the preachers. When peace came the movement spread over the continent of Europe, where Protestantism had assumed too much the type of the Savoyard Vicar, and had been content if it found in the pulpit a man in a black vestment, and saying what was expected of him. All this was changed when the apostles of English Evangelicalism lifted up their voice in France and Switzerland. Unhappily they cast these great truths into too narrow a mould. In the reaction against the spirit of worldliness, they were led into an exaggerated Puritanism, which allowed little scope for the higher culture.

Vinet was first struck with the asperities of this extreme dogmatism, which presented in great prominence the most sombre features of Calvinism. But when he saw the adherents of the religious revival bravely enduring in Switzerland a persecution which was as odious as it was petty, he learnt to respect them; and it was in defending them that he first became the unflinching advocate of liberty of conscience. He soon came to recognise that they were right on more than one point; that they were not mistaken in proclaiming the necessity of a moral and spiritual regeneration, and in protesting against a Christianity of mere routine, which was satisfied with a supernaturalism devoid of mystery, and which made mere virtue the substitute for holiness. Vinet received the spiritual impulse which he needed from this imperfect Methodism, though it was never able to hold his generous spirit captive in its narrow formulas. He formed his own belief, and always remained profoundly human, while holding fast the essential principles of revealed truth. We shall see that he acted the part of a true reformer in the lofty sphere of religious thought.

Vinet devoted the best years of his early life to the humble office of teacher of French, which he had accepted at Basle. He was as conscientious in the fulfilment of this duty as of all others; hence it was during these years he acquired that extensive literary erudition which made him afterwards a consummate critic. To this period of his career we owe his "Chrestomatie"—the best work of its kind, not only in the selection of pieces, but in the biographical and literary notices which precede them, and still more in the eloquent and exact *résumé* of French literature which Sainte-Beuve regarded as above all praise. Vinet was, as we have just said, mixed up at this period, in those struggles for religious liberty which were inevitable when a retrograde legislation was brought into collision with the first aggressive movements of the new religious zeal. The articles written by Vinet on this subject, and afterwards collected in a volume, are still as pointed and powerful as ever, for the very same questions which are discussed in them are still pressing for a solution from the democracy of our day. This is especially the case in Switzerland, where a false demagogy seems aiming to show how it could be the worst of all tyrannies. It was at Basle also that Vinet wrote his "Mémoire sur la liberté des cultes," to which the Society of Christian Morals at Paris gave the prize, at the warm recommendation of M. Guizot. In this work Vinet displays the maturity of his powers in the complete mastery of thought and style. It is a full, fervent, high-toned pleading for liberty of conscience, on the ground of respect for the human soul and for God, who alone has the right to command in matters of religion.

After the Revolution of 1830, the periodical *Le Semeur* was started. It was a sort of Protestant *Globe*, and was conducted with singular ability and firmness by M. Henri Lutteroth. It became at once the organ of the highest liberal and Christian culture of French Protestantism, and gave a fresh impetus to Vinet's mental development. His contributions to it were constant, and of the most various order. In it he published his very able literary articles on all the great works of the day — articles which placed him in the first rank of literary critics. In it he steadily carried on his campaign in favour of religious liberty, and published his "Études Apologétiques," which are perhaps the most able of all his works. He also often preached through its pages, and it thus became the medium of circulating his thoughtful and powerful sermons through all the Protestant Churches of the Old and the New World.

Appointed Professor of Literature in the Academy of Basle, he expanded his course by adding to it a series of public lectures on French Moralists, which remain a standard work. His reputation increased daily, though he himself would do nothing to court publicity, and steadily refused the invitations that constantly came to him from all parts of Switzerland

and France. The reason he gave for these refusals was "his incapacity for, and unworthiness of the proffered honour."

At the close of his stay in Basle, Vinet had become a close and exact thinker, and complete master of the fine and subtle harmonies of language. Few writers have ever shown such versatility of thought. This appears, not only in his expositions, but in his very turns of expression, and in his original application of metaphors derived from nature, art, and science. His style is not, of course, faultless: it is sometimes overladen; the lines of reasoning are lost in the too ample development; the plan is wanting in symmetry; the images do not always correspond. In many respects Vinet reminds us of Clement of Alexandria, not only in his breadth of view, but also in his manner, at once erudite and brilliant, of expressing his ideas. The great apologist of the third century called his writings "stromata," or "tapestries." This was a true description of his rather elaborate style, in which, like threads of many colours interwoven in one close fabric, we find the blended results of the most varied culture. I know no writer who, in this respect, more resembles him than Vinet. All this brilliance of language was the reflection of the ardent soul within. His writings are always full of feeling. Indeed, it may be truly said that the moral tone dominates to a degree very rare even the form in which his thoughts are conveyed.

His motto, whenever he took pen in hand, was this: "Let us write in the best manner possible." The following is found among the jottings in his memorandum book: "Responsibility of a writer, even when no fame attends his publications. He has sown, and that which he has sown will germinate in silence, and, whether he sleep or wake, will become a principle, an affection, a habit of mind in his readers."

In 1837 Vinet was called to Lausanne as Professor of Practical Theology, a branch which comprehends the oratorical art as applied to the pulpit, and what may be called pastoral morality—not easily distinguished from simple Christian morality, where there is no recognition of a narrow clericalism. It was not without regret that he quitted the town where his laborious youth had been passed in the midst of growing sympathies, and where he had the advantage of combining, to an unusual degree, the science of Germany with the culture of France. He returned to his native place at a time very favourable for his work. The political quarrels of the past seemed to have ended in a durable amnesty. Democracy in Lausanne was becoming established on a sound liberal basis, under a just Government, which was very desirous of promoting the intellectual development of the country.

The Academy of Lausanne was distinguished for the welcome it gave to illustrious foreigners. Misckiewitz, the great poet of partitioned Poland, held the Latin professorship. Melegari, an exile from Parma (afterwards a senator of the Italian kingdom, and its minister at Berne), filled the chair of Political Economy with an erudition equal to his popularity. Lastly, Sainte-Beuve had accepted the invitation to give there, in a course of public lectures, the first outlines of his "History of Port Royal." For the rest, Lausanne could supply its own requirements. M. Monnard, formerly a contributor to the *Globe*, and the intimate friend of Thiers and Mignet, gave instruction in French literature. M. Juste Ollivier, the national poet, was Professor of History. M. Charles Secrétan, one of the most brilliant representatives of the younger generation, which could count in its ranks such poets as Frédéric Monneron, and such able and eloquent writers as Adolphe Lèbre (first known to fame through his writings in the *Revue des Deux Mondes*), was about to commence the philosophical course, in which he endeavoured to show the harmony between the gospel and free speculation, and supplemented Vinet's work in the track opened by Schilling.. The theological faculty at that time commanded the services of M. Herzog, who afterwards published his great theological Encyclopædia; and of M. Samuel Chappuis, one of the most eminent of living Protestants, whose noble and cultivated intellect was always devoted to the service of what he regarded as the cause of truth. Unfortunately he had a rooted aversion to appearing in print, and thus his invaluable labours have been preserved to us only through the memoranda of his students.

Lausanne was for many years an intellectual centre not inferior to any of the German Universities. It diffused an atmosphere of liberty, and of faith broad and human, in the best sense of the word. The society of Lausanne had long enjoyed a reputation for intellectual taste ; in the eighteenth century it was characterised by a mental frivolity, largely to be traced, no doubt, to Voltaire's sojourn there. At the commencement of this century Mesdames de Charrière and de Montolieu continued this tradition of brilliant and racy conversation, while Gibbon raised the tone by his solid erudition. Coppet, also, was not far off, and Lausanne would catch at least the echo of the Decameron of French *esprit*, presided over by the illustrious exile, Madame de Staël. The society of Lausanne, no doubt, underwent a considerable change under the influence of the religious revival, but it still maintained its literary reputation. The greater seriousness of its tone took nothing from its breadth, and the *salons* in which Vinet and Sainte-Beuve appeared had no cause to envy the brilliant *réunions* of Paris. If conversation ranged over a narrower area, it was more solidly thoughtful, and great intellectual and moral questions were discussed under all their aspects, with an exhaustive thoroughness which gave a peculiar value to the results reached. These were years of extraordinary growth and fruitfulness in the spiritual history of Switzerland, and the memory of them lingers like a vision of sunset Alps towering above the blue Geneva lake.

The most abiding influence was that of Vinet, who was compelled by the prolonged absence of M. Monnard to add a course of literature to his theological lectures. After his death most of his lectures were printed. Among those most worthy of note we may mention his history of the Christian pulpit, Catholic and Protestant; his lectures on the rules of preaching—a course of sacred oratory, teaching how to dispense with rhetoric in the vulgar sense of the word; and his lectures on the gospel ministry. In addition to these we have his entire literary course; his essay on Pascal, his studies of the seventeenth and eighteenth centuries, and of the great French writers of the day, beginning with Madame de Staël and Chateaubriand, to whom he devoted an entire course.

I have listened to many great masters, but I never heard any who surpassed Vinet. Sainte-Beuve has paid a noble tribute to his teaching, and to that purely moral beauty which impressed him so vividly after the false glitter and glamour of pagan and papal Rome. I shall never forget how I felt on hearing him for the first time. I intended only to devote a few months to his course of instructions; but when I had once entered upon it, in 1842, I felt myself fixed there for the whole of my student years. Such an opportunity does not come twice in a lifetime. I never knew any teaching so suggestive as Vinet's, any which so surely communicated to heart and mind the living spark, without which all mere learning is comparatively vain. To inspire is more than to instruct. The teaching which imparts, not only increased knowledge, but the key of science, and above all the love of truth, and the method of laying hold of it, is the true training of the mind.

When Vinet entered the lecture-room he generally looked languid and exhausted. His great height gave him a sort of awkwardness, and his features, sharply cut but not classic, gave no indication of the treasure within. But after a few minutes all was changed, and there was singular aptness in Madame de Montolieu's shrewd remark, after meeting him one day, while he was quite young, at the house of another professor. She asked, "Who is that ugly man who becomes beautiful when he speaks?" His thoughts seemed to play over his face like a long pent-up fire, kindling it to light and warmth. In his deep and sonorous voice he poured forth a constant stream of original ideas, in language which was the luminous reflection of his thoughts. He threw his whole soul into his teaching. No student of his ever came out of the lecture-room with heart unmoved. All carried away, not simply the recollection of eloquent words, but a new impulse in the life. His last course, which he was unable to finish, was on the practical philosophy of Christianity. It has come down to us only in a fragmentary form. Had it been completed it would have been truly his "Génie du Christianisme." All who heard it are unanimous in saying that his genius was never more powerfully displayed. His death prevented its being prepared for publication, and thus we have lost a book of which our age might have been justly proud, and in which the author was prepared, as it were, to bind his sheaves.

The relations of Vinet with Sainte-Beuve, which commenced at Lausanne, were from the first those of intimate friendship. The great critic received from Vinet an impression which never wore away. It is calumny to say that Sainte-Beuve only watched with an amused curiosity the travail of this great soul, amid severely simple surroundings which reminded him of Port Royal. That such a representation does him injustice is evident from the letter which Sainte-Beuve wrote to Vinet after his return to Paris.

"I imagine," he writes, "that one of the great attractions of Paris, and indeed the only one which makes it worth while to live here, is that here you are in a good position for watching the comedy. But the worst of it is this comedy itself, in which you have always to look on, never to act, and have to accept this low world as a show, not as a field of labour. All this is so different at Lausanne. That is what moved my envy in a certain visit in the shade of the cathedral, where I saw a whole life of study, of sacrifice, of humble unremitting activity. Life here is all dissipation; men do a thousand things, and never the one important thing. . . . . Your letter touched and gratified me; but I have never any words in which to acknowledge your praises, feeling myself so unworthy of them, for I have sunk into a state of purely intellectual criticism, and am a sorrowful witness of the death of my own heart. I judge myself, and remain calm, cold, indifferent. I am a dead man, and can look upon myself as dead without being moved. Alas! there are causes for this, deep and of long standing. . . . . But here I am speaking to you like a father confessor. Reason sheds cold rays over this cemetery like a dead moon!"

The confession is significant. Sainte-Beuve is in this letter a far less flippant man than he chose to appear afterwards.

The letter shows also that Vinet was not afraid to go below the surface in his relations even with such men as Sainte-Beuve; he went straight to the soul. M. Rambert gives us a short correspondence between Vinet and Chateaubriand, in which the great *ennuyé* poet who, to use his own expression, "yawned out his life," tells the story of his disenchantment with a heart-aching bitterness. When a man has become sceptical to such a degree, in relation to all things human and earthly, he is not likely to have much faith in eternal things; for faith in the higher would fling its reflection over the lower world. It is beautiful to see with what a delicate touch Vinet endeavours to staunch the wounds of the old Réné. This sort of solicitude seems strange, and perhaps a little indiscreet, to polite society. With Vinet it is inseparable from the strong and pitiful love of mankind which is the animating principle of his life. He thought, moreover, that it was degrading to our relations with one another to avoid touching on the things that concern us most deeply—the great questions of the soul—and to treat Christianity as if it were a dead friend whose name is not to be mentioned for fear of re-awakening bitter regrets. This feeling he expresses very fully in his book, " La Manifestation des Convictions Religieuses," which, like his " Mémoire sur la Liberté des Cultes," was written in connection with a meeting of the Society of Christian Morals. He begins by maintaining that it is the duty of every sincere and thoughtful man to show his convictions, and that for the honour of the truth. He then describes, in some of the finest pages he ever wrote, the sufferings through which the truth has been triumphantly vindicated, and concludes that every hindrance to its free progress ought to be removed. He is thus led, in the second part of his book, to develop his favourite theory of the separation of Church and State. The same train of thought runs through his work on the origin of Socialism, which, in his view, has its root in the undue subordination of the individual to the State—

an error never more fatal than in the domain of religion.

The events which were transpiring at the time in the Canton de Vaud were well calculated to strengthen his convictions. The Revolution of 1845, though accomplished without bloodshed, was none the less lamentable in its results. It raised to power a clamorous and despotic demagogy which laid forcible hands upon the Academy and the Church, in the attempt to make the Church the victim of its caprices. It encountered a determined resistance, which does honour to the Christian conscience. A considerable portion of the clergy broke with a government which sought to make use of it merely as an electoral agent. A free and self-supporting Church was founded in a few days. It encountered at first a sharp persecution. Religious liberty was grossly violated. Vinet, who had been obliged to resign his office as Professor of Theology, and who had been soon after deprived of his chair of Literature, vigorously took up the defence of the new Church, which he had helped to organise. He gave several lectures in the theological faculty, which had just been founded outside the Establishment, but sickness soon laid him on a bed of pain from which he rose no more. He never ceased to write while life remained, and his last breath was spent in the cause of that religious and theological liberty for which he had so strenuously laboured. He died in the month of May, 1847, before he had reached his fiftieth year. The sorrow which his death spread throughout Switzerland and in all the Protestant Churches was too deep for words. His coffin, covered with flowers, was borne by his weeping disciples to the cemetery of Clarens. There he sleeps in the midst of that natural beauty which he so dearly loved. The spot is marked by a modest tombstone, on which are engraved the words : " They that turn many to righteousness shall shine as the stars for ever and ever."

The great consolation to his friends was that, though his voice would be heard no more, his thoughts would live on with an ever-widening influence for good.

It remains for us now to follow out the various lines of thought which he illuminated with his powerful genius.

· Let me preface the review of the general tendency and leading characteristics of Vinet's teaching with a personal reminiscence. A few months before his death I had an interview with him which I shall never forget. I had heard him in the morning deliver one of his most impressive sermons in a lower room of the Castle of Châtelard, where the worship of the Free Church was held under the pressure of the persecution raised against it. The reformed worship became more austerely simple than ever, in this its enforced banishment from its regular places of worship. On this occasion there was neither pulpit nor organ, but the preacher was in his very happiest vein.

There was a wealth of thought in the sermon worthy of Pascal himself, and an entire absence of the rhetorical, though the fire within would now and then reveal itself in flashes of eloquence. The subject was the sublime friendship which God seeks with the human soul, in which He thus honourably recognises His own image and the expression of His glory. As I was walking with Vinet the same evening to Châtelard, through the woods of Clarens, then pierced by shafts of quiet moonlight, he resumed the train of thought which had filled his mind in the morning. He dwelt with peculiar emphasis on the greatness which Christianity confers on human nature, and on that sort of baseness which impels man to reject this glory of humanity by which he becomes a partaker of the divine life. As one of the fathers has well said: "Christ became man to accustom us to become like God." This last conversation with my revered master has always lived in my memory as the most perfect expression of his inner life. The thought contained in the words just quoted ran as a connecting link, not only through all his teaching, both as a preacher and an apologist, but through all his labours as a literary critic and a liberal journalist, giving singular power and unity to his whole work. Vinet accepted it as a fundamental principle that the human soul is veritably the offspring of God, and bears His image even in its fallen and degraded condition; while in Christianity, so far from being absorbed and lost in the infinite, it is restored to its true self. The supernatural in the gospel, thus regarded, is the restoration of the truly natural, freed from all that has polluted and falsified it. A man who has not experienced this renovating influence is like the shipwrecked mariner, whom Plato describes so vividly, covered with slime and crawling sea foam. Christianity frees him from all this defilement. The Christian alone is the complete man.

This is a doctrine widely different from the *splendida vitia* of St. Augustine, from his systematic disparagement of human nature apart from faith. In Vinet's view, even fallen man is a being of a noble race. " Upon the heights of human nature," he says, in the introductory lecture to the practical philosophy of Christianity, " we find the ruins of an altar." Conscience bears witness to the divine presence in a man; this is the source at once of his greatness and of his misery. Between this innate sense of the divine and Christ, there is a pre-established harmony. "Conscience," says Vinet, " is only the abiding and ineffaceable impress of a powerful hand, which having once held us has now let us go—or rather, out of which an enemy's power has dragged us. The hand is gone ; the mark of its pressure remains." The human soul bears in its secret depths an inscription written, as it were, in that invisible ink which only the fire reveals. The gospel is the fire, and by its light we read the divine characters traced on our own souls. Vinet has embodied the same idea, which is the key to his whole religious teaching, in the following striking image :

> "We call to mind," he says, "the usages of ancient hospitality. Before parting from a stranger, the father of the family was wont to break a clay seal, on which certain characters were impressed, and giving one half to his guest, he kept the other himself. After the lapse of years, these two fragments being brought together again would recognise each other, so to speak, and would be a medium of recognition between the two men who held them, and by the evidence they bore to the relations of former days, would become the basis of new ones. Thus is it in the book of our soul: the lines there begun find their divine complement ; thus our soul does not, properly speaking, discover the truth, but may be rather said to recognise it. The gospel is believed when it has ceased to be to us an external, and has become an internal truth, when it has become a fact in our consciousness. Christianity is conscience raised to its highest exercise."

Upon this purely moral basis Vinet constructs the edifice of theology. So far from explaining away the supernatural to a mere rationalistic idealism, he shows how truly it is in harmony with the deep instincts of the soul. The divine humanity of Christ, and His voluntary sacrifice of Himself, are represented as the supreme satisfaction of the demands of conscience, which craves to find itself once more perfectly united to God, through the redeeming sacrifice.

Vinet's conception of religion was thus altogether distinct from a dry scholasticism, in which a closely-linked chain of doctrines fetters the mind without influencing the heart. Christianity is not essentially either a formulary or a code. It is a grand fact, or to speak more truly, it is a living person, truth incarnate. Christ, when He came to take His place among men, came to His own. It was vain to shut the door against Him; He is at home in the human heart, because it was made for Him. When it comes to itself it recognises this, and welcomes the truth of God which stoops to dwell with him, as Adam welcomed Eve, saying: " This is now bone of my bone and flesh of my flesh."

We can well understand that in a system like this, doctrine and morality are inseparable, even as the two meet together in the person of Christ and in the cross of Calvary. The greatest, the most amazing of all doctrines is that doctrine of the cross, which reconciles earth and heaven; and the highest morality is that very act of redemption which is the supreme sacrifice. Faith accepts both the doctrine and the morality. The Christian soul believes in Christ by uniting itself to Him, and learning from Him the secret of self-devotion. Thus that great controversy of faith and works, which has so sharply divided Christendom, is solved by being brought before a higher tribunal, where the two parties so long at enmity are reconciled. Faith appropriates the whole Christ by a moral act which engages all the energies of the soul, and renders it more and more conformed to His image, which stands forth radiant with the light of heaven against the dark background of the cross. It was in bringing out this aspect of the truth that Vinet accomplished his most important work as a Reformer of the faith. He did much to render it less narrow and more human, while he never fell into the error of confounding it with a rationalistic philosophy. No one was ever more deeply conscious of the wounds of humanity, and no one ever more faithfully interpreted the cry of the soul after the sovereign and divine remedy. He carried on and extended the work of Pascal, whose so-called scepticism was in reality only the passionate avowal of the insufficiency of a purely intellectual and doctrinal religion, or of a rigidly Cartesian philosophy.

Having thus laid down the premises of the great Christian thinker, it will be easy to deduce from them the broad and consistent liberalism which characterised all his writings.

Vinet had first of all a firm belief in moral liberty in its highest application, I mean in the relations of man to God. The negation of liberty always seemed to him emphatically *the* error. He was thus led to modify considerably the implacable idea of the Divine sovereignty to which such prominence is given in Calvinism, and from which, with an apparent inconsistency, it has deduced the doctrine of civil and religious liberty. The inconsistency is only on the surface, however, for the very doctrine which humbles man before the supreme majesty of God, vindicates his dignity in relation to all inferior powers, and especially to the hierarchy. The Calvinistic dogma of predestination was, perhaps naturally, evolved in the reaction of the sixteenth century, and adopted as a controversial weapon, but it is, nevertheless, a dangerous exaggeration which has too long been a clog on the progress of the Reformation. It is well for us to realise that these questions, which seem to deal with purely abstract matters, have their counterpart in history, and that, in fact, they have to a great extent shaped it. Looking back to Luther's first protests, we should be ready to say, "A mere monkish quarrel." But this monkish quarrel inaugurated the greatest and most formidable schism in Europe.

"Only a theological dispute," some may be ready to say, referring to the discussions on grace and freewill. And yet we have but to read the history of Holland and of the Anglo-Saxon peoples, or "Les Provinciales" of Pascal, in order to see how important has been the bearing of these problems on the history of the modern world. Vinet, in conjunction with some of the most eminent divines of Germany, proclaimed that great reconciliation between human liberty and Divine sovereignty, which opens a new career to the Reformation. He used this happy phrase to convey his meaning: "Grace is a divine eloquence, which carries man's free-will captive by persuasion."

Principles like these strike at the root of all external authority in matters of religion. It is very evident that if man has in his conscience a sufficient criterion of truth, if he is by his very nature in harmony with it, truth cannot be forced upon him under any pretext, by a power outside himself. What necessity can there be for constraint, where there is already affinity and latent sympathy? Undoubtedly the conscience is often dulled by evil passions; it needs to have these hindrances removed, and to be itself aroused from its stupor, but this is a moral act. Hence the intervention of the will in the formation of the belief, not to enforce the blind acceptance of that which the intellect repudiates, not to annul or suspend the operation of the rational faculties, but to raise man above all that would lead him into exile, all that would hinder the pursuit of his true ideal, and would prevent his recognising the supreme embodiment of good presented in the gospel.

Vinet was thus led to sap the very foundations of that system of external authority, which celebrated not long ago its most decisive and dangerous victory. It must not be supposed that he would leave Christian thought to drift without an anchor or a helm. On the contrary, the authority for which he pleads is all the more powerful because it is voluntarily accepted. The magnetic needle does not need to be turned to the pole by force, it tends towards it by a necessity of its nature, and thus becomes the mariner's guide. So it is with the soul; it has a tendency towards the pole of truth, all the more sure because it is spontaneous, and a tendency, which once recognised, it feels itself bound religiously to obey. It is not true, then, to say that it is left to drift over the wide ocean of thought. Conscience is its compass; and truth accepted, its polar star. Vinet gives the fullest and most correct statement of his views on the false authority, as opposed to the true, in his work on Pascal.

He does not repudiate this false authority under one form only; he denounces it as unsparingly in his own communion as elsewhere. He is as impatient of the yoke of an intolerant orthodoxy, as of that of the hierarchy. He would have the Christian thinker free himself from all merely human tradition, and form his own faith from immediate contact with the truth at its very source. The honest seeker will not find the truth embodied in the form of a *systematic creed* even in the Bible itself, which speaks with supreme authority on matters of faith. It was not the purpose of God to spare man the wholesome effort of seeking for and eliciting the truth for himself. This conception of religious truth and of the method of its attainment, altogether excludes those arbitrary solutions, and that imperious insistence upon certain formulas of faith, which would crush all opposition, as resistance to lawful authority to be summarily dealt with. Such denunciations may become a Bossuet, as the proud representative of a power, the sacred titles of which he deems none can dispute. The Christian apology, in this view of it, is the armed guard of the sanctuary, the office of which is to stamp out all rebellion. Doubt is, on this theory, a refractory subject, to be curbed by authority, not to be convinced by reason. It needs to be rebuked from the pulpit, in such tones as a master might use to an intractable scholar. This proud assumption of authority runs through all the lofty eloquence of the French pulpit in the seventeenth century, which achieved at that time some of its most magnificent effects.

Vinet's teaching is in striking contrast to all this. He is a brother, stretching out a hand to his brethren in distress. Himself, so lately battling with the same stormy winds, he is full of sympathy with his struggling brethren, and longs to lead them into the port of peace. Is he not, indeed, still a seeker after truth, like themselves? for who can boast that he has attained to absolute truth, unless he be under the same illusion as the child who deems that he can grasp the ocean in the hollow of his hand? In the introduction to the first volume of his sermons, Vinet thus explains his position: "As one conscious of his own weakness, I address myself to the weak. I have thought that those, who are still in the infancy of their faith, want some one who, placing himself at their standpoint, should speak to them less as a preacher than as a man who is himself but a few steps in advance of them, and who is anxious to use for their benefit the slight advantage this may give him."

To us it seems that, in an age like ours, this is the safest and most effective method of teaching. We are reminded of Corneille's beautiful line—

Désarme d'éclairs ta divine éloquence.

The lightning dazzles rather than enlightens. No pomp of sacerdotalism carries half so much weight as the frankly human utterance of an honest and earnest heart. Do we not learn this lesson from the life of the Great Master, who left the seat of Moses in the temple to the scribes and Pharisees, while He taught by the well of Sychem, in the streets of Galilean villages, or from the deck of the fishermen's boat?

Vinet's breadth of view gave him a noble vantage-ground as a literary critic. He looked upon literature as the most genuine expression, not only of social conditions, but of the human heart. The secret of the power of literature is, that it embodies in a tangible form, that which is essentially the mind of the age. It is the revelation, all the more reliable because it is often unwitting, of the psychological condition of the generation which produces it. Vinet always regarded it in this light. Hence his criticism was never slight or superficial, but always conscientious and exact. He never entered on the study of great writers, simply with a view to finding proofs in support of his own beliefs. Literature, thus treated, becomes only a series of texts for one endless sermon. No one had a keener relish than Vinet for the pure beauties of literature, and he delighted in kindling the same enthusiasm in others. With a few strokes of his powerful pen, he would characterise our great writers, but he always recognised the man in the author. He never ridiculed. We always feel that he approaches a fellow-man with respect; and when he finds that which is unworthy, he treats it not as a satirist, but as a good physician, anxious to relieve, if possible, the ills which grieve his compassionate heart. His studies of the nineteenth century are among the finest pages of the moral history of our era, into which he had a singularly clear insight.

Vinet was not so absorbed in the conflict of ideas as to become indifferent to the not less ardent controversy which was agitating the political world at the same time. He was a staunch Liberal on every question. It was impossible that he should be otherwise, with his views of the destiny of man. Believing, as he did, that man was called to fulfil in the free exercise of his highest faculties, a truly divine vocation, he could not admit that he was subject to any other yoke than that of the protecting law of liberty, which is the true guardian of peace and order in the State. The more exalted the origin and destiny of man, the surer basis is there for his rights as a member of society. A sacred buckler is over him, and any wrong done to him is sacrilege. Hence Vinet's deep love for liberty. Speaking of it in a letter to a friend, he says: "As long as I live, my heart will beat true to the cause of freedom."

"Even though liberty were fraught with all imaginable perils," he says again; "while slavery promised all peace and tranquillity, I would still prefer liberty, for liberty is life, and slavery death. We are well aware that in many minds this word liberty awakens all sorts of misgivings, that in some ears it sounds like the trumpet blast of civil discord. But surely such fear is weakness. Has any word ever been more abused? But in this it only shares the fate of all holy and sublime things. From the very beginning of the world, the conflict has been going on between slavery and liberty. The sixty centuries of its history have been but one long day of battle. The history of liberty has been assured ever since the great Leader of mankind placed Himself at the head of this sacred battalion, which gains strength by the blows which it receives even more than by those which it gives."

Vinet thus always kept in view the close connection between liberty in its outward manifestations and its sacred source. "Liberty has need," he said, "of a religious basis." He shared De Tocqueville's conviction: "The man who does not believe, is of necessity a slave." That which filled him with the keenest apprehension for France, which he dearly loved, was the fact that the tree of its liberal Constitution, with all its fresh and luxuriant foliage, had no deep roots. This state of things wrung from him a cry of alarm. "Only think," he exclaimed, "of so much liberty, and no beliefs!"

We have mentioned De Tocqueville. Vinet was in full accord with this great and noble man, who was one of the first, after Benjamin Constant, to repudiate the proceedings of the Revolutionists, refusing to follow the school of Rousseau, and to identify liberty with the sovereignty of the people. He maintained that despotism was not lightened by being exercised by many tyrants instead of one, and that it made not the slightest difference whether the rights of the individual were crushed by a giant with a single club, or by a Briareus with a hundred arms. The characteristic of true liberalism is that it limits the power of the State with a view to the protection of individual liberties, and makes the State the legal guardian of the rights of the citizen. France owes much to De Tocqueville, for his efforts in the cause of decentralisation,—a cause which has unhappily been forsaken of late by its former defenders. Vinet did equally effective service in the same direction, by enforcing a religious respect for the individual. It is just because man is a moral being that every individual has an infinite value, and that it can never be lawful to sacrifice him for the public cause, as if he were a mere integral part of a great whole. It was under the influence of this broad and enlightened liberalism that Vinet, on the eve of the Revolution of 1848 (which he did not live to see), attacked the principle of Socialism, with characteristic acumen and vigour.

While Vinet was thus the champion of all liberties,

he was the indefatigable and incomparable advocate of religious liberty, carried to its furthest consequences. To this subject he devoted some of his noblest works —his "Mémoire" of 1823, his volume on "La manifestation des Convictions religieuses," and a constant succession of pamphlets and articles, called forth by the current polemics of a little democracy, which had small regard for the rights of conscience. In this cause also, he served under the same banner as De Tocqueville, and had soon such eminent allies as MM. De Laboulaye and Jules Simon. No one did more than Vinet to uplift that noble standard which, unhappily, even now—eighty years after the French Revolution, and three centuries after the Reformation —rallies around it so few followers on the Continent of Europe.

There are two bases on which liberty of conscience may be philosophically maintained. The first is the impossibility of establishing religious truths by direct evidence, which takes away from the State all right to impose or to defend them by force ; the second is respect for conscience, on the ground of God's exclusive right of control over it. We accept both lines of argument. We hold that religious and philosophical truth cannot be established by direct evidence—a statement which Vinet, who laid such stress upon the moral character of faith, would certainly not have disputed. It was on the second ground, however, that he mainly took his stand, in opposing stedfastly all coercion in matters of religion, as the most odious abuse of power. In his view, there was no worse offence against God than the attempt to interpose the rude hand of the State between Him and the human soul. He says: "It is impossible, on any hypothesis whatever, to conceive the slightest relation between political science and the science of the Infinite, between politics and the faith of the heart, between the police and the conscience. The sacred realm of conscience is the unassailable stronghold of individual rights,— rights which belong to every man absolutely and undividedly, and for which he is accountable to God alone. Lest any should mistake his meaning, and confound him with the defenders of the illusory liberty for the right, Verny adds: "Liberty of conscience is not merely the competence to decide between one religion and another; it is also essentially the right not to accept any."

This, then, was Vinet's motto—liberty for all men, under all circumstances; liberty not only for the faithful, but for the unbelieving—nay, even for the great contemners of conscience. Let those inconsistent Liberals, who are tempted to excuse the attacks made on the Ultramontanes in Prussia and in Switzerland, reflect on the following noble words: "If ever toleration can find a worthy occasion for its exercise, it is in relation to the intolerant."

Vinet did not rest satisfied with generous theories: he desired to see the recognition of liberty in practice, as well as in principle. Religious liberty was inseparable, in his view, from liberty of worship and of outward profession, under the single condition of respect for the laws and for public order. He went even further—he desired to see the independence of worship secured by the separation of the Church from the State. It was not enough for him that the Church should not persecute ; he was equally averse to its position as the protector of religion, for, by such protection, it acquires a privilege, and casts its gold or its sword into that scale of the sanctuary, which ought not to be turned by any but the highest moral considerations. To expect religious liberty in a State which has an established religion of its own, is a chimera. The Church is an association of souls, based upon individual convictions freely arrived at. Such an association cannot lawfully identify itself with the State, which is a purely civil institution, in which all citizens have equal rights by birth. From such an unholy alliance one of two results must follow : either the Church will become a mere external organisation, within whose easy enclosure souls will be lulled into a false security ; or it will be a refractory force, always at issue with the State, and compromised in the purity of its character alike by success or failure.

It may be objected that Vinet went too far in his depreciation of the State, and failed to recognise sufficiently its high vocation as the representative of law. All we ask of the State is that it should bear in mind this its noble function, and refuse to lend itself to the violation of the most sacred form of law —that which is enshrined in the human conscience. The State will never be further from atheism than while scrupulously fulfilling its secular duties: it is really atheistic when it presumes to put itself in the place which belongs to God alone, in the government of souls.

Even if we admit, however, that Vinet may have taken an inadequate view of the high functions of the State, we must still regard as truly sublime his eloquent vindication of the great cause of spiritual independence, which Mirabeau had already illumined with some of the lightning flashes of his genius, as when he said "religion is no more national than conscience."

In our estimation, Vinet has no rival among his contemporaries in the vindication of these principles, unless it be Lamartine. We recall his noble utterances on the subject of the Concordat, and his irrepressible indignation at the very thought of a religion placed under the control of any imperial power whatsoever, or of a sovereign democracy. The separation of the Church and State would be, as he deemed, the fitting consummation of what he called the religious phase of the French Revolution. Vinet, De Tocqueville, Lamartine—these are names which impart a truer than any mere heraldic dignity to a great idea, which the superficial and bigoted adherents of routine regard as among the abominations of a rabid Radicalism.

It is now more than thirty years since the great thinker of Lausanne died, and how amply has the course of events during that period fulfilled his forecast. Those tendencies to absolutism in religion and politics, which he never ceased to denounce, have been carried in every direction to their furthest issues. As we see how deeply men's minds have been troubled by the insolent pretensions of those who would force upon the Church a fictitious unity, we feel the full value of Vinet's motto: " Liberty is the one way to unity." What an unrestricted application he himself gave to this principle, we may judge from the following words: " Protestantism," he says, " is with me only a starting-point ; my religion lies beyond it. I may, as a Protestant, hold Catholic opinions ; and who knows whether I do so or not? That which I repudiate, utterly, is the right of any human power to control my beliefs."

How grandly does this exalted liberalism of Vinet's, based upon the purest religion, contrast with the social theories which the materialistic school deduces from its philosophical principles—theories which daringly apply to humanity the doctrine of the survival of the fittest, and declare with a cynical indifference that the weak must give place to the strong. Was not Vinet right when he said that materialism throws all its weight into the scale of tyranny? The world has never yet seen any despotism so terrible as that which would hold it in its grasp, if these deadly systems, to which some of the most distinguished psychologists of the day lend the support of their genius, were ever to become dominant in the minds of men. Let us fully realise our position. We are lost if Christian spirituality does not win the day; and it will only win it if it is faithful to those principles of broad and honest liberalism which Vinet consistently advocated. We are sick at heart of those ostentatious appeals to liberal principles, made by the worst enemies of liberty, when they are anxious to secure a vantage-ground for trampling it under foot. They have taken the surest means to dishonour their cause, and, more than that, to bring discredit on the idea of religion, of which they are the unworthy representatives. Religion loses all its force and dignity when it is dissociated from the idea of freedom.

Vinet has left a noble heritage to be entered upon by this generation. To give full liberty to religion, and to restrict the authority of the State to its proper civil sphere—this was the object of his unrelaxing efforts.

We are fully convinced that no other solution of the ecclesiastical problem is possible, and that till this is accepted, we shall see the perpetual renewal of those disastrous and dangerous struggles for exclusive power and privilege to persecute, which are equally dishonouring to the Churches and prejudicial to the State.

There are few writers who can be studied with more advantage at the present time than Vinet. We are thankful to M. Rambert for bringing before us this type of a lofty and liberal Christianity, which vindicates the gospel from many of the calumnies cast upon it, by showing what it is in its true spirit, in contrast to those miserable travesties which are often presented to us in its name.

VERNY AND ROBERTSON.

VERNY AND ROBERTSON.

"*Ces questions, coupables amusements des esprits légers, insondables douleurs des âmes profondes*" (Verny. Sermons, p. 358).

THE names of Verny and Robertson recall two of the most remarkable representatives of the Church of our day, both removed by death in the fulness of their manhood, after passing through a crisis in their spiritual life, in which they only achieved the victory after a long and painful struggle. Both started from the most rigid orthodoxy; but they soon grew ill at ease in a vesture which was too narrow for their spirits. The questions of the day pressed upon them, and having been taught to confound theology with religion, or rather a particular theology with the very essence of Christianity, they thought they had lost their faith, when they could no longer hold fast this form of sound words. The anguish of mind which both suffered at this crisis of their mental history shows how dearly they loved the truth. To them it was no mere theory to be held or dropped, but the very gist of life, without which existence would be aimless and worthless. They were among the trembling seekers after truth; but their quest was pursued all the more sorrowfully because they had to begin it afresh after having once already, as they had supposed, found and grasped the hidden treasure. This it was which made their position peculiarly painful. But their ultimate success was certain, for they used the means by which alone a full assurance of truth can be finally reached. They did not treat the grave doubt which had arisen in their hearts as a demon to be exorcised, nor did they try to banish it by an unintelligent surrender of reason to authority. They had too much respect for truth to hold it so cheap. They were careful, however, not to allow the doubt to extend to their moral and religious life; they held fast those immutable convictions of right and wrong to which conscience appeals. These supplied a fixed point on which the lever of inquiry might rest. Above all, they held constant fellowship with the living God, the source of all purity and light. They thus escaped that moral scepticism which is a disease of heart and brain, smiting both with sterility, and against which conscience raises its accusing voice. Both Verny and Robertson, as we shall see, came out from the spiritual conflict with their faith purified and enlarged, and established upon a more solid basis.

I am far from saying that either had arrived at the

complete apprehension of Christian truth. I shall have to draw attention to more than one point on which their creed appears to me deficient; but it bears the unquestionable impress of the gospel of Christ, and, in many respects, it is peculiarly adapted to the wants of our generation. Nothing is likely to be of more use in the present day than the example of men like these. All the disciples of Christ are not required to pass through the same experiences. There are many who never know any other conflict than that against sin; once born into the new life, doubts no more arise in their hearts. Their convictions are solid and genuine, based upon their personal experience of the truth. There is a cast of mind to which doubt is impossible, and which instinctively ignores all the problems of religious thought. We admit that such a spiritual attitude is perfectly legitimate: all we ask is that it should not be exacted of all Christians, and that a happy, natural disposition should not be confounded with faith. We must recognise the existence also of minds of another order, more disposed by habit and constitution to the analysis of ideas and doctrines, and which, while they bow in reverence before the cross, want to test the firm foundations of their faith. To such minds there must come painful crises of self-questioning in times like ours, when so many difficult problems constantly present themselves, and when, in the great heritage of thought received from past generations, we are called upon to distinguish between what is eternal truth and what is merely human tradition. Let it be observed, moreover, that this cannot be accomplished, as in the times of the Reformation, by one of those great religious movements which destroy by replacing, and the negations of which are but as it were the keen point of powerful affirmations. The fire, which burns up the straw and the stubble, mixed with the true material in the Christian building, comes straight from heaven, and it begins by kindling a new and intense life in the believing soul.

There has been nothing of this sort in our day. The change in theology, which our generation has witnessed, has been wrought by a spirit of inquiry, rather subtle than fervent, and working under a cold and cloudy sky. It is a spirit in harmony with the age; but one which is full of danger to the Christian life. Hence the permanent interest that attaches for us to the spiritual history of such men as Verny and Robertson. In them we see true faith coming forth victorious from the agonising conflict with doubt. From them we learn that inquiry does not necessarily result in the frivolous negations of Rationalism, which are the bane of our modern Protestantism. That which strikes us, indeed, in this so-called liberalism, is not so much the poverty of its results, as that self-satisfaction which it displays so ostentatiously, in the midst of the ever-widening religious and theological desert which it creates around itself. We find no trace of that spirit of earnest inquiry which is ever characteristic of the ardent lovers of truth. The calm complacency of the Rationalistic school has no parallel, unless it be in that of a certain orthodox school, which believes it has comprehended the inexhaustible treasure of revelation in a few well-defined formularies. The evolutions of the young theological Left remind us of the feats of brilliant skaters. They go curvetting and gliding over the brittle surface, beneath which lie depths of which they never think—the deep mysteries of heaven and hell, of human sin and of Divine love. Verny and Robertson were utter strangers to this smiling and superficial theology, neither on the other hand did they make shipwreck upon the barren rock of universal doubt. In reading their writings—those of Robertson especially—I am reminded of the impressive, sternly mournful pages in which M. Scherer has related the tragic story of Montaigu, a type easy to recognise, and nobler a hundred times than the blatant triflers of one section of the theological Left. The adaptation of the monologue of Faust to our present circumstances is very pathetic.

Robertson has described, in terms not less eloquent, the night of anguish in which the faith he had held as a mere tradition, slipped from him. Only he goes on to tell us how he again found Christ. He was not satisfied, like Faust and Montaigu, with listening to the Easter bells, and yielding to a mere reverie of poetic sadness. He heard, at the same time, a deeper tone, the voice of conscience, which he never allowed to be stifled by his intellectual doubts. He heard, too, in the depths of his heart, another voice, yet more sublime and tender, the voice of the God of the gospel; and thus he came out of the struggle with a yet firmer grasp of those beliefs, which are the safeguards of the moral, no less than of the religious life. In his biography we have the description, not only of the night of windy storm and tempest, but also of the faithful star which guided him into the port of peace.

I.

The volume of Verny's Sermons brings vividly before us the thinker and the preacher, but no written words can do full justice to his peculiar genius, to that versatility and freshness of mind which lent such a charm to his unstudied intercourse with his friends. In such free conversation, he poured forth the treasures of his knowledge, and the still richer treasures of his own heart and mind, with a readiness and richness of utterance rarely equalled. His was an ardent and highly sensitive nature. His eyes would fill with tears under the influence of some strong emotion, when a moment before he had been indulging in bright, humorous sallies, sometimes not unmixed with a touch of irony. The reason why he did not write more was no doubt this, that he was never wholly himself, pen in hand. In his pulpit preparations, he was obliged to adopt a very exact method, lest he should be carried away by his constant habit of rapid, impulsive improvisation. He had to keep within rigid bounds, those floods of impetuous eloquence which were always ready to burst forth. Hence the fine aroma of his genius can never be fully appreciated by those who know him only through his writings. The pious urn, in which his remains are presented to us to-day, contains only the cold ashes of his powerful intellect. This is, however, no mean memorial, and we are deeply grateful to the family of the author for this valuable contribution to our religious literature.

The short biographical notice with which the Sermons are prefaced, gives us the principal phases of Verny's life, especially in its moral and religious aspect. He began at the bar. His dedication to the ministry was the result of his own well-considered choice, and not a career pre-determined for him by his family. He always carefully avoided any assumption of the clerical, either in speech or manner, and was never betrayed into anything like religious cant. The knowledge he gained of life and of men, in his legal apprenticeship, was the best preparation possible for the ministry. Most of the leading preachers among the Catholic clergy have been engaged in some civil career before entering the seminary, and have thus acquired a manliness which education in a clerical hot-house can never give.

It was at Mulhouse, when acting as Principal of the College in that town, that Verny became a new man. He says himself: "It was Vinet who removed the cataract from my eyes." He could not have come under a healthier influence, or one more adapted to his noble and vigorous nature.

Vinet remained through life his most dear and venerated friend. We understand that the correspondence between these great men has been preserved. We may hope that it will one day be published, for what could be more rich in interest than the interchange of two such minds on the highest themes of thought and feeling.

At this time, about the year 1834, no difference of opinion had yet arisen to overshadow the dawn of the religious awakening in Protestant France. It is easy to trace in the early writings of Vinet a fresh current of thought, distinct from the prevailing orthodoxy; but this current was then like the Rhone in the Lake of Geneva, a distinct, but not as yet divergent, stream. Verny, therefore, could be at this time a disciple of Vinet, without any marked dissidence from the then prevailing mode of thought.

On his nomination to the pastorate of the Lutheran Church of Paris, he at once took his place among the excellent men who were at that time the leaders of the orthodox religious movement, and he contended, side by side with them, against the mitigated Rationalism which still widely prevailed. He appears even to have preached emphatically the particular doctrine of his Church as to the Lord's Supper, although he was never an advocate of the rigid exclusiveness which characterised it subsequently, especially in Alsace. A contributor to the periodical, the "Semeur,"[1] and closely associated with Vinet, who conducted it with so much judgment and generous large-heartedness, he was entirely free from the sectarian spirit which can see nothing beyond its own narrow sphere, and looks suspiciously on everything that will not fall in with its petty theories.

A crisis in Verny's life, however, was approaching— a crisis rendered inevitable by the intellectual and religious atmosphere of the day in which he lived.

In our time we are disposed to look on the religious revival through a softening haze of distance, which gives it an unreal breadth of horizon. We do it more simple justice when we recognise it as it actually was, in all its rough but vigorous originality. The services rendered by it are so great, that we can afford to acknowledge that it was narrow and incomplete, without lessening its claim to our devout thankfulness. To say that its theology was well-considered, that it had a due regard for the liberty of Christian thought, that it adequately recognised the claims of science, would be to put fiction in the place of history. There

---

[1] In reference to the "Semeur," see remarks in the Article on Vinet.

has been a disposition recently to resent the assertion, that the theology of the revival is identical with that of the seventeenth century. What, then, are the differences between the two? The current notions of that period as to verbal inspiration, expiation, and many other points, are much more nearly allied to the Confession of Dort than of Rochelle. This theology is purely and simply the almost literal translation of the English theology of the commencement of the present century, and this, in its turn, is the legitimate offspring of the narrow dogmatism of the seventeenth. Undoubtedly, from a moral point of view, the difference was great; a Divine fire of enthusiasm and of charity glowed through this meagre theology; but in order to recognise the actual progress of the revival since the time of the Swiss *Consensus*, we must draw a distinction between theology and faith, which the foremost representatives of the revival resolutely disallowed. In the fervour of their belief and the narrowness of their knowledge, they could not conceive of a possible history of doctrine. To them it seemed that the orthodoxy of the day had been the invariable belief of all true Christians, and that "the good sound doctrine" had been professed on all points by Christian antiquity; that it had been re-discovered intact by the Reformers, and brought into full relief in all its integrity by the fathers of the revival. I appeal, in support of this statement, to the writings of the venerable Gaussen, and to the course of argument constantly adopted in the "Archives du Christianisme," conducted by the venerated Frédéric Monod, whose name is identified in our warmest memories with the purest disinterestedness, the most sincere faith, and courageous candour. I appeal, yet further, to the protests of the elder M. Bost, whose powerful vindication of the distinction between theology and religion was not a mere fighting the air. Neither the "Semeur" nor Vinet himself had as yet taken sufficiently firm ground against this dangerous tendency of the time, the effect of which was to confound eternal truth with transitory forms, the human system with the Divine substance. It was an error fraught with manifold perils, for it compromised eternal things in the variations of theological formularies ; and it held fast, as the seamless vesture of Christianity, a worn and patchwork robe, altogether unworthy and inadequate to enfold its spirit of immortal youth.

I lay stress upon this point, because it explains, not only the spiritual crisis through which Verny passed, but also the particular form of his new theology, with its merits and defects. Always eager after knowledge, he kept himself well up in all the movements of religious thought, and especially followed carefully the discussions of German theology. Here all questions were boldly approached, and the argument called forth by Strauss' "Leben Jesu," brought to the front the most widely differing views. The evangelical School, led by men like Neander and Nitzch, brought forward, under the banner of evangelicalism, ideas which would have been regarded as of very questionable orthodoxy on the French side of the Rhine. There was no passing with impunity in that day the terrible Styx, which divided the peaceful shores of uncontested beliefs from the stormy strand of daring speculation. It was not without a sharp wrench, that faith was separated from its formula. It seemed, indeed, at one time, as if faith itself must be uprooted in the process. So it was with Verny. The conflict in his case was sharp and agonising. How could it be otherwise, in a nature so strong as his, to which truth was no mere matter of curious speculation, but the great aim and end of life? To him, to lose Christ was to lose all that gave strength and joy to his spiritual being—his ideal, his hope. What was his agony when it seemed to him that this heavenly Friend, this Divine brother, was slipping from his embrace, was growing dim to him in clouds of bewildering thought? The burden of his ministry aggravated his distress. He felt compelled to give it up for a time, for he was not made of the same stuff as those Savoyard vicars, who go on with a mass in which they no longer believe, and babble through a creed which they have ceased to accept. This sublime duplicity had not yet been introduced into the category of cardinal virtues. Verny, himself, tells us how he found his way into the light out of this dense darkness. He held fast to the sacred convictions of his moral nature, and never ceased for an instant to wait upon God. We may quote part of a letter, written by him from Germany, as a report from the field of battle. It is easy to predict from it the victory that was at hand.

"The grace of God," he writes to his wife, "is with me. I have not ceased to pray; I pray still. And I hope—I know—that through all this doubt and anxiety, I shall reach light and peace. This struggle is for my good, and I cannot doubt that the goodness of God has yet happy days in store for me in His service. I am not trying to constrain myself to become a Methodist again, *nolens volens*, to please my friends. No; I desire to be sincere before God and man. To profess again the strictly orthodox views would be, I feel, to act a lie. By meditation and by the study of Scripture, I must endeavour to frame a theology, which I can bring before God with the approval of my conscience. This is a painful and difficult task; but I will not shrink from it. I desire above all things to be sincere and true.

"I most assuredly shall not, through fear of offending such and such person, hold myself bound by an orthodoxy which in me would be hypocritical. But I shall hold fast with all my strength, that which God has given and confirmed to me: faith in Himself, in His grace, His mercy, His love which pardons all sin and heals all wounds. There is, I feel it, something above ourselves; there is an eye that sees, an ear that hears, a mercy which pities and brings relief to perplexed and anguished hearts. I feel so deeply, I see so clearly, that out of God is no peace, no joy, no true life. All misery, all trouble, all bitterness come from seeking satisfaction apart from Him. I must renounce self utterly, must make a complete surrender of my own will, my own glory, and only live in Him. Then all will be well."

We find the reflection of this great spiritual crisis in Verny's life, in a funeral sermon preached by him for one of his dearest friends, who was prematurely cut off just as he was entering on a brilliant literary career. This friend was Adolphe Lèbre, so well described by Vinet in the letter of introduction sent by him to Verny. "I have never known," says Vinet, "a more sincere and devoted lover of truth. He has the mind of a philosopher, and the heart of a Christian." We ourselves, who had the privilege of his intimacy, know how well deserved was this encomium. Lèbre lives in our memory as one of the purest and most elevated of thinkers. To him too the darkness came, and, less happy than others, he never saw the light again till it dawned upon him in the eternal morning beyond the grave. He died before his beliefs had recovered their equilibrium. A too vivid imagination added much to his actual sufferings, and a terrible disease carried him off in a few days.

Never, however, did his heart swerve from his loyalty to Christ. An extract from an unpublished letter, written by Lèbre himself, will best bring him before the reader. His intimacy with Verny, at this period of his life, gives to the following passages a real bearing upon the subject before us. They are not a digression, for they throw much light upon the spiritual attitude of the two friends at this crisis, and they help us to understand perfectly the manner in which Verny spoke at the grave of Lèbre.

"You doubt," writes Lèbre to a young student. "I do not wonder at it. It is impossible in our day to go fairly into scientific questions without encountering doubt. We are in a transition period. A reformation much more broad and deep than that of the sixteenth century is in preparation. Catholicism and Protestantism will perish in it: a new era is at hand for the whole world. That kind of doubt which redoubles its watchfulness in obedience, its ardour in prayer, and which is full of holy aspirations, is alone of God; the other kind of doubt leads to license of the will, to sinful self indulgence; it degrades the soul and does the work of sin and death. It destroys the past, and it would blot out the future, if God allowed it to triumph. The doubt which comes from God works sorrow, but it works also life. It destroys nothing in the past, but that which is imperfect and transitory. It gives life to all that deserves to live. It rends the soul, but it lifts it higher and makes it greater, for it springs from new and loftier aspirations. You doubt: this is a reason to be all the more submissive to conscience, to obey it more strictly, to strengthen the soul in the love of good and the hatred of evil, to watch over it with holy trembling. When doubt attempts to enter the domain of conscience, to attack foully the eternal principles of right; or when you discover that the metaphysical scepticism will in the end shake your moral convictions and dull your conscience; whenever, in a word, doubt would urge you to a less high, pure, and noble practice; when it would weaken your love for the right or your power to do it; when it would make you indulgent to your own selfishness, and exempt you from sacrifice and self-devotion—then, be sure, it conceals a mortal error. Reject it! Listen to nothing that would lower you : it cannot be the light of truth. And if your selfish, carnal, evil heart finds a secret pleasure in it, take alarm and resolve to flee from it. Seek the truth with your whole heart, and you will find it. Begin by making it a law to obey that which you know to be right, to hold evil in abhorrence, to follow in everything the voice of duty.

"In scepticism the conscience is often very dull, but obey all that still remains clear. Follow your generous instincts, all high and noble desires. Make it your aim to become manly in the true sense of the word. I mean, try above all things to do right, to deny self and live for others. Lastly, do not stifle, by an evil, petty, miserably distracted or dissipated life, the light that yet remains within you. Follow its leadings, and from day to day they will grow clearer and stronger. Be faithful also to prayer. You will feel the need of this in order to resist temptation. You ought to feel the need of this help also in that search after truth which is at once so difficult and so simple ; in which the upright heart always succeeds, while the heart that is not honest goes ever further and further astray. Pray according to your faith ; God will hear you. Say to Him, as did one of those mighty Christians who passed through a long period of doubt before he could grasp the truth for which he longed : 'My God, whatever Thou art, enlighten me ; make Thyself known to me. Give me to seek Thee and to desire Thee. Give me to live aright.' The light came little by little, and at length he believed. Oh! dear soul, if with sincerity and perseverance you will do this, I shall rest calmly about you. I do not know when you will see your prayer answered ; but I have this certainty, that it will be answered. You are, perhaps, alarmed at this way, but you shall not walk in it alone. Whenever we have a sincere desire after God, He is with us ; He aids, He sustains us. Why should we fear the difficulties of the road ? We have the most helpful, the most faithful of friends, who knows all our weakness, who pities it, who sends us inward peace and joy of conscience to strengthen us, who measures out the work of each day as we are able to bear it. He has towards us a heart full of love, tenderer than a mother's. As soon as we set out on our way back to the Father's house, He runs to meet His prodigal child. The faintest sigh of the soul that is seeking Him is more precious to Him than the persevering efforts of the self-righteous. He is full of goodness, of strength, of pity, of gentleness, of all tender mercies. He is only severe to those who have no desire after that which is good. Let us trust in God to help us in the good fight, and He will give us the strength in which we shall conquer. You feel melancholy, perhaps, at the thought of a Christian life. It seems to us sometimes as if it were sacrificing our youth. But what an illusion! It is only Christianity which can give the true youth, for it alone gives the true love. Oh, what a power does it give of sacrifice; what a passion of devotion; what an acquaintance with the infinite; what worship of all that is noble, generous, elevated, pure; what a life of the heart, what a glorious expansion of our whole soul, what an impulse to our hopes which rise immense, eternal! The joys and festivities of our youth are but the image of the joys and festivities of the Christian life; that is the true, immortal youth, the other is but a transitory shadow. So far from drying up the fountains of the spring, Jesus Christ opens in the heart that receives Him wells of living water. All that is noble and beautiful, the fire of the heart and of the imagination, devotion, poetry—all are purified and ennobled by love. The sinful pleasures of youth religion does proscribe; but these you will not regret. The youth which we have by nature soon withers; beneath it lurks a secret decrepitude, some seed of death, some lie; it is but an imperfect figure of the true youth. That is the true youth which love gives—the infinite love of God and of our brothers. It does not fade; it is renewed every morning; it bears each day flowers of heavenly beauty; and when the body totters and the mind fails, the soul remains ever young—because it loves. Selfishness under all its forms,—the absence of self-devotion, the pettiness of a life which makes enjoyment its aim, rather than duty; the neglect of our generous instincts; pleasures, even the highest, such as the pursuit of study, when they make us forget that our great concern is not to live for ourselves; everything that takes away the sense of the solemnity of life; everything that shuts us up within ourselves, and makes us the captives of self-indulgence, not to speak of those excesses and sins which are reproved of all: selfishness, in a word, under whatever name, is old age and death. Ah! I have proved only too well that age creeps quickly on, where there is unfaithfulness to the nobler instincts; but thanks to Christianity, all that narrows the heart, all that dries it up and takes from it its freshness, its elasticity and generous warmth, is resisted, and in the end fully overcome. For myself, I feel I owe it to Christianity alone that I am still young; without it I should have fallen by this time low indeed."

The reader will now easily understand how the

death of Lèbre called forth from Verny one of the noblest efforts of his eloquence. He touches the bleeding wounds of the soul that has passed away with a tender sympathy, learnt in the same school of suffering, through which he himself had recently been brought.

"And now, why should I be silent," says the preacher, "on the subject which is in all our thoughts to-day, and which, by the side of this grave, may well appear supremely important ? This faith became beclouded. You know the demands, the doubts, the conflicts of our age : it would be childish to pretend to ignore them ; it would be untrue to deny their influence and weight. More than one of the historical pillars on which Christianity rested has been shaken ; more than one of the formularies, under which till now it has passed current in the world, has failed to stand the stern ordeal of philosophic thought, or to verify itself by the standard of a true exegesis. We must go even further. I say, that more than one legitimate cry of unsatisfied spiritual need rises in our day, to which our old systems seem to make no response, to which our old institutions have neither succour nor sympathy to offer. Who will dare to pronounce a sentence of sweeping condemnation on all these aspirations and efforts ? Who will dare to say that all these movements, without distinction, are sinful in their origin, that the love of truth, of the truth of God and of His kingdom, has no place in them ? that they are not signs of the times, signs precursive of a new spiritual advent of the Lord ? These questions, which superficial minds treat as trifles, but which present to deeper thinkers mysteries, the depths of which they try in vain to sound, laid hold of the mind of Lèbre in the course of his studies. He doubted. Yes ; but with a sincere doubt. His doubts were not the mere exercise of reason, proud and cold; nor were they the sophistries of a heart impatient of the holy law of God, and eager to give free course to its passions. They were the agonising cry of his soul after a purer, more powerful, more efficacious light. He doubted. Yes ; but his doubt was a hunger and thirst after righteousness. It was but a fortnight yesterday that he poured out for the last time, to the friend who now renders him this parting service of love, the sorrows of his soul ; and how can I better sum up those confidences, or should I rather say those unutterable groanings of his spirit, than in the words of the Psalmist : 'As the hart panteth after the water-brooks, so panteth my soul after thee, O God. My soul thirsteth for God, for the living God. When shall I come and appear before God ?' He doubted. Yes ; but his doubt has received the consecration of suffering and death. His nights of toil, the turmoil of his brain, the tumultuous agitation of his heart, had been long spending his strength. None remained to contend with his last sickness, and he sank under it.

"Is doubt like this still to be called doubt ? It is

faith, my friends; the faith of those who pray, 'Lord, I believe; help thou mine unbelief.' Here, then, for my own consolation and yours, let me give my testimony that the faith of our friend, while shaken in some of its expressions, forms, and applications, still remained stedfast in its secret depths. The great travail of his soul was to find a form more in harmony with his deep faith. The grace of God which had received him, set its seal upon him, and to the very end Lèbre bore that ineffaceable impress. He loved. Love was the life of his heart; love to God and man —the love which forgets and renounces self. Is not love like this the fruit and the witness of the truth? St. Augustine says: 'If love is not desired with all the strength of the soul, it is absolutely impossible to be found; but, when it is sought in a manner worthy of it, it can never be missed by those who love it. It is love which desires, love which seeks, love which knocks at the door, love which reveals—love, finally, which abides in that wh h is revealed.' Such love dwelt in the heart of our friend; it was in this loving spirit that he yearned after and sought the truth, and had he lived, this same love would have crowned his search with success. And that love—never did I express the hope with a more joyful confidence—that love has now drawn back the veil that hid the truth from him, and has satisfied the thirst of his soul."

Verny could apply to himself that which he said of Lèbre. Only in his case, the light came more quickly.

Though still somewhat overcast, like all earthly brightness, it yet shone clearly enough for him to live and die by, and even to fulfil his work as a preacher.

We find in all Verny's sermons from this time, a more categorical affirmation of the great facts of revelation. The belief in the supernatural he retained unimpaired; indeed, it enters into his very conception of Christianity as a religion of liberty. This is admirably expressed in his sermons on the religion of nature, and the religion of the Spirit. We may cite the following passage :

" We said just now, in speaking of the personality of God and of His absolute freedom in the work of creation—*this is essential.* In the same way, we would say here of the eternal pre-existence of the Saviour, and His absolute freedom in the work of redemption—*this is essential*; for if sin is indeed the effect of such a bondage as we have been describing ; if, as the Scripture affirms, and, as our deepest experience teaches us, it is transmitted and perpetuated by a fatal law ; if every sinful action, being itself the result of antecedent sin, becomes in its turn the cause of fresh transgression ; if every generation of mankind, being conceived and born in sin, conceives and gives birth in its turn to another sinful generation ; and if the Saviour came to break this chain, He could not be Himself a mere link in it. In order to grasp it with a powerful hand, and to break it in the midst, He must occupy a position outside of the common race of man, and must draw His strength from a higher source. If He is to heal the diseased tree of humanity, He must not be Himself one of its branches, though the strongest and fairest, for the worm is at the root of all. He must not be an out-growth of humanity and of history; He must not be borne along without any volition of His own on the stream of time, with those floods that sweep away the generations of mankind. He must not be, like one of us, born without choice of our own in a certain age, by the conditions of which our lot is determined.

"No! He must make a new beginning; He must be the Head and Father of a new humanity, a new history. He must be, as St. Paul says, 'the second Adam.' He must needs come freely, because He would, and solely because He would."

It is clear that Verny does not regard the supernatural or the miraculous as the mere scaffolding of the Christian building. It is, in his view, of the very essence of Christianity, which, being a religion of redemption, implies a sovereign manifestation of Divine freedom, in order to break, as he says, the iron chain of sin and its consequences. After such a declaration, the Radical School of theology must renounce all claim to Verny as in any degree belonging to it, since its cardinal doctrine is the negation of the supernatural.

Verny's sermon on "La Religion des Faibles," gives us the ground of this firm belief in the supernatural.

He regards humanity as verily poor, blind, and naked. Evil is not a mere phase, it is a mortal sickness of the soul; and his heart cries out for pardon and restoration. Jesus Christ is not to him, therefore, simply the model of perfection, the bringer-in of the true religion. He is also Himself the object of that religion, the Son of God who has brought life anew to the world; in a word, He is the Saviour. Verny speaks of Him with holy emotion, with ardent enthusiasm, in tones of adoration, in which we seem to catch the deep utterance of his heart rather than any formal ascription of praise. His sermons have the true ring of evangelical piety. They are in harmony with the great chorus of the Church universal.

On one point Verny's preaching seems to me inadequate. It would, indeed, ill become me to condemn him by the standard of traditional orthodoxy on the doctrine of redemption. It does appear to me, however, that he did not sufficiently recognise how completely the relation of humanity to God has been changed by the sacrifice of the cross. He regards it rather as a sublime and overwhelming proof of the love of God, than as the redemption of our souls. He says: "It was to the life that man had lost by his own fault, in which he could not reinstate himself by his own efforts, for which he had no longer either will or desire, that God in His mercy would recall him. For this purpose it was that He sent to men the Son of His love, the Son who is one with the Father, and who, like the Father, has within Himself the fulness of the Divine life. He sent Him that men, seeing Him, might be re-awakened to think of, and aim to fulfil their original destiny; that, as they beheld His obedience in suffering, even to the death of the cross, His participation in all the sorrows of sinful humanity, they might have in Him a certain pledge that, in spite of their transgressions, they were not for ever excluded from their ancient heritage. Finally, that by accepting this pledge, embracing Christ, cleaving to Him, entering into communion with Him by faith, they might be brought back into fellowship with the Father and with the life of the Father."

It would be unfair to take this passage as a summary of Verny's views, or to look in a sermon for the exactness of a theological formulary.

The deficiency, to which we have alluded, is one which Verny would very probably have supplied, had he treated exhaustively that great subject which has called forth so much discussion in more recent times. It cannot be denied, however, that he went too far in his reaction against the tendency to confound religion with theology. He was abundantly justified when he appealed to the history of religious thought, in our own time alone, as conclusive against such a system, and asked whether the partisans of an implacable orthodoxy would put out of the Church such men as Neander and Nitzch. He was equally right in his protest against the claim to identify the doctrine with the life, as if piety had but one side, and as if there might not be blessed incongruities, so that a Christian heart might be beating where we should little have expected it.

We fully endorse the saying, quoted by him in his sermon at the Pastoral Conferences in Paris, in the year 1846: "There is a faith which saves, but there is no dogmatism which saves." He failed, however, to define with sufficient distinctness, apart from all human systems, what is that saving faith which is the essence of Christianity. He calls it the life of God—life eternal. This is true; but that life requires certain conditions, without which it vanishes away. It is based upon positive facts; its essential feature is a great miracle, wrought by the Son of God who "died for our sins, and rose again for our justification." These facts and miracles are the foundation of Verny's preaching—they are its constant theme. Why not lay it down, then, as a settled point, that these are above all dogmatisms and systems; that they belong not to theology, but to religion? "I know well, indeed," said Verny, "that there is a point at which we must stop. He who believes not that life is come into the world in Jesus Christ; he who thinks he can go to the Father otherwise than by the Son; in a word, he who confesses not Jesus Christ, the Son of the living God, is not a Christian. But this point we cannot yet fix; we are still too much in the strife of words and of parties." I think that, even at that time, it was possible to define this capital point of Christianity, and that practically Verny did so in all his preaching. Might he not still say to-day that we are in the midst of disputes of words and parties, when an entire section of the Protestant Church maintains that Jesus, instead of being " the way, the truth, and the life," is only a pattern, a teacher; the type, and not the object of religious worship? Verny would have maintained to-day, as he did twenty years ago, the claims of religious science and its legitimate rights; but he would also have said, as we say, that Christian theology implies Christianity, and that Christianity, without the supernatural element, which it has so stedfastly affirmed, has lost all its specific character. The counsels of broad comprehension which Verny gave in 1843, as the sovereign remedy for the divisions of the Protestant Churches, would have quite another significance in an age when the very foundations of the most elementary faith are overthrown. Even at that time they were exaggerated; but, to do them justice, we must bear in mind the exaggerations in the opposite direction, which had to be refuted before it was possible to make any progress whatever in the study of theology.

I do not question that it was his anxiety to secure the largest possible liberty to Christian thought, which made Verny, for a time, the determined opponent of the great principle of the severance of Church and State. He was afraid of premature action at a time when men's minds were so unsettled. He preferred to keep the boundaries of the Church still undefined, and to receive into it a mixed multitude, whom he hoped to leaven gradually by the influence of true teaching, rather than by a strict definition of doctrines to separate the heterogeneous elements. On this point he was mistaken, as the course of events only too clearly proved. But his great mind was not long held in the bonds of a prejudice unworthy of it. The course taken by events in 1848 led him to abandon his theory of national religions, though he did not see it his duty to break with the Church to which he belonged. This he himself stated to me in unmistakable terms. He showed himself uniformly one of the most faithful and ardent defenders of religious liberty. The independence of the Church in relation to the civil authority was with him a fundamental principle. I remember well the hot indignation with which he stigmatised the famous decrees which, in 1852, gave to the established Protestant Church a new organisation, about which it had not been properly consulted. "No one is satisfied," he said to me, "except those who think of nothing but eating and drinking." These words had, in truth, a wider application than to the recent arbitrary decision in ecclesiastical matters; they characterised the entire system and prevailing state of mind in a country worn-out with repeated struggles for liberty, and ready to seek repose in a state of sluggish acquiescence. Verny denounced, in terms of unmeasured reproach, the promoters of the re-organisation of the Church by means of the civil power. "Even in Russia," he said, "if a poor *curé* had prepared in the dark such a clandestine blow, he would have been overwhelmed with indignant protestations." The vehement orator was careful to add, that he meant nothing personal, but the dart remained none the less rankling in the wound.

Verny has not anywhere given a full exposition of his theological views. Apart from the distinction between theology and religion, between dogmatism and faith, on which he constantly insists, he contents himself with a broad and admirable exposition of the great truths of the faith, dwelling largely upon the spirituality and high morality of the gospel, and combating Pharisaism under all its disguises. Freedom of action in God and in man is one of the points to which he attaches most importance, in an age inclined to a pantheistic philosophy. He never represents pardon as the sum of salvation. To him, salvation is the coming back to, and possessing God. He is consumed with this holy longing; and it is at the foot of the cross that he finds the ever-flowing spring of eternal life. There is an intense earnestness about all his words. He believes firmly in the fundamental harmony between the needs of the soul and the gospel—a harmony constantly broken by sin, but restored by Jesus Christ. His noble sermon, "La prophétie de la conscience," is a model of sound apology. It breathes the very spirit of Pascal and Vinet. His views on inspiration are remarkable for their breadth, yet they do not detract anything from the authority of Scripture, which, like that of the Divine Master has nothing in common with the pretensions of the Scribes and Pharisees.

It would be difficult to speak too strongly of Verny's merits as a preacher, though he never rose to the very highest rank of pulpit oratory. His was not the splendid and impassioned eloquence of Adolphe Monod, nor the inexhaustible fulness of Vinet; but his qualities were nevertheless of rare eminence. His language, without being too ornate, was always brilliant and full of life, altogether free from conventionalism, and characterised by a strong and manly simplicity. In his sermons we find instruction and edification admirably combined. The thinker was faithfully mirrored in the preacher. All his sermons, though free from technical formalities, were based upon a solid exegesis, the thoughts being linked closely together by a natural chain of argument. But over this substantial framework was spread a strong and brilliant fabric dexterously wrought of many colours. This is the secret of all true preaching. The preacher must come into close contact with his subject, grasping it with all his force, or he will be sure to fall into endless and wearisome repetitions, and into meditations which are such in name only. Preaching, which is mediocre through the mere negligence of the preacher, is painful enough to hear; but it becomes a solemn mockery when the special sanction of the Holy Spirit is invoked upon it. It is generally under this form of an appeal to direct inspiration, that indolence grants itself a plenary indulgence. It ought to be well aware, that only a few good souls accept the same view of it, and that it is answerable before God for all the *ennui* which becomes thus associated with holy things.

The sermons of Verny, which have been published collectively, are perhaps rather edifying than consoling. They rarely appeal to the feelings. The sorrows of the heart—those only excepted which arise out of the earnest search after truth—are allowed little place in them. Must we gather that the great preacher was disposed to take his stand among the optimists of the Church? Nothing could be farther from the truth. If the minor key is seldom heard in these sermons, this is accounted for by the choice of subjects. No one had more earnest aspirations than Verny after the realisation of that high ideal of holiness and love, which Christianity holds up before us. All who were present at the Pastoral Conferences in Paris, in the year 1851, can bear witness to this. Verny proposed as the subject for discussion: "The interval which exists between the gospel law and the Christian life of our days." Never in the pulpit or elsewhere did I hear him speak with more power than on this occasion. It was more than eloquence, it was a sublime outpouring of the Christian conscience. He rebuked with terrible irony, not sparing himself, all our inconsistencies, our moral cowardice, the poverty of our dwarfed, cautious, worldly piety, which has nothing of the grandeur of self-sacrifice, which has forgotten what heroism with its divine follies means. He showed how fatally easy it is to speak of the cross, to exalt it without knowing what it is to bear it; and to enlarge in a facile way on the austere morality, the very essence of which is the offering up of selfish ease. He asked where are now to be found those extraordinary vocations, which reveal the Spirit of God moving over the sluggish waters of our existence, and preventing our religious life from becoming a mere routine. He dwelt upon the great duties of Christians towards the poor, the sacred legacy of Christ to the Church, which she has not truly accepted till she has emptied herself to clothe the naked and to feed the hungry. I can only reproduce in cold outline, that which Verny poured forth with burning eloquence that day, when the depths of his spirit were stirred within him. No sermon ever touched me so much, or made me feel more self-condemned. Nor did I ever see that assembly, composed of such various elements, so moved as by one impulse, and lifted for the moment to such a height as to lose sight of its habitual differences. To all who were present this was a moment never to be forgotten.

All Verny's great qualities as a Christian and as a pastor, are conspicuous in his last sermon preached before the higher Consistory at Strasburg. It was never finished, for he died in the pulpit like a valiant soldier standing in the breach. With what breadth of view he described the Church, which he regarded not as some magical institution, existing apart from the living faith of its members, but as a holy society of men, united by the same faith, hope and love, that they might have a fellowship of feeling and of action, of repentance and worship, of joy and sorrow ; but, above all, that they might carry on the work of salvation among their fellowmen. With deep feeling he dwelt on the motive which urges all Christians to activity, the same compassion which " made the eye of Jesus fill with tears, whenever He thought of the multitudes scattered abroad as sheep having no shepherd." " If ever," he went on, " the Church should descend to the level of a popular institution, instead of being an argument in favour of the truth of God, it would become a hindrance to the power of the gospel. Instead of forcing men to cry, ' See how these Christians love one another,' it would lead them to exclaim, ' See how worldly and carnal they have become!'" I know few passages finer than those in which Verny dwells on the good and the evil which may be the hidden motives of our religious activity. He shows us the evil spirit that may be disguised beneath " the doctor's hood, or the pastoral vestment ; that may creep into the academic desk, whether orthodox or heterodox—a spirit sometimes sombre, sometimes sardonic, petrifying holy things in cut and dried formularies, or seasoning them with insipid pleasantries. This spirit mounts the pulpit stair behind the preacher, and whispers in his ear to say nothing that may startle his hearers, to play on their feelings rather than on their conscience, to preach to please men rather than God." It was just as the preacher was describing, in living characters, the good spirit—the spirit of love, of faith, of devotedness; the spirit which makes us realise the kingdom of God upon earth, in humiliation, in poverty, in oppression, it may be, but with the certainty that by-and-by we shall realise it in the excellent glory, the eternal blessedness of the presence of Christ in heaven—it was at this moment that he fell as if struck by lightning, caught away from those who loved him, from the Church, from his sphere of invaluable service, by that sovereign and mysterious will, which teaches us by such providences, that God is not dependent even on His most faithful servants.

We may well believe that had Verny lived, he would have been led, without abandoning his true liberality, to take a more decided attitude in relation to the negative school of our day, which is as daring in speculative, as it is cautious in practical matters. He would have rejoiced in the noble efforts of the Lutheran Church in the sphere of practical activity and philanthropy, while he could never have approved that rigid adherence to old confessions which would make the Reformation a lifeless mummy, instead of a principle of progress and perpetual rejuvenescence —that is to say, a Reformation continually carried on.

II.

The life of Robertson presents the same features of spiritual conflict as that of Verny, only intensified by the greater force and fervour of his nature. The influence of Robertson increases every day; he stands acknowledged as one of the greatest minds of the age, and as the happy exponent of its best aspirations. His theology is not exempt from the imperfections of a transition period. It should rather be regarded as representing in its noblest phase an era of deep religious agitation. Robertson's was one of those intense and ardent souls which seem to bring to a focus all the scattered rays in the surrounding atmosphere. By this concentrated light we learn to read not only the man, but the age; hence the peculiar interest attaching to such lives. The biography of Robertson by Mr. Brooke opens to us a delightful study of character. It is rich in extracts from the correspondence of the great preacher, and reveals throughout the heart and hand of a true friend. We shall endeavour to characterise first the man, and then his style and method as a writer and preacher.

Frederick Robertson was born in London, on February 3rd, 1816. His early wish was to follow his father's profession, and enter the army. This was more than a mere childish fancy for a red coat. His energetic nature made him eager for a course of manly activity and noble peril. His desire was on the point of being fulfilled, for his commission as a cavalry officer reached him a few days after he had entered at Oxford. This step had been taken by him, not only in obedience to the will of his father, but also under a higher impulse, which coincided with deep religious impressions. The sacrifice, however, was very great; and he retained through life a deep and settled regret that he had not been able to follow his first choice. His University course was not brilliant. His individuality was too strongly marked for him to reap the fruits of rapid culture; he came slowly to maturity. Depth is usually incompatible with brilliant facility at the decisive age of moral and intellectual development. He appears, however, to have profited largely by the noble classical studies which are the glory of England. To these he owed the strength and vigour of his style. Plato, the poet of metaphysics, the philosopher of the ideal, and Aristotle, the incomparable analyst and master of severe dialectics, were his favourite classic authors. The influence of both is traceable in his sermons, in which a subtle psychology is clothed in images of singular beauty. At Oxford he led a very secluded and serious life. His piety was deep and fervent; but he had not as yet formed any theological opinions of his own. He had accepted without questioning the current doctrines of English evangelicalism, and preached them with scrupulous fidelity during the early years of his ministry at Winchester. It was under this form that eternal truth had been first apprehended by him, and he had not as yet separated the form from the substance. We shall see how severe was the struggle in which he at length shook off the yoke of strict orthodoxy. In order to understand aright this crisis in his life, we must take a rapid survey of that English evangelicalism which exerted at the time so great an influence, and won such wide and, to a large extent, well deserved respect. When, in connection with the peculiar views of this religious party, we consider the intellectual and moral idiosyncrasies of Robertson, we shall easily understand how inevitable was the reversion of feeling and opinion which cost him so much suffering.

English evangelicalism was born of the great re-awakening of faith and piety which, at the close of the last century, shook off the lethargy of the Church, and told with powerful effect upon the prevailing infidelity of the age. The severe struggle against Napoleon, in which England was engaged for so many years, had also an influence favourable to the revival of serious religion. The impulse thus given produced magnificent results. The great evangelical and missionary societies, among which the British and Foreign Bible Society occupies the first rank, were founded within a few years, and wrought wonders, not the least of which was the inexhaustible generosity by which these noble efforts were sustained. Unhappily, this great progressive movement took a practical direction only, and was not accompanied, as in the Reformation of the sixteenth century, by a deep and powerful impetus in the domain of thought. Hence it led, in the main at least, to a lamentable theological narrowness, which only increased as the first fervour of the Revival died away.

It would be unjust to bring home this charge indiscriminately to all the eminent men who lent their support to the cause of evangelicalism. We could easily refer to writings issuing from that school which breathe a more liberal spirit, to preachers and influential laymen, who were distinguished for a wise and healthy tolerance of diversity. But, while we would carefully guard against the injustice of passing a sweeping condemnation without exception, it cannot be denied that the prevailing doctrinal type in what was called the Low Church (for we speak of this only) was singularly cramped and meagre. It borrowed all that was most dogmatic in the confessions of the Reformation period, without reproducing the logical vigour and theological breadth of the sixteenth century. The Low Church theology took cognisance only of immediate practical results, and made no provision for the demands of speculative or contemplative minds.

It was like the over-busy Martha, unable to comprehend the pre-occupied Mary, who sat at the Master's feet and heard His word. Hence the severe judgment passed by orthodox England upon Protestant Germany, which she always suspected of heresy, and whose science and philosophy awakened scruples and suspicions, even before they had led to any dangerous result. Simple faith, said the English evangelicals, did not concern itself with all these things. It was content with the good, sound doctrine which it had received in the religious Revival, and was absorbed in its propagation. This good and sound doctrine unquestionably contained the essential truths of Christianity: hence it was accompanied with a sincere earnestness, and did a vast amount of good, as we ourselves should be the first to own. But it presented these truths under a very imperfect and inadequate form, and it made the mistake of confounding this form with the gospel itself. It went on, therefore, to proscribe all free inquiry which did not coincide in its results with the *credo* of the Church. Hence it formed a Church which was, on a small scale, a garbled copy of the Church of Rome, claiming infallibility in fact, though not in name, and equally ready with its excommunications and denunciations. This *credo*, of which there was no recognised formulary, but which formed the basis of all the utterances of the Low Church party, may be described in a few words.

The plenary and literal inspiration of Scripture ; expiation by the sufferings of the Son of God, enduring all the pains of hell in our stead ; the imputation, purely external, of the sacrifice of the cross by a faith doctrinal rather than mystical ; Sabbatarianism of the strictest type ; and, as the top-stone of the system, the predestination of a small number of elect souls, and the often morbid development of millennarian views — this was the framework of evangelicalism, animated and warmed, for the most part, by a noble piety, but always and everywhere insisted upon as the Alpha and Omega of Christianity.

To deviate from this was to break with the great tradition of orthodoxy, which, it was asserted, had been handed down from the earliest ages of Christianity. That which the evangelicals preached was emphatically salvation by a doctrine. Heaven must be seen through this narrow loophole, or the soul was declared to be in darkness, alienated from the divine life, and an object of distrust and suspicion.

The evangelical school was, we repeat, admirable in its practical Christianity; it cannot fail to command our respect as we watch its operation in country parishes, or among men and women animated with the purest zeal in winning souls for Christ, and indefatigable in their efforts to relieve the sufferings of their fellow-men. Far be it from us to pronounce such sweeping condemnation upon the evangelicals as they are ever ready to pronounce upon others. But we need not extend the same forbearance to the violent and bitter organs of this school in the religious press, nor can we justify in any degree those intolerant polemics which merely denounce all that in any way runs counter to their prejudices; or approve the clamour raised in excited religious meetings, where the remonstrances of conscience are drowned in party cries. It is necessary for us to note this harsh and haughty attitude assumed by some of the leaders of the party, in order that we may do justice to the reaction provoked by it. Their ignorance was on a par with their vehemence. One of the most eminent representatives of strict English orthodoxy, was one day branding in the most severe terms the whole modern theology of Germany, in the presence of the illustrious Tholuck. He quietly asked if the speaker was acquainted with German theology except by hearsay. The reply was a frank avowal that he knew nothing of that which he so severely condemned, and a confession of the unfairness of such a judgment. A similar act of humiliation would well become the columns of the *Record* and many another blatant organ of the same opinions.

It will be easily understood how this blending of intolerance and ignorance on the highest and most legitimate themes of Christian thought, would be likely to exasperate beyond measure young and generous minds, to make them impatient of all human systems, and disgusted with the *odium theologicum* which would vent its spleen in such narrow judgments.

If we now look at Robertson as he was when he entered on the clerical office, we shall see at once that it could not be long before the ties which bound him to the evangelical party would be broken. He had accepted the first system of vital Christianity which presented itself to him, but he had accepted it, as a whole, without careful examination. He had simply laid hold of the saving truths which it contained. The germ of a higher spiritual development was already implanted within him. His mind, enamoured of Plato and Aristotle, took a speculative turn, and he necessarily applied this powerful analytical instrument to traditional beliefs. His fondness for speculative and metaphysical studies might have become a snare to him, if the moral principle had not been at the same time so vigorous. It was this which soon made the narrowness of orthodoxy intolerable to him. On the day of his consecration (July 12, 1840) all present noticed how pale and trembling he was. His was not one of those self-satisfied natures, which lightly take up the burden of the ministry, with the formulary on their lips that divine grace is all-sufficient. It is, indeed, all-sufficient, but only where the whole heart is surrendered to its influence. "*Cor meum sicut immolatum tibi offero.*" This, which was Calvin's motto, might truly be said to be Robertson's also. He writes at this period: "Every day convinces me more and more that there is one thing, and but one, on earth worth living for—and that is, to do God's work and gradually grow in conformity to His image, by mortification, and self-denial, and prayer."[1]

Robertson knew the secret sorrows of soul conflict, and he adopted voluntarily ascetic habits of life as a process of self-discipline. We find in his journal the following prayer, in which all others centred: "Bring into captivity every thought to the obedience of Christ. Take what I cannot give—my heart, body, thoughts, time, abilities, money, health, strength, nights, days, youth, age—and spend them in Thy service, O my crucified Master, Redeemer, God! Oh, let not these be mere words! Whom have I in heaven but Thee? And there is none upon earth that I desire in comparison of Thee. My heart is athirst for God, for the living God. When shall I come and appear before God?"[2]

It was in this spirit that he passed the first year of his ministry, devoting himself unreservedly to the duties of his office. The consciousness of his shortcomings, in view of the ideal he had set before himself, was often so overpowering that he longed to die, though he was deeply beloved by his flock, especially by the humbler and poorer portion, to whom he chiefly devoted himself. His deep melancholy struck Dr. Malan, in an interview which Robertson had with him

---

[1] "Life and Letters," vol. i. p. 61.   [2] Ibid. p. 66.

at Geneva, when he was compelled to travel on the continent for the sake of his health. This eloquent apostle of the assurance of salvation in the juridical sense, said to him: "My dear brother, you will have a sorrowful life and a sorrowful ministry." "It may be so," Robertson writes; "but present peace is of but little consequence. If we sin we must be miserable; but if we be God's own, that misery will not last long: misery for sin is better worth having than peace."[1]

From Winchester, Robertson removed to Cheltenham, in January, 1841. His great gifts as an orator, of which we shall presently speak more fully, now began to attract much attention. He was never ambitious of a facile popularity, and rebuked unsparingly the worldliness of a fashionable resort.

"It gave me pleasure," he writes, "to hear that what I said on Sunday had been *felt*, not that it had been admired." We find in his papers a sort of pledge made with himself, which gives us a glimpse into the deep earnestness of his soul, and shows also that his theological views were already beginning to waver.

"*Resolves.* To speak less of self and think less. To try to despise the principle of the day—'every man his own trumpeter'—and to feel it a degradation to speak of my own doings as a poor braggart. To be systematic in visiting, and to make myself master of some system of questions for ascertaining the state of the poor.

---

[1] "Life and Letters," vol. i. pp. 82, 83.

To aim at more concentration of thought. To perform rigorously the *examen* of conscience. To try to fix my thoughts in prayer without distraction. To listen to conscience, instead of, as Pilate did, to intellect. *To try to fix attention on Christ, rather than on the doctrines of Christ."*[1]

From this time, the humanity of Christ fills a prominent place in Robertson's meditations. We feel that the icy veil of a traditional scholasticism has fallen, and he has come face to face with the living Saviour. We find these significant words in a letter to an afflicted friend:

"I feel that sympathy from man, in sorrow such as yours, is almost mockery. None can feel it, and certainly none soothe it, except the man Christ Jesus, whose infinite bosom echoes back every throb of yours. To my own heart, that marvellous fact of God enduing Himself with a human soul of sympathy is the most precious, and the one I could least afford to part with, of all the invigorating doctrines which everlasting truth contains. That Christ feels now what we feel— our risen, ascended Lord—and that He can impart to us in our fearful wrestlings all the blessedness of His sympathy, is a truth which, to my soul, stands almost without a second. I do pray that in all its fulness this may be yours—a truth to rest and live upon."[2]

---

[1] "Life and Letters," vol. i. p. 100. [2] Ibid. p. 102.

Words like these show how far removed was Robertson's faith from the barren dogmatism in which Jesus only occupies a chapter or a paragraph in the development of the system. A ray of fresh light has fallen, kindling to a glow the cold metaphysics of the Councils of the fourth century. This inspiration of the heart bears within it the germ of a new and fuller theology; but Robertson will only come to apprehend this through much anguish of soul.

The paltry and irritating discussions in relation to the Puseyite movement, which agitated the religious world of Cheltenham, did much to hasten his enfranchisement from the fetters of party. On a subject of this kind, narrowness and bigotry find full scope; and it is then seen how much pettiness and malice may lurk under a piety otherwise sincere. Everything seems legitimate in what is called the good cause. Slander may use its tongue unrebuked, when those who are to be injured are the enemies of the Lord. The noble banner of the gospel is trailed in the dust. Religious discussion in a small town generally leads to gossip and ends in bitter personalities. Each individual is classed and labelled by the spirit of party, and the transition is fatally easy from the infinitely great to the infinitely small. We can well imagine what a noble mind would feel in this stifling atmosphere, and with what deep disgust a man like Robertson would listen to the miserable squabbles on a subject which, however important in itself, has been so degraded by the littleness of its advocates, as to be hopelessly compromised. Robertson's biographer says: " His conception of Christianity, as the religion of just and loving tolerance, and of Christ, as the King of men through the power of meekness, made him draw back with horror from the violent and blind denunciation which the 'religious' agitators and the 'religious' papers of the extreme portion of the evangelical party indulged in under the cloak of Christianity. 'They tell lies,' he said, 'in the name of God; others tell them in the name of the devil—that is the only difference.'"[1]

Under this impression he detached himself gradually from the *Recordite* party, a step to which he was also impelled by his recent theological studies, into which he had entered with a new spirit of free inquiry. With his ardent and conscientious nature this inquiry could not be carried on without much anguish of soul. There came a moment when his faith seemed to be crumbling to the very base. Happily the rock—his moral life—escaped unharmed. Feeling that he could not preach in such a state of mind, he sought leave of absence, and it was among the mountains of the Tyrol that the darkest hours of his spiritual history were passed. He has described to us, as none other could, this terrible phase of his experience. We will give it in his own words:

"It is an awful moment when the soul begins to

---

[1] "Life and Letters," vol. i. p. 108.

find that the props on which it has blindly rested so long are, many of them, rotten, and begins to suspect them all ; when it begins to feel the nothingness of the many traditionary opinions which have been received with implicit confidence, and in that horrible insecurity begins also to doubt whether there be anything to believe at all. It is an awful hour—let him who has passed through it say how awful—when this life has lost its meaning, and seems shrivelled into a span ; when the grave appears to be the end of all, human goodness nothing but a name, and the sky above this universe a dead expanse, black with the void from which God Himself has disappeared. In that fearful loneliness of spirit, when those who should have been his friends and counsellors only frown upon his misgivings, and profanely bid him stifle doubts, which for aught he knows may arise from the fountain of truth itself; to extinguish, as a glare from hell, that which, for aught he knows, may be light from heaven, and everything seems wrapped in hideous uncertainty, I know but one way in which a man may come forth from his agony scatheless ; it is by holding fast to those things which are certain still—the grand, simple landmarks of morality. In the darkest hour through which a human soul can pass, whatever else is doubtful, this at least is certain. If there be no God and no future state, yet even then it is better to be generous than selfish, better to be chaste than licentious, better to be true than false, better to be brave than to be a coward. Blessed beyond all earthly blessedness is the man who, in the tempestuous darkness of the soul, has dared to hold fast to these venerable landmarks. Thrice blessed, because *his* night shall pass into clear, bright day. I appeal to the recollection of any man who has passed through that hour of agony, and stood upon the rock at last, the surges stilled below him, and the last cloud drifted from the sky above, with a faith, and hope, and trust no longer traditional, but of his own—a trust which neither earth nor hell shall shake thenceforth for ever."[1]

Robertson had chosen the true method for recovering a genuine faith. By holding fast those moral certainties which we have no right ever to allow to be shaken, he kept in his hands the indestructible cable which would raise him again out of the abyss. It mattered little that the vessel in which he had till then sailed, went to pieces in the storm; the shipwrecked mariner came safe to land. Had he once been untrue to conscience, he would have perished miserably, for he would have let go the rope—the one means of escape. When we have once lost the sense of a certainty *within* which can never be shaken, the soul has nothing to hold by, and is drifted hither and thither on the desert strand, like seaweed without root. So long as conscience asserts itself, we have an

---

[1] "Life and Letters," vol. i. pp. 111, 112.

inward witness for the divine, and when the divine is again presented to us we are able to grasp it. Robertson often dwelt on this thought, so fully verified in his own experience. Writing from Heidelberg to a friend, he says: "Some things I am certain of; and these are my *Ursachen*, which cannot be taken away from me. I have got so far as this: moral goodness and moral beauty are realities, lying at the basis and beneath all forms of the best religious expressions. They are no dream, and they are not mere utilitarian conveniences. That suspicion was an agony once. It is passing away. After finding littleness where I expected nobleness, and impurity where I thought there was spotlessness, again and again I despaired of the reality of goodness. But in all that struggle I am thankful to say the bewilderment never told upon my conduct."[1]

Robertson was not content with keeping a firm hold of the axioms of conscience. He boldly faced the investigation of the questions which troubled him and, like Verny, he went to Germany. Timid believers seek to stifle doubt by a practical exercise of faith, and flee scientific inquiry as they would the plague. They do not see that in this way they put unbelief in the place of doubt; for the man who is afraid of his own thoughts, and dares not look scientific objections in the face, is an unbeliever. It is by

---

[1] "Life and Letters," vol. i. p. 121.

the strangest perversion that the stultification of the mind can be mistaken for sanctification, and that the abnegation of intelligence can be supposed to be a Christian virtue. There are pious ignorant people; but ignorance is not in itself pious. It is an outrage to Christianity to make it appear that it cannot bear the free air, and still less the stormy wind, of heaven to blow on it. Christianity is the stalwart oak, which can give ample shelter to all the birds of heaven, and must not be treated like the tender exotic of the hothouse. The fear of German theology, so often expressed in the camp of extreme orthodoxy, is not a scruple of faith, but a leaven of unbelief and a cowardly distrust of the truth.

Robertson's stay in Heidelberg did him good. He came back confirmed, not indeed in his attachment to evangelicalism, but in his Christian convictions. In the absolute holiness of Jesus Christ he found more and more the perfect realisation of the ideal of his conscience. Thus he became himself again, and his religious character acquired the strength and settledness which belong only to a man who has thoroughly tested his beliefs. His closer acquaintance with Germany—the classic ground of Christian learning—was of much advantage to him. There he found, side by side with the representatives of the boldly speculative school, which made the negation of conscience their starting-point, another school, full of religious vigour combined with a large-hearted liberality, prepared to treat religious questions without any bias of party, aiming in the midst of much obscurity at a salutary reformation of evangelical theology, and anxious above all things to introduce a moral element into religious speculation. This was the very thing which Robertson sought—the eternal substance of Christianity under an enlarged form. He might then abandon the formularies which were so painful to him, and recognise that they were human and transitory. It was no longer necessary to shut his eyes in order not to see fatal objections. These objections only applied to a particular theology, and did not affect the essence of Christianity. Great as was the light which the young preacher thus received at Heidelberg, he did not commit himself to any school. He was not to be, like many others, the mere translator of Germany; he was to represent the aspirations of modern theology in his own way, and in harmony with the needs of his own country.

On his return to England, he was appointed pastor of the church of St. Ebbe's, Oxford. He was now a married man and the father of a family, and the slender income of his parish was insufficient for their maintenance. He feared, too, that in this position he would be obliged to mix himself up, more than he wished, with the ecclesiastical squabbles over Puseyism; and it was his great desire not to be in any way a party man. We cannot but regret, however, that he did not continue to preach in that seat of learning.

He was singularly adapted for preaching and teaching in a University town, though he always fulfilled his humbler pastoral duties with unflagging devotion. Perhaps he might have found more helpers in this learned city, and his life might not have been shortened, as it was, by excessive toil. He made his mark at Oxford as everywhere else, though his stay there was so short; and he was deeply regretted when he left St. Ebbe's for Trinity Chapel, Brighton. Here he reached his highest development, both of genius and character. Here also he endured the bitterest experience of moral isolation. A secret presentiment warned him of the trials which awaited him. Nevertheless, he felt it his duty not to refuse the reiterated invitations, and in the year 1847 he took up his residence at Brighton.

He found much to sustain and compensate him under the manifold trials of his life, in the splendid site of the town. He was a passionate lover of nature; the view of the sea and its solemn sound were to him sources of exquisite delight, which he describes in his own marvellous language. Robertson reached at this period the full maturity of his moral and intellectual nature. His correspondence, and the recollections of his friends, help us to appreciate to some extent the wealth of his mental resources and his powerful originality.[1]

---

[1] See especially chap. vii. vol. i. of the "Life and Letters."

He belonged to the order of minds which have an intuition so intense and keen that it amounts to positive suffering. The poetic faculty is, in such natures, a sort of clairvoyance; it is like faith, the vivid realisation of things unseen, only it does not deal exclusively with the invisible things of eternity. It apprehends that which lies hidden beneath superficial semblances, and sees, unveiled, those elements of the awful and the sublime which underlie all life, but which vulgar minds never recognise except in those sudden convulsions when the subterranean fire bursts forth, so to speak, in molten lava. Such sensitiveness brings exquisite suffering to those who are endued with it; if it intensifies the joys, it adds a double poignancy to all the sorrows of life.

Men in whom imagination predominates over the moral life, generally find a sort of selfish consolation in the mere rendering of their vivid impressions in eloquent and poetic forms. Literary glory and the delights of art amply compensate them for the pain of a too exquisite sensibility. But it is not so with those to whom the moral life is everything, and who live for God. In their case, the God-like compassion which they feel for their fellow-creatures, is painfully intensified by the vividness with which they realise all their difficulties and perplexities. This is the secret of the sublime melancholy of Pascal, and of the strong relief in which all the figures, especially those of a sorrowful cast, stand out on his powerful pages. Robertson belongs wholly to the same order of mind. His fervid language seems the outpouring of a heart consumed with a holy fire ; it was his nature to realise the difficulties of others with an intensity that became an agony to himself.

" My misfortune or happiness," he says, " is power of sympathy. I can feel with the Brahmin, the Pantheist, the Stoic, the Platonist, the Transcendentalist, perhaps the Epicurean. I can suffer with the Tractarian tenderly shinking from the gulf blackening before him . . . I can also agonise with the infidels, &c."[1]

This temperament was at once the bane of his life and the source of his power as a writer and speaker. It made him realise, in all their bitterness, the sufferings of humanity ; it gave a terrible poignancy to all his mental struggles, and magnified the misconceptions and unjust judgments passed upon him into actual torture to his over-wrought sensitiveness. His sufferings were unquestionably morbidly acute, and brought his life to an untimely close. Every sermon that he preached cost him some of his heart's best blood. But the anguish was not unrelieved. We should do injustice to Robertson's nature and school of thought, if we did not recognise that, with his ever-growing faith and deepening love, the sacred joys of

---

[1] " Life and Letters," vol. i. p. 183.

his heart and mind were such as meaner souls can never know. And surely, even in our day, there are many who would still make Achilles' choice, and deem it better to live *much* in the highest sense than to live long.

Robertson's strong feelings did not expend themselves merely in sympathy. Cowardice, hypocrisy, vice of any kind, stirred him to vehement indignation, and his language when rebuking them burst forth, to use his own expression, like liquid fire. He could also exercise at times a severe self-repression. He was one of those strong men who regard effusiveness as a sign of weakness. A pressure of the hand and a look convey more to such than any sentimental demonstrations by speech or action. It was this power of repression which gave such strength and simplicity to Robertson's style, and such concentration of thought, illumined by the flashes of a vivid imagination. He had always a horror of mere excitement, as so easily mistaken for the reality of piety and devotion. He knew that Christianity was like a marvellous musical instrument, which can be made to give forth exquisite harmonies under the touch of the skilful player; but he felt, too, how easy it is to practise self-deception under such influences, and to talk much of Christian heroism without bringing it to bear on the daily life. There is an illusive poetry of the cross. It is far more easy to sing about it than to carry it. Robertson was fully alive to this danger. He knew but too well that preaching, however tender and forcible, was but as a tinkling cymbal, unless it reached the springs of the life. He says:

"Nothing is more dangerous than the command of a pen which can write correct sentiments, such as might befit a martyr or an angel. And the danger is, that the confusion between a commonplace life and that of an angel or a martyr is hopeless. For, when the same sublimities proceed from both, who is to convince us that we are not beatified martyrs or holy angels? . . . How dare I talk of sacrifice? And how little there is of it in my life! one perpetual succession of enjoyments! It has often struck me that Christ never suffered sentimentalisms to pass without a matter-of-fact testing of what they were worth and of what they meant."[1]

Robertson dreaded the intoxication of success, and had a horror of becoming a fashionable preacher.

"If you knew," he wrote to a friend, "how sick at heart I am with the whole work of parle-ment, talkee, palaver, or whatever else it is called; how lightly I hold the 'gift of the gab;' how grand and divine the realm of silence seems to me in comparison; how humiliated and degraded to the dust I have felt in perceiving myself quietly taken by gods and men for the popular preacher of a fashionable watering-place; how slight the power seems to me to be given by it of winning

---

[1] "Life and Letters," vol. ii. p. 194.

souls; and how sternly I have kept my tongue from saying a syllable or a sentence, in pulpit or on platform, *because* it would be popular." [1]

This asceticism, which was such a safeguard to a brilliant nature like Robertson's, was perfectly compatible with great breadth of general culture. He delighted in all that was noble and true in art and literature, as well as in nature, connected himself with every great social and political movement of the age, and indulged the high ambition of bringing every thought into captivity to the obedience of Christ. In his correspondence we find him passing from a fine description of a sunset at sea, to a subtle analysis of a drama of Shakespeare or a poem of Wordsworth; taking up questions of popular education or philosophy, but ever reverting to his great theme, the truths of Christian theology and ethics. Unity underlies all the variety—one spirit runs through all his thoughts. He is not the austere representative of a mummified tradition, or of clerical authority; he does not play the farce of an imperturbable assurance; but his influence is all the greater, because it is derived purely from his moral qualities.

His correspondence gives us in his own words the broad outlines of his too brief ministry at Brighton. He devoted himself by preference to the humbler members of his church, thus he became the cherished

---

[1] " Life and Letters," vol. i. p. 196.

friend of the poor and the suffering. He had too clear an insight into the conditions of the age not to understand that the social question was one of supreme importance, and that the practical solution of it must be sought primarily in the better education of the working classes. The Revolution of 1848, which occurred soon after his settlement at Brighton, confirmed him in his wise and generous determination to devote himself unsparingly to the cause of popular education. He took a very active part in the foundation of a Working Men's Institute with a library and public lectures, and by this means he exercised a most happy influence over the artisans of the town, with whom, however, he never hesitated to break a lance when necessary. He vigorously opposed the attempt to introduce bad books into the library.

Robertson greatly offended the Tories by speaking with what they considered an irreverent candour of the beginnings of royalty, in a course of expositions of the Book of Samuel. It might well be supposed that he would have little sympathy with the narrow Conservatism which, at the critical times of the nation's history, fell into a state of imbecile terror and had nothing but resistance to offer to aspirations however legitimate. Of this futile policy Robertson wrote:

"What has ever made democracy dangerous but Conservatism? The French Revolution! Socialism! Why, men seem to forget that these things come out of Toryism, which forced the people into madness!

What makes rivers and canals overflow? The deep channel cut ever deeper, or the dam put across by wise people to stop them?"[1]

Robertson was repeatedly accused of Socialism: he scorned to refute the foolish calumny. Nothing could be more opposed to the general tenor of his teaching than Utopian schemes, the very basis of which was the extinction of individuality and the suppression of liberty. He was none the less anxious to bring the various classes of society nearer to each other, by the operation of that true practical charity, the first principle of which is respect for the poor.

"I knew a young lady," he says, "who used to go down to —— and lecture the poor people upon their dirt and uncomfortable habits and houses, and—hear it heaven and earth!—they did not repent of their evil ways, and reform at the voice of that angelic visitation! It is just possible that, never having *seen* cleanliness or comfort, they did not know *what* she wanted them to aim at or how to begin. Mrs. Fry would have bought them a bit of soap, and washed a child's fingers with her own hands as a specimen, and drawn out a little set of rules, and paraded the family once a week, half in fun, half good-humouredly, to see that her orders were obeyed; and she would have gone on for a year, and if at the end of a year she saw a little dawn of improvement, she would have thanked God

---

[1] "Life and Letters," vol. i. p. 150.

and taken courage. But fine young ladies think that an elegant cut of a riding-whip through the air in the last Belgravian fashion is to electrify a Celtic village, and convert a whole population of savages to civilised tastes and English habits. The patient drudgery which does God's work, however, is not learned in Belgrave Square. Well, the aristocracy of the next world will be the Frys, the Chisholms, and the people who do not care for being smart, and are not afraid, like their Master, to 'lay their hands' upon the wretches whom they would rescue."[1]

Socialism was not, however, the main charge brought against Robertson. His bold and uncompromising preaching came into constant collision with the opinions of the current orthodoxy, though he never went beyond the categorical statement of his views. Thus, while vast crowds still thronged to hear him, he was painfully conscious of moral isolation; and as time went on this feeling became increasingly bitter and hard to bear.

"Of one thing," he writes, "I have become distinctly conscious—that my motto for life, my whole heart's expression is, "None but Christ;' not in the (so-called) evangelical sense, which I take to be the sickliest cant that has appeared since the Pharisees bare record to the gracious words which He spake, and then tried to cast Him headlong from the hill at Nazareth; but in

---

[1] "Life and Letters," vol. ii. p. 154.

a deeper, real sense—the mind of Christ; to feel as He felt; to judge the world and to estimate the world's maxims, as He judged and estimated. This is the one thing worth living for. To realise that, is to feel 'None but Christ.' But then, in proportion as a man does that he is stripping himself of garment after garment, till his soul becomes naked of that which once seemed part of himself. He is not only giving up prejudice after prejudice, but also renouncing sympathy after sympathy with friends whose smile and approbation were once his life, till he begins to suspect that he will be very soon alone with Christ. More awful than I can express. To believe that and still press on, is what I mean by the sentence 'None but Christ.' I do not know that I can express all I mean, but sometimes it is to me a sense almost insupportable of silence and stillness and solitariness."[1]

These sentiments are expressed with a force, bordering on coarseness, in the following words:

"In proportion as I adore Christ (and I do think my whole soul thrills and trembles at the thought of Him, when I understand, or fancy I understand Him, and feel my own heart acquiescing in His life and views of life and God, and acknowledging them to be revelations), exactly in that proportion do I abhor evangelicalism. I feel more at brotherhood with a deranged, mistaken, maddened, sinful Chartist, than I

---

[1] "Life and Letters," vol. i. p. 154.

do with that religious world which has broken popery into a hundred thousand fragments, and made every fragment an entire, new, infallible Pope, dealing out quietly and cold-bloodedly the flames of the next world upon all heretics who dispute their dictum, in compensation for the loss of the power which their ancestor by spiritual descent pleasingly exercised, of dispensing the flames of this world. Luckily, the hope remains that they are not plenipotentiaries of the place with which they seem so familiar. More and more, day by day, one's soul feels itself alone with God, and resolved to listen for His voice alone in the deeps of the spirit."[1] Robertson was manifestly unjust in thus implicating the whole of a great religious party in the blame which really attached only to some of its leaders. But upon these the rebuke falls with no undue severity.

The incidents in Robertson's life are few and unimportant; its dramatic interest lies in the inward conflict, which was incessantly renewed. However keenly wounded in his deepest affections, he made no sign of suffering; his soul was too proud, too noble to betray its secret anguish. His sermons give scarcely any indication of the conflicts within; few could guess how deeply agitated was the soul that could express itself with such quiet strength. Yet every word was perfectly sincere; the calmness was

---

[1] "Life and Letters," vol. i. p. 158.

no mere mask, it was a manly self-conquest. He was like the young Spartan who kept a quiet face while the wild beast was gnawing at his vitals, and would have deemed it dishonour to betray his agony. The publication of Robertson's life was, therefore, a revelation to the readers of his sermons. It showed how much every sermon had cost him. It is a most interesting study to place the sermons side by side with his private correspondence. This we shall attempt to do before pronouncing our final opinion upon him as a theologian and a preacher.

Some of the organs of an implacable bigotry, which persecuted him with their unfair representations of his teaching, called forth from him repeated outbursts of indignation. Of one of these periodicals he said:

"The *Record* has done me the honour to abuse me for some time past; for which I thank them gratefully. God forbid they should ever praise me! One article alone contained four unscrupulous lies about me, on no better evidence than that some one had told them who had been told by somebody else. They shall have no disclaimer from me. If the *Record* can put a man down, the sooner he is put down the better. . . . The evangelicalism, so called, of the *Record*, is an emasculated one, snarling at all that is better than itself, cowardly, lying, and slanderous. It is not worth while to stop your horse and castigate it, for it will be off yelping, and come back to snarl. An evangelical clergyman admitted some proof I had given him of the *Record's* cowardice and dishonesty, but said: 'Well, in spite of that, I like it, because it upholds the truth, and is a great witness for religion.' 'So,' said I, 'is that the creed of evangelicalism? A man may be a liar, a coward, and slanderous, and still uphold the truth!"[1]

The attacks against Robertson became more and more numerous. He would often be visited in his study on Monday by persons with long, alarmed faces, who seemed, however, well satisfied with themselves for having been so shocked. These benevolent censors found exquisite consolation in expressing their fears for him with many ominous shakings of the head. Sometimes his patience failed under the ordeal, especially when he felt that the attack was as malicious as it was ignorant. One Monday morning a solemn gentleman introduced himself as having been of great service to young clergymen. He arraigned the sermon he had heard in Trinity Chapel the day before: spoke of the dangerous views and the impetuosity of young men; offered himself as a weekly monitor, and enumerated, in conclusion, the perils and inconveniences to which popular preachers were subject. Mr. Robertson, who had remained silent, at last rose. "Really, Sir," he said sternly, "the only inconvenience I have experienced in being what you are pleased to call me, a popular preacher, is intrusion,

---

[1] "Life and Letters," vol. ii. p. 128.

like the present." And he bowed his censor out of the room. He had recognised instinctively in his visitor the malice prepense of an implacable bigotry.

The lady theologians who pronounce sentences against which there is no appeal, and who promulgate with touching eagerness, the decrees of excommunication issued in orthodox circles, greatly annoyed and wearied Robertson. They were always accusing him of neology, a convenient and elastic word to be used by those ignorant persons who regard science as the smoke of the abyss. He was also accused of German theology, and this was a grave cause of suspicion to those who were strongly inclined to believe that truth is English and the devil German. These absurdities were of no real importance, but they set on foot misrepresentations which had the painful effect of alienating from Robertson many upright and pious souls, for whom, in spite of the unintentional injustice, he still retained a deep love and respect. The sense of moral isolation is always peculiarly painful to men of Robertson's temperament ; and he felt it in even an exaggerated degree. He learnt great lessons, however, in this severe school. His sermons on the kingdom of truth, and on the Loneliness of Christ, give us, in a matured form, the fruit of these bitter but salutary experiences. Though he did not know Vinet, he vindicated with an eloquence almost equal to that of the author of " Les convictions religieuses," the inalienable claims of truth, and its purely moral power, which does not derive its support from might or authority or from mere force of argument, but which appeals to the heart and conscience, and requires to be received with uprightness and with the resolve to bring the life into agreement with the doctrine. Robertson, in his sermon on the scepticism of Pilate, truly represents false authority as a principle of doubt. He says:

"Fanaticism and scepticism—these are the two results which come from all claims to infallibility and all prohibition of inquiry. They make bigots of the feeble-minded who cannot think; cowardly bigots, who, at the bidding of their priests or ministers, swell the ferocious cry which forces a government, or a judge, or a bishop, to persecute some opinion which they fear and hate; turning private opinion into civil crime: and they make sceptics of the acute intellects which, like Pilate, see through their fallacies, and, like Pilate too, dare not publish their misgivings.

"And it matters not in what form that claim to infallibility is made; whether in the clear consistent way in which Rome asserts it, or whether in the inconsistent way in which churchmen make it for their church, or religious bodies for their favourite opinions; wherever penalties attach to a conscientious conviction, be they penalties of the rack and flame, or the penalties of being suspected, and avoided, and slandered, and the slur of heresy affixed to the name, till all men count him dangerous, lest they too should be put out of the synagogue—and let every man who is engaged in persecuting any opinion ponder it—these two things must follow, you make fanatics, and you make sceptics; believers you cannot make." [1]

In his sermon on the Loneliness of Christ, the bitter anguish of a loving heart, when it feels itself alone in the midst of its fellows, is described with a power and pathos which rise to the height of true poetry :

"It is a solemn thing, doubtless, to be apart from men, and to feel eternity rushing by like an arrowy river. But the solitude of Christ was the solitude of a crowd. In that single human bosom dwelt the thought which was to be the germ of the world's life : a thought unshared, misunderstood, or rejected. Can we not feel the grandeur of those words, when the Man, reposing in His solitary strength, felt the last shadow of perfect isolation pass across his soul : 'My God, my God, why hast Thou forsaken me'?" [2]

Robertson describes no less impressively the ineffable joy found even in solitude by the soul, when it can exclaim : " Yet I am not alone, for the Father is with me." He characterised very happily his peculiar mission in its noble and in its painful aspect, perhaps, also, in its incompleteness, when he said :

"I believe the path in which I work is the true pass across the mountains, though the thought and the hand of the master engineer are wanting to make it a

---

[1] "Sermons," First Series, pp. 298, 299.
[2] Ibid. pp. 229, 230.

road broad and safe for the people and the multitude to travel in." [1]

Such was he indeed—the one to go first down a steep and slippery descent, a pioneer in the path of progress. He was never to know the joy of marching on with the great body of the army to the thrilling strains of martial music. The danger to one in such a position is that of becoming self-absorbed and estranged from sympathy with his fellows—a mischief far more serious than that of being excommunicated by a narrow party spirit. Robertson escaped this greater evil, and retained through life a generous breadth of heart and mind.

"It is really time, now," he wrote, "after eighteen centuries, that we should get some better conception than we have of what Christianity is. If we could but comprehend the manifested Life of God, Christ in His earthly career, how He looked on things, and felt and thought, what He hated and what He pitied, we might have some chance of agreement. As it is, I suppose we shall go on biting and devouring one another, and thinking—alas! for the mockery!—that we have realised a kingdom of God upon earth. To understand the life and spirit of Christ appears to me to be the only chance of remedy; but we have got doctrines about Christ instead of Christ; and we call the bad metaphysics of evangelicalism the gospel, and the tem-

---

[1] "Life and Letters," vol. ii. p. 185.

porary, transitory forms of Tractarianism the Church. To know Him, the power of His resurrection, and the fellowship of His sufferings, that is all in all; and if the death and life of Christ are working in a man, he is our brother, whether Tractarian or Evangelical, if we could but believe that very simple proposition." [1]

We find this idea dwelt upon at length in the sermon on the Dispensation of the Spirit. Starting from the same standpoint as Vinet in his noble discourse on the invisible Christ, Robertson says:

"The outward humanity is to disappear, that the inward union may be complete. . . . For this reason the ascension was necessary before Pentecost could come. The Spirit was not given, we are told, because Jesus was not yet glorified. It was necessary for the Son to disappear as an outward authority, in order that He might reappear as an inward principle of life. Our salvation is no longer God manifested in a 'Christ without us, but as a Christ within us, the hope of glory.' . . . The operation of this Spirit of God creates a living unity—spiritual not formal; not sameness, but manifoldness. There may be a unity shown in identity of form, but it is a lifeless unity. There is a sameness on the seabeach—that unity which the ocean waves have produced, by curling and forcibly destroying the angularities of individual form, so that every stone presents the same monotony of aspect. There is no life

---

[1] "Life and Letters," vol. ii. p. 186.

in such unity as this. But as soon as you arrive at a unity that is living, the form becomes more complex, and you search in vain for uniformity. What is the unity of the human body? Is it not this? The unity of a living consciousness, which marvellously animates every separate atom of the frame, and reduces each to the performance of a function fitted to the welfare of the whole—its own, not another's: so that the inner spirit can say of the remotest and in form most unlike member, 'That, too, is myself?'"[1]

We will now pass rapidly in review some of the collateral labours of Robertson's ministry not directly connected with his theological work. It is very interesting to see how, while never neglecting his proper vocation, he threw himself into the great general interests of the day. We have already spoken of his influence among the poorer classes, and of the part taken by him in founding the Working Men's Institute at Brighton. For the benefit of this institution he gave a very admirable lecture on the influence of poetry upon the people. When called to preach at the Assizes, he showed how much thought he had given to this important phase of our social life. His remarks on punishment were altogether free from that maudlin sentimentality which fails to recognise the majesty and wholesome severity of law. We are surprised, however, to find him approving the punishment

---

[1] "Sermons," Third Series, pp. 30, 40.

of death. It was before the Assizes that he preached his very fine sermon on the Kingdom of Truth, in which he brings face to face the prevaricating judge and the Divine prisoner. At the time of the political elections, Robertson, who belonged heart and soul to the Liberal party, preached a sermon on the election of the Apostle Matthias. He carefully abstained, as he was bound to do in the pulpit, from any allusion to his private opinion; but he used the opportunity given him by the excited feelings of the moment, to define very distinctly the principle of Gospel morality, which ought to guide citizens in the fulfilment of so important and delicate a duty. He never hesitated to give variety to his sermons by drawing largely upon the literary and historical culture of the time. His sermons on the Romans, the Greeks, and the Barbarians, regarded in their relations to primitive Christianity, are of extreme interest. His sermon on the Religion of India is no less remarkable; it is a sort of apologetic history, more in the nature of a lecture than of a sermon, but animated throughout by the power of a living faith.

The sermons in which he takes up the great characters of Old and New Testament history, are richly poetical. He draws the moral features of his heroes with a firm and faithful touch; and, contrary to the usual practice of his countrymen in their religious literature, he gives the true historical setting, painting in the background in solid and sober colours.

He treats with equal depth and originality all the main points of Christian morality. Among his best known sermons are those on "The Power of Sorrow," "Sensual and Spiritual Excitement," "Purity," "Unity and Peace," "Christian Casuistry," "The Law of Christian Conscience," "The Lawful and Unlawful Use of Law," "The Irreparable Past."

The very choice of subjects like these was itself an innovation. As a specimen of the richly poetical form which his thought often assumed in these discourses, which were studies of sacred history and morality rather than of theology, we may quote the following passages from his sermon on Jacob's Wrestling. The method of treatment is most suggestive. Robertson says:

"Putting aside the form of this narrative, and looking into the heart and meaning of it, it will become apparent that we have before us the record of an inward, spiritual struggle, as real now in the nineteenth century as then; as real in every earnest man as it was in the history of Jacob.

"We take these points:

" 1. The nameless secret of existence.

" 2. The revelation of that secret to the soul.

" I observe that this desire of Jacob was not the one we should naturally have expected on such an occasion. He is alone—his past fault is coming retributively on a guilty conscience—he dreads the meeting with his brother. His soul is agonised with *that;*

and *that* we naturally expect will be the subject and the burden of his prayer. No such thing! Not a word about Esau: not a word about personal danger at all. All that is banished completely for the time, and deeper thoughts are grappling with his soul. To get safe through to-morrow? No, no, no! To be blessed by God—to know Him, and what He is—that is the battle of Jacob's soul from sunset till the dawn of day.

"And this is our struggle—*the* struggle. Let any true man go down into the deeps of his own being, and answer us—what is the cry that comes from the most real part of his nature? Is it the cry for daily bread? Jacob asked for that in his *first* communing with God—preservation, safety. Is it even this—to be forgiven our sins? Jacob had a sin to be forgiven; and in that most solemn moment of his existence he did not say a syllable about it. Or is it this—'Hallowed be thy name'? No, my brethren. Out of our frail and yet sublime humanity, the demand that rises in the earthlier hours of our religion may be this—'Save my soul;' but, in the most unearthly moments, it is this — 'Tell me thy name.' We move through a world of mystery; and the deepest question is: What is the being that is ever near, sometimes felt, never seen—that which has haunted us from childhood with a dream of something surpassingly fair, which has never yet been realised—that which sweeps through the soul at times as a desolation, like the blast from the wings of the Angel of Death, leaving us stricken and silent in our loneliness—that which has touched us in our tenderest point, and the flesh has quivered with agony, and our mortal affections have shrivelled up in pain—that which comes to us in aspirations of nobleness, and conceptions of superhuman excellence? Shall we say It or He? What is It? Who is He? Those anticipations of Immortality and God—what are they? Are they the mere throbbings of my own heart, heard and mistaken for a living something beside me? Are they the sound of my own wishes, echoing through the vast void of nothingness? or shall I call them God, Father, Spirit, Love? A living Being within me or outside me? Tell me Thy Name, Thou awful mystery of loveliness! This is the struggle of all earnest life.

"We come now to the revelation of the Mystery.

"It was revealed by awe. Very significantly are we told that the Divine antagonist seemed, as it were, anxious to depart as the day was about to dawn; and that Jacob held Him more convulsively fast, as if aware that the daylight was likely to rob him of his anticipated blessing, in which there seems concealed a very deep truth. God is approached more nearly in that which is indefinite than in that which is definite and distinct. He is felt in awe, and wonder and worship, rather than in clear conceptions. There is a sense in which darkness has more of God than light has. He dwells in the thick darkness. Moments of tender, vague mystery often bring distinctly the feeling of His presence. When day breaks and distinctness comes, the Divine has evaporated from the soul like morning dew. In sorrow, haunted by uncertain presentiments, we feel the infinite around us. The gloom disperses, the world's joy comes again, and it seems as if God were gone—the Being who had touched us with a withering hand, and wrestled with us, yet whose presence, even when most terrible, was more blessed than His absence. It is true, even literally, that the darkness reveals God. Every morning God draws the curtains of the garish light across His eternity, and we lose the Infinite. We look down on earth instead of up to heaven ; on a narrower and more contracted spectacle—that which is examined by the microscope when the telescope is laid aside—smallness, instead of vastness. 'Man goeth forth to his work and to his labour until the evening;' and in the dust and pettiness of life we seem to cease to behold Him : then at night He undraws the curtain again, and we see how much of God and eternity the bright distinct day has hidden from us. Yes, in solitary, silent, vague darkness, the Awful One is near.

"This morning, my young brethren, we endeavoured to act on this belief—we met in stillness, before the full broad glare of day had rested on our world. Your first communion implored His blessing in the hour which seems so peculiarly His. Before the dull and deadening and earthward influences of the world had dried up the dew of fresh morning feeling, you tried to fortify your souls with a sense of His presence. This night, before to-morrow's light shall dawn, pray that He will not depart until He has left upon your hearts the blessing of a strength which shall be yours through the garish day, and through dry, scorching life, even to the close of your day." [1]

We have quoted so much at length from this sermon, because it exhibits at once the strength and the weakness of Robertson's preaching; we shall speak more particularly of both in our summary of his character and work.

He took part, as we have said, in all the great theological controversies of his time. Catholicism was already beginning to assert a strange ascendancy over the aristocratic classes in England. This fact was not to be got rid of by the cry, "No Popery," raised on all hands by the orthodox of every shade. Robertson rightly felt that this tendency to return to a discarded form of religion, could only be accounted for by the existence of unsatisfied religious needs, and that it was of far more importance to discover what these were, and to try to meet them, than to indulge in embittering controversy. The only argument which really carries conviction, is that which

---

[1] "Jacob's Wrestling," Sermons, First Series.

takes away from error the admixture of truth by which it lives, and thus allows it no *raison d'être*. This course Robertson pursued with a rare power of intuition, which saved him from the unfairness of party spirit, as is shown by his liberality with respect to Ireland. He declared boldly that the bill for Catholic Emancipation had put an end to a monstrous system, and desired to see it carried out to its fullest issues, since he held that it was only by religious liberty and equality that Ireland could ever be really attached to England, and an effectual barrier be raised against Ultramontanism.[1]

On the other hand, he makes no concession whatever to the Catholic system. How radical was his disapproval of its principles appears in the following passage from a letter to a friend, who was tempted to forsake the Church of liberty and of the Spirit for the Church of external authority:

"Do you believe in God? Dare you not trust yourself like a child to Him? Oh, what is your baptism worth if it has not taught you that blessed central truth of all—that He is your Father? Dare you so stifle His voice in your soul, which comes in the simple rushings of earnest thought, and then call it conscience? Are you sure that you may not be shutting out a ray from Heaven, although you fear that it is a meteor from Hell? . . . I tried no arguments

---

[1] "Life and Letters," vol. ii. p. 141.

against Romanism, for I feel that Romanism is only an infinitely small and sensualistic embodiment of truths—a living human form shrunk into a mummy, with every feature there hideously like life, especially when it, by force applied from without, by wires or galvanism, moves humanly. . . . God made the soul to correspond with truth. Truth is its own evidence, as the lightning flash is, as the blessed sunlight is. . . . . Alas! alas! you do not believe that you have a soul—you do not believe in God—you do not believe that His Spirit can find your soul—you believe in the dial, and not in the sun—you are not alone with Christ—you do not feel the solitary yet humbling grandeur of being in this vast universe alone, as He was, with your Father. His life is not the pattern of your life, and His divine humanity is not the interpretation of the mysteries of your solitary being. You cannot walk the valley of the shadow of death fearlessly, as David did, because 'Thou art with me.' You must have a crowd of —— and a number of other good men by some hundred thousands to assure you that you are not alone. All this universe is God's blessed sacrament, the channel of His Spirit to your soul, whereof He has selected two things as types of all the rest: the commonest of all elements, water, and the commonest of all meals, a supper, and you cannot find Him except in seven! Too many or else too few; but even in that protest against the Protestant limitation of grace to two channels I recognise a truth, only distorted and petrified as usual.

"Oh, be brave and wait! These are dark days—lonely days—and our unbelieving impatience cannot bear to wait, but must rashly and by impetuous steps of our own, plunge after the *ignis fatuus* of light. Peace at once! Light at once! I cannot wait my time and I will not! I do not say all this as one who is utterly unable to comprehend 'the delusion of people who cannot be content with the sound and excellent principles of our incomparable liturgy.' I only comprehend too well the struggles and the agonies of a soul that craves light and cannot find it. And as to our 'incomparable Church,' why it does not require a prophetic spirit to see that in ten years more she must be in fragments, out of which fragments God will re-construct something for which I am content to wait, in accordance with His usual plan, which is to be for ever evolving fresh forms of life out of dissolution and decay. If not in my time, why then I still wait. I am alone now, and shall be till I die, and I am not afraid to be alone in the majesty of darkness which His presence peoples with a crowd. I ask now no sympathy but His. If He should vouchsafe to give me more I shall accept it gratefully; but I am content to do without it, as many of His best and bravest must do now. Why cannot you live with Him? . . . I have no superstitious evangelical horror of Romanism, but—Alas! alas! for the substitution of an artificial created conscience for the sound and healthy one of humanity, whose tides are distinct and unmistakable in their noble music, like those of Nature's ocean in its irresistible swell!"

Vinet justly said that the special doctrines of Catholicism are like the buoys which mark the spot where some precious cargo has been swallowed up by the sea; a man must dive very deep to discover the treasure. Robertson did so dive. Thus, both in his letters and sermons, he shows that the adoration of the Virgin, who is but the personification of the tenderness and compassion of Christianity, gained ground after the metaphysics of the fourth century had thrown a veil over the true humanity of Jesus Christ.[1] The multiplication of sacraments, which is erroneous if we regard them as ecclesiastical institutions, yet expresses the very legitimate desire to set an impress of sacredness upon the entire life. The idea of apostolical succession conceals a sublime truth —namely, that there ought to be, as it were, an unbroken lineage of prophets and heroic saints through all the ages. Luther is the true successor of St. Paul.[2]

Much excitement had been caused throughout England by the petitions for the opening of the Crystal Palace on Sunday, the only day when the

---

[1] " Life and Letters," vol. ii. pp. 23, 24. See "The Glory of the Virgin Mother," Sermons, Second Series, p. 229.
[2] " Life and Letters," vol. ii. pp. 161, 162.

working classes could visit it. A vast array of petitions on the other side was sent up from all parts of the country. Robertson, though opposed to the opening, did not feel it his duty to take part in this movement; because it seemed to him to be based on an entirely Jewish Sabbatarianism. According to his custom, he preached on the subject, and established with singular logical clearness the true principles on this important question; showing that the legal distinction between one day and another had been abolished by Christianity, but that nevertheless the observance of Sunday meets the wants of the Christian soul and of the Church. Writing to one of his opponents, he says: "Historically the Lord's day was not a transference of the Jewish Sabbath at all from one day to another. St. Paul, in Rom. xvi. 5, 6, speaks of a religious non-observance of the Sabbath."[1]

He showed further that it is possible to imagine a state of mind and soul in which the thought of God should have so thoroughly permeated the life that there would be no longer any necessity for setting apart one particular day for worship. It must be admitted, however, that this is a height of spirituality most rarely attained, and that no one who comes short of it has any right to deprive himself of a means of grace essential to the well-being of his soul, and to the maintenance of piety in the world. He wrote

---

[1] "Life and Letters," vol. ii. p. 112.

again to a friend: "I must reverse all my conceptions of Christianity—which is the mind of Christ—before I can believe the Evangelico-Judaic theory; which is that Mr. —— may, without infringement of the Fourth Commandment, drive his carriage to church twice every Sunday, but a poor man may not drive his cart; that the two or three hours spent in the evening by a noble lord over his venison, champagne, dessert, and coffee, are no desecration of the command; but the same number spent by an artisan over cheese and beer in a tea-garden will bring down God's judgment on the land. It is worse than absurd. It is the very spirit of Pharisaism, which our Lord rebuked so sternly."[1] He insists strongly, nevertheless, on the benefit of the Sunday, and declares that no one who loves his country could consent to encourage the regular and public violation of that day. He cannot approve, however, of legislative measures, taken in the name of a patched-up Judaism, to restrict the liberty of souls. Any one who knows England can understand what indignation words like these would excite.

Another question arose, on which the conflict of opinion ran no less high. I refer to the Gorham case. It is well known that Mr. Gorham, as a clergyman of the Church of England, had taught doctrines altogether opposed to the notion of baptismal regenera-

---

[1] "Life and Letters," vol. ii. p. 113.

tion. A sharp discussion arose, which led to legal proceedings. The futility of such measures, where questions of doctrine are concerned, was soon made evident. The Court of Queen's Bench gave a decision which settled nothing, but which inclined decidedly to the side of baptismal regeneration. Robertson, in his correspondence, and in his two sermons on the subject, took an intermediate position. He could not sanction the superstitious idea which attributes to the material element a magical virtue over the soul, but neither could he accept the strict notion of Calvinism, that baptism receives its value only from conversion. According to Robertson, baptism does not *make* but *declares* us sons of God; recognising in the redeemed of Christ this Divine adoption. It is the proclamation of pre-existing rights, just as the ceremony of coronation does not confer the royal dignity, but declares it to the world.

Robertson showed himself, in relation to this question, the almost bitter enemy of all religious forms which are based upon an individual profession of faith. This injustice arises from a leading defect in his theology. He had too much confidence in human nature as it is, and did not sufficiently recognise its fallen state, and the radical change wrought in it by sin. Of this we shall have to speak further when we come to analyse his theology, so faithfully reflected in his preaching.

III.

There were three theological questions which chiefly exercised Robertson's mind.

1. The method of arriving at certainty on matters of religion, a problem inseparable from the question of inspiration.

2. The true idea of redemption and expiation.

3. The nature of Jesus Christ, and His relation to the Father.

On all these points he repudiated the exaggerations of current theology, but he also failed to hold the even balance of truth, and was carried by the strength of his reaction against what seemed to him the errors of orthodoxy, too far in the opposite direction.

In relation to the first question—certainty in matters of religion—his teaching was as far removed as possible from anything like Rationalism. The tendency of ultra-orthodoxy is, in truth, more rationalistic than such a faith as Robertson's. That school does, in fact, regard revelation rather as the communication of certain mysteries about God, than as the living manifestation of Him in a Divine history, finding its centre in the person of Jesus Christ. It seeks an intellectual rather than a moral adherence, and attaches paramount importance to doctrines, the authority of which it establishes on the ground of an inspired book and of attested miracle. I know, indeed, that it seeks to correct this latent Rationalism by forbidding inquiry, and insisting on the blind acceptance of orthodox dicta; but the fact remains that with a certain orthodox party revelation is regarded as essentially a system of doctrine.

Robertson starts from quite other premises. He differs both from the Jew, who requires a sign, and the Greek, who seeks after wisdom. In other words, he does not derive his faith from sight; either the sight of the eyes or that of the reasoning mind. It is something both higher and deeper. It is the communication of the Divine Spirit to the spiritual and higher nature in man. He says, "If there has been a single principle which I have taught more emphatically than any other, it is that not by reason—meaning by reason the understanding—but by the spirit—that is, the heart, trained in meekness and love by God's Spirit—truth can be judged of at all. I hold that the attempt to rest Christianity upon miracles and fulfilments of prophecy is essentially the vilest rationalism; as if the trained intellect of a lawyer, which can investigate evidence, were that to which is trusted the soul's salvation; or, as if the evidence of the senses were more sure than the intuitions of the spirit, to which spiritual truths almost alone appeal."[1]

One of his finest sermons is devoted to this subject—the sermon on "God's Revelation of Heaven." We

---

[1] "Life and Letters," vol. ii. p. 149.

quote his own beautiful language on the verse, "Eye hath not seen, nor ear heard, neither hath it entered into the heart of man to conceive, the things which God hath prepared for them that love him."

"There is a life of mere sensation. The degree of its enjoyment depends upon fineness of organisation. The pleasures of sense arise from the vibration of a nerve, or the thrilling of a muscle — nothing higher.

"The highest pleasure of sensation comes through the eye. She ranks above all the rest of the senses in dignity. He whose eye is so refined by discipline that he can repose with pleasure upon the serene outline of beautiful form, has reached the purest of the sensational raptures.

"Now the Corinthians could appreciate this. Theirs was the land of beauty. They read the apostle's letter, surrounded by the purest conceptions of art. In the orders of architecture, the most richly graceful of all columnar forms receives its name from Corinth. And yet it was to these men, living in the very midst of the chastely beautiful, upon whom the apostle emphatically urged, '*Eye* hath not seen the things which God hath prepared for them that love him.'

"Let us not depreciate what God has given. There is a rapture in gazing on this wondrous world. There is a joy in contemplating the manifold forms in which the All Beautiful has concealed His essence, — the living garment in which the Invisible has robed His mysterious loveliness. In every aspect of Nature there is joy; whether it be the purity of virgin morning, or the sombre gray of a day of clouds, or the solemn pomp and majesty of night; whether it be the chaste lines of the crystal, or the waving outline of distant hills, tremulously visible through dim vapours; the minute petals of the fringed daisy, or the overhanging form of mysterious forests. It is a pure delight *to see.*

"But all this is bounded. The eye can only reach the finite beautiful. It does not scan 'the King in his beauty, nor the land that is very far off.' . . .

"No scientific analysis can discover the truths of God. Science cannot give a revelation. Science proceeds upon observation. It submits everything to the experience of the senses. Its law, expounded by its great lawgiver, is, that if you would ascertain its truth you must see, feel, taste. Experiment is the test of truth. Now, you cannot by searching find out the Almighty to perfection, nor a single one of the blessed truths He has to communicate. . . .

"Eternal truth is not reached by hearsay—'*Ear* hath not heard the things which God hath prepared for them that love him.'

"No revelation can be adequately given by the address of man to man, whether by writing or orally, even if he be put into the possession of the truth itself. For all such revelations must be made through words; and words are but counters — the coins of intellectual exchange. There is as little resemblance between the silver coin and the bread it purchases, as between the word and the thing it stands for. Looking at the coin, the form of the loaf does not suggest itself. Listening to the word, you do not perceive the idea for which it stands, unless you are already in possession of it. . . .

"Now see what a hearsay religion is. There are men who believe on authority. Their minister believes all this Christianity true: therefore so do they. He calls this doctrine essential: they echo it. Some thousands of years ago men communed with God; they have heard this and are content it should be so. They have heard with the hearing of the ear that God is love—that the ways of holiness are ways of pleasantness, and all her paths peace. But a hearsay belief saves not. The Corinthian philosophers heard Paul—the Pharisees heard Christ. How much did the ear convey? To thousands exactly nothing. He alone believes truth who feels it. He alone has a religion whose soul knows by experience that to serve God and know Him is the richest treasure. And unless truth come to you, not in word only, but in power besides—authoritative because true, not true because authoritative—there has been no real revelation made to you from God. Truth is not discoverable by the heart—'neither have entered into the heart of man the things which God hath prepared for them that love him.'

"The heart. Two things we refer to this source: the power of imagining, and the power of loving.

"Imagination is distinct from the mere dry faculty of reasoning. Imagination is creative — it is an immediate intuition; not a logical analysis—we call it popularly a kind of inspiration. Now imagination is a power of the heart — great thoughts originate from a large heart—a man must have a heart or he never could create.

"It is a grand thing when, in the stillness of the soul, thought bursts into flame and the intuitive vision comes like an inspiration; when breathing thoughts clothe themselves in burning words, winged as it were with lightning—or when a great law of the universe reveals itself to the mind of genius, and where all was darkness, his single word bids light be, and all is order where chaos and confusion were before. Or when the truths of human nature shape themselves forth in the creative fancies of one, like the myriad-minded poet, and you recognise the rare power of *heart* which sympathises with and can reproduce all that is found in man.

"But all this is nothing more than what the material man can achieve. The most ethereal creations of fantastic fancy were shaped by a mind that could read the life of Christ, and then blaspheme the adorable. . . .

"There is more in the heart of man—it has the power of affection. The highest moment known on earth by the merely natural, is that in which the mysterious union of heart with heart is felt. . . . .

This is the purest, serenest ecstasy of the merely human — more blessed than any sight that can be presented to the eye, or any sound that can be given to the ear: more sublime than the sublimest dream ever conceived by genius in its most gifted hour, when the freest way was given to the shaping spirit of imagination.

"This has entered into the heart of man, yet this is of the lower still. It attains not to the things prepared by God—it dimly shadows them. Human love is but the faint type of that surpassing blessedness which belongs to those who love God.

"We pass therefore to the Nature and Laws of Revelation. . . .

"Now the Spirit of God lies touching, as it were, the soul of man—ever around and near. On the outside of earth man stands with the boundless heaven above him: nothing between him and space—space around him and above him—the confines of the sky touching him. So is the spirit of man to the Spirit of the Ever Near. They mingle. In every man this is true. The spiritual in him, by which he might become a recipient of God, may be dulled, deadened by a life of sense, but in this world never lost. All men are not spiritual men; but all have spiritual sensibilities which might awake. All that is wanted is to become conscious of the nearness of God. God has placed men here to feel after Him if haply they may find Him, albeit *He be not far* from any one of them. Our souls float in the immeasurable ocean of Spirit. God lies around us: at any moment we may be conscious of the contact.

"The *condition* upon which this Self-Revelation of the Spirit is made to man, is love. These things are 'prepared for them that love Him,' or, which is the same thing, revealed to those who have the mind of Christ." [1]

It appears to us that Robertson does not sufficiently recognise the direct, special, mystical operation of the Spirit of God in illuminating the soul. He relies too much on the original relations of man with God, and overlooks to some extent the necessity for the reparative work of redeeming love. This is the defect that runs through all his teaching. We would guard against being misunderstood. He very distinctly recognises the miraculous, and in the sermon on the doubt of Thomas, lays special emphasis on the fact that the resurrection of Christ alone put to flight the persistent doubt of humanity as to the future life.

With regard to the divine authority of the Scriptures, he repudiated strongly the idea of verbal inspiration. He insisted that the co-existence of the human element with the divine was indispensable in Holy Scripture, and showed what difficulties would have been presented by a revelation couched

---

[1] "God's Revelation of Heaven." Sermons. First Series.

in the language of exact science, at a time when such a mode of representation would necessarily have been regarded as erroneous. His sermon on inspiration is not a theological dissertation; it dwells chiefly on the practical and positive aspect of the question, showing how everything in Scripture tends towards Christ, and how all receives from Him its sacred evidence and its beneficent authority. He dwells with fervid eloquence on the universal and incomparable power of the Bible.

"The Jews," he says, "have been for eighteen hundred years a byword and a reproach. . . . Yet the words which came from Israel's prophets have been the life-blood of the world's devotions. And the teachers, the psalmists, the prophets, and the law-givers of this despised nation spoke out truths that have struck the key-note of the heart of man; and this not because they were of Jewish, but just because they were of universal application.

"This collection of books has been to the world what no other book has ever been to a nation. States have been founded on its principles. Kings rule by a compact based on it. Men hold the Bible in their hands when they prepare to give solemn evidence affecting life, death, or property; the sick man is almost afraid to die unless the Book be within reach of his hands; the battle-ship goes into action with one on board whose office is to expound it; its prayers, its psalms are the language which we use when we speak to God; eighteen centuries have found no holier, no diviner language. If ever there has been a prayer or a hymn enshrined in the heart of a nation, you are sure to find its basis in the Bible. The very translation of it has fixed language and settled the idioms of speech. Germany and England speak as they speak because the Bible was translated. It has made the most illiterate peasant more familiar with the history, customs, and geography of ancient Palestine than with the locality of his own country. Men who know nothing of the Grampians, of Snowdon, or of Skiddaw, are at home in Zion, the lake of Gennesareth, or among the rills of Carmel. People who know little about London, know by heart the places in Jerusalem where those blessed feet trod which were nailed to the cross. Men who know nothing of the architecture of a Christian cathedral, can yet tell you all about the pattern of the Holy Temple. Even this shows us the influence of the Bible. The orator holds a thousand men for half an hour breathless—a thousand men as one listening to his single word. But this word of God has held a thousand nations for thrice a thousand years spellbound; held them by an abiding power, even the universality of its truth; and we feel it to be no more a collection of books, but *the* Book." [1]

The doctrine of expiation was an absorbing subject

---

[1] "Sermon on Inspiration." First Series, pp. 302, 303.

of thought with Robertson, as is evident both from his correspondence and his sermons. It must be admitted that this was a subject very imperfectly treated in the current literature of the religious revival in England. Salvation was represented as the payment of an infinite debt by infinite suffering. I need not repeat the observations already made in reference to this view. It is idle to attempt to defend the dangerous exaggerations of the evangelical school. In order to justify this great religious movement, its champions appeal to the writings of its most moderate theologians, much in the same way that the more elevated minds among the Catholics quote Bossuet's "Exposition de la Foi." But in judging of the distinctive and characteristic principles of a theology, we must test it, not by the writings of wise and able men, who present it softened, modified, all but transfigured through the medium of their own genius, but by its effects on the preaching and current literature of the day, and on the religious life of the people. It is certain that the popular doctrine of expiation, in circles where evangelical views predominated, was as we have described it. It taught that the Divine anger was appeased by the momentary damnation of Christ. Faith was simply the acceptance of a purely external imputation. This it was that chafed and irritated a conscience like that of Robertson, and led him into an exaggerated reaction against his early convictions. In one of his letters he says: "It appears to me that Protestantism throws upon the intellect the work of healing, which can only be performed by the heart. It comes with its parchment, signed, sealed, and delivered, making over heaven to you by a legal bond, gives its receipt in full, makes a debtor and creditor account, clears up the whole by a most business-like arrangement:

Cr. *Dr.*
Infinite. Infinite.

"And when this Shylock-like affair, with its scales and weights, is concluded, it bids you be sure that the most rigorous justice and the most wanton cruelty can want no more. Whereupon selfishness shrewdly casts up the account and says: 'Audited, I am safe!' Nay, it even has a gratitude to Him who has borne the pain instead; a very low kind of affection; the same, differing only in degree, which young Peel felt for Byron, when he volunteered to accept half the blows which a young tyrant was administering. The love which is only gratitude for escape from pain is a very poor love. It does not open the heart wide, and accordingly, basing his hopes only on a *quid pro quo*, a sinner's penitence is half selfish, and has rarely in it any of that glorious *abandon* which, whether wisely directed or not, has so marked the Roman penitence, and which we explain away by saying, it is work done to win heaven by merit. The Protestant penitent, if the system succeeds, repents in his arm-chair, and does no noble deed such as boundless love could alone inspire. He reforms, and is very glad that broken-hearted remorse is distrust of God, becomes a prosaic Pharisee, and patronises missionary societies, and is all safe, which is the one great point in his religion."[1]

In these strong utterances we must make allowance for Robertson's peculiar temperament. This is clearly not a calm and impartial judgment; it is a passionate outburst of indignation against the most obnoxious aspect of the extreme orthodox school. In another letter he says: "The difference between my views and those of the current orthodoxy does not lie in the question of the atonement—we agree in this—but in the question *what* in that atonement was the element that satisfied God? They say pain. I say, because I think the Scriptures say so, the surrender of self-will, as is clearly and distinctly asserted in John x. 17, and also in Hebrews x. 5, 6, 7, 10, where the distinction is drawn between the sacrifices of blood and suffering, which were mere butchery, and the sacrifice which atones, in this special point; that one is moral, an act of *will;* the other immoral, merely physical, and therefore worthless."[2]

Robertson frequently treated this great subject in his sermons. We find the fullest expression of his views in the sermon entitled, "Caiaphas' View of Vicarious Sacrifice." He takes as his text the

---

[1] "Life and Letters," vol. i. pp. 304, 305.
[2] "Life and Letters," vol. ii. p. 139.

remarkable words, "Ye know nothing at all; nor consider that it is expedient that one man should die for the people, that the whole nation perish not. And this spake he not of himself, etc."

The preacher shows that there is a false and perverted sense of these words, and it is in this sense that Caiaphas uses them; while they have at the same time a true and Divine meaning, which is that accepted by St. John. We would gladly quote the whole of this remarkable sermon, one of the most original and powerful which Robertson ever preached, but space forbids. We may cite one passage, in which he describes the spirit of Caiaphas and of all the men of his school.

"The first falsity in the human statement of the truth of vicarious sacrifice is its injustice. Some one said, The accused is innocent. The reply was, Better that one should die than many. 'It is expedient for us that one man should die for the people, and that the whole nation perish not.' It was simply with Caiaphas a question of numbers: the unjust expediency of wresting the law a little to do much apparent good. The reply to that question was plain. Expediency cannot obliterate right and wrong. Expediency may choose the best possible when the conceivable best is not attainable; but in right and wrong there is no better and best. Thou *shalt* not do wrong. Thou *must* not: you may not tell a lie to save life. Better that the whole Jewish nation should perish than that a Jewish legislature should steep its hand in the blood of one innocent. It is *not* expedient to do injustice. . . .

"No man would justify the parent, pursued in his chariot by wolves over Siberian snows, who throws out one of his children to the pack that the rest may escape while their fangs are buried in their victim. You feel at once expediency has no place here. Life is a trifle compared with law. Better that all should perish by a visitation of God than that they should be saved by one murder.

"I do not deny that this aspect has been given to the sacrifice of Christ. It has been represented as if the majesty of Law demanded a victim; and so as it glutted its insatiate thirst, one victim would do as well as another—the fairer and the more innocent the better. It has been exhibited as if Eternal Love resolved in fury to strike, and so, as He had His blow, it mattered not whether it fell on the whole world or on the precious head of His own chosen Son.

"Unitarianism has represented the scriptural view in this way; or rather, perhaps, we should say, it has been so represented to Unitarians; and from a view so horrible no wonder if Unitarianism has recoiled. But it is not our fault if some blind defenders of the truth have converted the self-devotion of Love into a Brahminical sacrifice. If the work of redemption be defended from parallels drawn from the most atrocious records and principles of heathenism, let not the fault be laid upon the Bible. We disclaim that as well as they. It makes God a Caiaphas—it makes Him adopt the words of Caiaphas in the sense of Caiaphas. It represents Him in terms which better describe the ungoverned rage of Saul, missing his stroke at David, who has offended, and in disappointed fury dashing his javelin at his own son Jonathan.

"You must not represent the atonement as depending on the justice of unrighteous expediency.

"This side of viewing the truth was the side of selfishness. It was not even the calm resolve of men balancing whether it be better for one to die or many; but whether it is better that He or *we* should perish. It is conceivable, in the case supposed above, that a parent in the horrible dilemma should be enough bewildered to resolve to sacrifice one rather than lose all; but it is not conceivable that the doubt in his mind should be this, Shall *I* and the rest perish, or this one?—yet this was the spirit in which the party of Caiaphas spoke. The Romans will come and take away *our* place and *our* nation.

"And this spirit, too, is in human nature. The records of antiquity are full of it. If a fleet could not sail, it was assumed that the deities were offended. The purest and tenderest maiden of the royal household was selected to bleed upon the altar: and when the sharp knife passed to her innocent heart, this was the feeling in the bosom of those stern and unrelenting warriors—of the blood and of the stock of Caiaphas—better she should suffer than we.

"This *may* be the way in which the sacrifice of Christ is regarded by us. There is a kind of acquiescence in the atonement which is purely selfish. The more bloody the representation of the character of God, the greater, of course, the satisfaction in feeling sheltered from it. The more Wrath instead of Love is believed to be the Divine name, the more may a man find joy in believing that he is safe. It is the theory of the Siberian story: the innocent has glutted the wolves, and we may pursue our journey in safety. Christ has suffered, and I am safe. He bare the agony, I take the reward. I may now live with impunity; and, of course, it is very easy to call acquiescence in that arrangement humility, and to take credit for the abnegation of self-righteousness; but whoever can acquiesce in that thought chiefly in reference to *personal safety*, and, without desiring to share the Redeemer's cross, aspire to enjoy the comforts and benefits of the Redeemer's sacrifice, has but something of the spirit of Caiaphas after all, the spirit which contentedly sacrifices another for self—selfishness assuming the form of wisdom.

"We pass now to the prophetic or hidden spirit, in which these words are true. I observe, first, that vicarious sacrifice is the Law of Being. . . .

"The Highest Man recognised that law, and joyfully embraced it as the law of His existence. It was the consciousness of His surrender to that as God's will, and the voluntariness of the act, which made it sacrifice. Hear Him: 'No man taketh my life from me: I have power to lay it down, and I have power to take it up again.' 'This commandment have I received from my Father.' . . .

"We go beyond this, however. It was not merely a sacrifice, it was a sacrifice for sin. 'His soul was made an offering for sin.' Neither was it only a sacrifice for sin—it was a sacrifice for the world's sin. . . .

"Let no man say that Christ bore the wrath of God. Let no man say that God was angry with His Son. We are sometimes told of a mysterious anguish which Christ endured, the consequence of divine wrath, the sufferings of a heart laden with the conscience of the world's transgressions, which He was bearing as if they were His own sins. Do not add to the Bible what is not in the Bible. The Redeemer's conscience was not bewildered to feel *that* as His own, which was *not* His own. He suffered no wrath of God. Twice came the voice from heaven, 'This is my beloved Son in whom I am *well pleased.*' There was seen an angel strengthening Him. Nay, even to the last, never did the consciousness of purity and the Father's love forsake Him. 'Father, into thy hands I commend my spirit.'

"Christ came into collision with the world's evil, and He bore the penalty of that daring. . . .

"The Redeemer bore imputed sin. He bore the penalty of others' sin. He was punished. Did He bear the anger of the Most High? Was His the hell of an accusing conscience? In the name of Him who is God, not Caiaphas, *never*. . . .

"The second idea which it behoves us to master is the world's sin. The Apostle John always viewed 'sin as a great connected principle; *One;* a single world-spirit—exactly as the electricity with which the universe is charged is indivisible, imponderable, one, so that you cannot separate it from the great ocean of fluid. The electric spark that slumbers in the dewdrop is part of the flood which struck the oak. Had that spark not been there, it could be demonstrated that: the whole previous constitution of the universe might have been different, and the oak not have been struck. . . .

"To conclude. Estimate rightly the death of Christ. It was not simply the world's example—it was the world's Sacrifice. He died not merely as a martyr to the truth. His death is the world's life. Ask ye what life is? Life is not exemption from penalty. Salvation is not escape from suffering and punishment. The Redeemer suffered punishment; but the Redeemer's soul had blessedness in the very midst of punishment. Life is elevation of soul—nobleness—divine character. The spirit of Caiaphas was death: to receive all, and give nothing: to sacrifice others to himself. The spirit of God was life: to give and not receive: to be sacrificed and not to sacrifice. Hear

Him again: 'He that loseth his life, the same shall find it.' That is life: the spirit of losing all for love's sake. That is the soul's life, which alone is blessedness and heaven. By realising that ideal of humanity, Christ furnished the life which we appropriate to ourselves only when we enter into His spirit.

"Listen! Only by renouncing sin is His death to sin yours—only by quitting it are you free from the guilt of His blood—only by voluntary acceptance of the law of the cross, self-surrender to the will of God, and self-devotion to the good of others as the law of your being, do you enter into that present and future heaven, which is the purchase of His vicarious sacrifice." [1]

Robertson is admirable in his attacks upon the hard, judicial theory of the atonement; but his exposition of his own system gives a very inadequate view of the work of redemption. From this it would appear that Christ saves us simply by realising in His own person the ideal of humanity, and by the holy constraining influence of His love upon the heart. I find no place in such a system for redemption, properly so called—for that agonising travail of soul, in which Christ bore upon His heart the sin of the world. His obedience is not sufficiently represented as a reparation of the revolt of the first Adam.

Robertson rightly repudiated the horrible idea of

---

[1] "Caiaphas' View of Vicarious Sacrifice." Sermons, First Series.

the direct curse of the Father resting upon the Son, but passes over in silence the mysterious desertion, the anguish of soul which the Master endured, and in which He realised through his perfect sympathy with us, all the bitterness of our sin, and recognised God's righteous anger against it. Robertson represents the work of Christ as the initiation of a course of reparative effort rather than as the one unique work which it is ours simply to assimilate by a living faith. That such was really his view appears from another sermon on the same subject, in which the principal virtue of the cross is made to be that it sets before us an ideal of perfection, and fills us with an ardent desire to be conformed to it. Using a beautiful figure, he compares fallen man brought into contemplation of the sublime sacrifice of the cross, to Correggio standing before a canvas of Raphael's and exclaiming, " And I, too, am a painter ! " This is one aspect of the truth ; but we must not forget that while thus re-creating in the soul the divine ideal, the cross at the same time recalls to us the depth of our spiritual degradation, the impotence of our own efforts after goodness, and awakens the yearning for pardon and deliverance. But for this hope which it holds out, it would only aggravate our misery by setting before us an ideal for ever unattainable, and revealing to us with pitiless clearness the moral depths to which we have fallen.

Eloquent as Robertson is in the description of human suffering, he does not sufficiently recognise the infirmity and hopeless weakness of fallen man. Hence, while he rightly rejects that notion of prayer which regards it as a purely external and magical influence, a sort of Aladdin's lamp, capable of procuring for us whatever we desire, he too much disregards its character as a positive making request to God. His sermon on the prayer in Gethsemane contains many great and helpful thoughts on the necessity of bringing our mind into harmony with the mind of God, and submitting our will to His. But even this is a grace which we need to obtain, like every other. Prayer has an effect not only upon ourselves, but upon God. It is an active power. The cry of the poor beggar craving help from Christ is not an illusion. In order to receive, we must ask; for asking is at once the acknowledgment of our own emptiness and of the fulness of God. In relation to this subject, as to all others, there is a very valuable element of freshness and suggestiveness in Robertson, which only needs to be supplemented. All that he has written or said on justification by faith contains important truth. We have seen, in his sermon on Caiaphas, how he protests against such a notion of salvation as would imply that Christ had died for us, to save us from the necessity of crucifying ourselves. Like Vinet, he maintains the closest connection between sanctification and justification. God sees the development of the germ in the germ itself, as he sees the great river Thames, which bears on its bosom the mighty ships of the Atlantic and Indian Oceans, in the tiny scarcely perceptible rivulet from which it springs.

Robertson's attention was more deeply fixed upon the person than upon the work of Christ. No disciple ever loved the Master with a more fervent love; his language rises into poetry at the very mention of His name. He lives by His life; he is never weary of meditating on His perfections; he truly worships Him. He has therefore nothing in common with the Unitarian school. All his thoughts and feelings he refers to Christ; through Him he seeks constant access to the Father. Christ is the centre of his religious life. On every page of his writings we find expressions which implicitly recognise the unique relation existing between the Son and the Father, and the eternal divinity of Jesus Christ. It is upon His humanity, however, that he dwells most fully. This is to him no fiction, but a grand reality. He holds that Christ passed through the moral conflict without even the shadow of sin resting upon Him; but He does not admit that He possessed any peculiar inherent virtue, which rendered him unassailable by the same temptations to which we are exposed. Robertson expressed with characteristic vigour the legitimate necessity felt by the theology of the day, to escape from the metaphysical docetism which substituted a rigid Byzantine Christ for the living Son of Man. His sermon on the childhood of

Christ, on His loneliness and His sympathy, bring out this aspect of truth with peculiar beauty. We may quote, as expressing his deepest and most sacred convictions, part of a letter to a friend on this subject. He says:

"Unquestionably, the belief in the divinity of Christ is waning among us. They who hold it have petrified it into a theological dogma without life or warmth, and thoughtful men are more and more beginning to put it aside. How are we then to get back this belief in the Son of God? By authority, or by the old way of persecution? The time for these has passed. The other way is to begin at the beginning. Begin as the Bible begins, with Christ the Son of Man. Begin with Him as God's character revealed under the limitations of humanity. Lay the foundations of a higher faith deeply in the belief of His humanity. See Him as He was. Breathe His Spirit. After that, try to comprehend His life. Enter into His childhood. Feel with Him when He looked round about Him in anger; when He vindicated the crushed woman from the powerless venom of her ferocious accusers; when He stood alone in the solitary majesty of truth in Pilate's judgment-hall; when the light of the Roman soldiers' torches flashed on Kedron in the dark night, and He knew that watching was too late; when His heart-strings gave way upon the cross. Walk with Him through the marriage-feast. See how the sick and weary came to Him instinctively; how men, when they saw Him, felt their sin, they knew not why, and fell at His feet; how guilt unconsciously revealed itself, and all that was good in men was drawn out, and they became higher than themselves in His presence. Realise this. Live with Him until He becomes a living thought—ever present—and you will find a reverence growing up which compares with nothing else in human feeling. You will feel that a slighting word spoken of Him wounds with a dart more sharp than personal insult. You will feel that to bow at the name of Jesus is no form at will of others, but a relief and welcome. And if it should ever chance that, finding yourself thrown upon your own self, and cut off from sects—suspected, in quest of a truth which no man gives—then that wondrous sense of strength and friendship comes—the being alone with Christ, with the strength of a manlier independence. Slowly, then, this almost insensibly merges into adoration. Now what is it to adore Christ? To call Him God? to say, Lord, Lord? No. Adoration is the mightiest love the soul can give—call it by what name you will. Many a Unitarian, as Channing, has adored, calling it only admiration; and many an orthodox Christian, calling Christ God with most accurate theology, has given Him only a cool intellectual homage."[1]

Much exception was taken to Robertson's warm admiration for Channing. But the extract just given

[1] "Life and Letters," vol. ii. pp. 170, 171.

shows that he knew how to distinguish between Channing's feelings as a man, and the opinions of his party.

In Robertson's conception of the incarnation, the dogma of the two natures was altogether dropped. He believed firmly that it was possible for the human to become divine; or, rather, he recognised the divine in the primeval idea of humanity, which finds its eternal realisation in Christ.

In his sermon on the Trinity he fully develops these views, which are shared, as we know, by an important section of contemporary theologians, and which, if we except their tendency to exaggeration, can claim in their support the teaching of the second and third centuries. We would not venture to say that Robertson did not approach too daringly the mysteries of the Divine Being, when he said that before the world was there already existed in the mind of God that which we may call the *humanity* of Deity, that which the scripture calls the Word, the Son, the express image of the Father. In his sermon on the Trinity we read: " The Unitarian maintains a divine humanity — a blessed, blessed truth. There is a truth more blessed still — the humanity of Deity. Before the world was, there was that in the mind of God which we may call the humanity of His divinity. It is called in scripture the Word; the Son; the Form of God. It is in virtue of this that we have a right to attribute to Him our own feelings; it is in virtue of this that scripture speaks of His wisdom, His justice, His love. It is through this humanity in the mind of God, if I may dare so to speak of Deity, that a revelation became possible to man. It was the Word that was made flesh ; it was the Word that manifested itself to man. It is in virtue of the connection between God and man that God made man in His own image ; that through a long line of prophets the human truth of God could be made known to man, till it came forth developed most entirely and at large in the incarnation of the Redeemer." [1]

Robertson seems to have anticipated the ideas worked out by Beyschlag in his paper before the Kirchentag of Altenburg, which gave rise to so much stormy discussion. It must be admitted, however, that he never called in question, as did the German theologian, the eternal pre-existence of the Word. It is true that he speaks of the obscurity of the doctrine of the Trinity, and of the impossibility of attaching an exact and definite meaning to our common language, when it is used in relation to those unfathomable depths, which we cannot comprehend within our narrow formulas. We may well say in relation to subjects like these, as the apostle said, "We see through a glass darkly." Robertson gave exaggerated expression to his real belief when, in the Sermon on Absolution, he said that man has the

---

[1] " Sermon on the Trinity." Third Series, p. 56.

power as man to forgive sins, because he is the representative of God, and because of the essential harmony existing between the human and the divine nature. This is unquestionably an exaggeration amounting to error. It is the Father who has been offended by the prodigal son; and in this sense the Pharisees were right when they said, "Who can forgive sins but God only?" Their error lay in their failing to recognise in Christ the true representative of God.

Here, again, we notice the same deficiency to which we have already referred in Robertson's teaching. The idea of moral perfection throws into the background the idea of pardon. The religion he presents to us is rather that of a realised ideal than that of redemption and restoration.

Such a doctrine does not meet the conditions of our weakness; it is too high for us; we cannot attain to it. The love of God has stooped lower than Robertson thought. Robertson treats us as strong men; God knows that we are but feeble children. It is well to have a strong and rapid steed to bear us over the rough places on the way, but first of all the poor traveller, sick and sore wounded, needs some one to stoop and lift him up and to bind up his wounds like the good Samaritan.

It will not, I hope, appear hypercritical, if I still further take exception to Robertson's too persistent avoidance of all beaten tracks. There are sacred resting-places for the Christian soul which ought not to be neglected; there are rudiments of the faith which cannot with impunity be passed over in silence, however familiar they may be supposed to be. Robertson constantly contents himself with alluding to the fundamental points of Christian teaching without expounding them. This is a mistake. At other times he falls into the error of a too minute and subtle analysis. But with these exceptions, we know no writer more genial, none more nervous, none whose words are more stimulating to thought and reflection. He had a fertile and graceful imagination. His illustrations are original, and altogether free from conventionality. We never find in his pages that profusion of familiar metaphors—flowers, stars, storms, cataracts—which are the hackneyed properties of a meretricious rhetoric. Anglo-Saxon imagery, from the time of Shakspeare, has been distinguished by a vigorous realism, clear in colour, firm in outline. Few writers have understood its use better than Robertson. His delivery did full justice to his eloquence. He gave free expression to the results of his profound and careful study. His striking face, resonant voice, restrained but vigorous action, and above all, that strong tension of his whole being which made every word instinct with his own deepest life— all this tended to produce an ineffaceable impression upon his hearers. But in such spending the life soon exhausts itself, especially when the soul of the preacher is all the while the scene of a long wrestling like Jacob's, from which he comes forth again and again wounded though victorious.

Beside the volumes of sermons, Robertson has left behind a series of expositions of the epistles to the Corinthians, a reminiscence of those consecutive studies of various portions of Scripture which he was accustomed to give in his Sunday afternoon service. This mode of teaching seems to us peculiarly admirable, giving as it does a full and comprehensive view of the real intention of the sacred writers, instead of breaking up passages of scripture into disjointed fragments, of which the preacher may be often tempted to make a fanciful and unreal application.

We observe in this volume on the Corinthians the same defects and the same merits as in the other sermons. The form in which the truth is presented is in this case more simple, though always original and suggestive. His meditations on the resurrection are of peculiar depth and beauty.

Robertson's physical strength began to decline rapidly in the summer of 1853. He suffered from an irritation of the brain which produced terrible exhaustion. Rest seemed for the time to restore him, but the respite was very short. It was found necessary for him to have a curate; the candidate whom Robertson preferred was refused to him by his ecclesiastical superior, on the ground of unfounded charges against him. Robertson was fully determined not to accept any other, for he felt that in doing so he should seem to lend credence to the calumnies unjustly circulated against a good man.

This controversy, in which Robertson showed the rare nobility of his character, was not terminated at the time of his death, and no doubt hastened his end by deferring the help he absolutely needed, and thus aggravating his bodily suffering by mental distress. He died August 15th, 1853. His last words were, "Let me rest. I must die. Let God do His work."

He was followed to the grave by the deep regrets of His church, especially of the younger portion, whose hearts he had completely gained, and of the poor, to whom he had ever been a faithful friend. Robertson left behind him an unsullied memory, and an influence which has been increasing year by year, as his published sermons have won their way in all the thoughtful Christian homes of England.

CONCLUSION.

WE have seen in the case of both Verny and Robertson, how deep and severe the mental conflict may be in our day, even in the case of those who hold fast their faith in Christ. The severity of the struggle has in no way abated in the years that have elapsed since their death. Both in England and France souls are deeply agitated by religious questions, as is manifest from the reaction in the direction of Catholicism, and from the development of that lofty Christian stoicism, of which "Ecce Homo" is at once the noblest and most brilliant expression.

It would be childish to shut our eyes to the fact that that which constitutes the danger of these theories, which are acquiring such an ascendancy in our day, is the inadequacy of the orthodox creeds. We draw from this only one conclusion—that it is essential that we should press forward, in the fullest exercise of faith and of freedom, the development of our theology. It is not for us to slumber calmly while the problems of the age are placed before us for solution. All those who have obtained for themselves the answer to the question, "What must I do to be saved?" all who are living by the life of Christ, have found for themselves a sure abiding place. But they are not to fall asleep in it; rather are they bound to unite their efforts to give satisfaction to the spiritual needs of other souls, and primarily to the legitimate aspiration after a closer union of the religious with the moral element. In this way they will be saved from falling into exaggerations, which are the sure indication of some spiritual unsoundness.

We believe firmly in a Church of the future, which, unlike ancient Rome, shall gather into itself the good elements of all existing Churches, which shall give us in worship true adoration without the forms of idolatry, and in doctrine moral vigour and definiteness of teaching without an arid dogmatism.

Upon this lofty height will meet the pilgrims who

have climbed the hill by many paths. And still behind this summit there will rise another, and again another and another loftier still, till we shall have reached the mountains radiant with the eternal sunlight of perfect love, on which we shall know as we are known.

So the search after fuller truth, with all the diversities that it brings with it, must recommence after each great fusion of thought and feeling wrought under some mighty impetus in the religious life. This is the law of history, and we freely accept it; for after all, what we seek is only to arrive at a fuller knowledge of ourselves, and a fuller apprehension of the truth we have already grasped. He who has Christ has in Him all things. Let us not misinterpret the struggles and turmoils of these periods of transition. I can think of no more fitting conclusion to these studies of earnest lives than words used by the noble Lèbre, whose death drew such an eloquent tribute from the heart of Verny. It is a quarter of a century since he wrote the words, and yet they are more appropriate to-day than ever: "Those in whose souls the great travail of the future is being carried on ought to seek solitude as did the ancient prophets, but like them, also, they ought to fill the solitude with their prayers, and to walk with bowed souls before God. It is theirs with deep humility and holy fervour to seek the help of God for themselves and for the whole world."

www.ingramcontent.com/pod-product-compliance
Lightning Source LLC
Chambersburg PA
CBHW051742300426
44115CB00007B/669